Louise

Letters, Reflections, Stories
A Life To Remember

Louise Fluke Brownson Conery Beattie
Edited by Ann Brownson Keiffer

ShadowDancePress and Pete's Publishing

Copyright © 2019 Ann Brownson Keiffer

ISBN-13: **978-0-9893801-5-7**

ACKNOWLEDGMENTS

Thank you to my mother for sharing her heart with us.

Thank you to Bob for being my one-man
google for dates, times and context.

Thank you to Tina, the keeper of family treasures,
for rounding up binders, notebooks, and photographs.

Thank you to Molly for encouraging Mom to write
and for supporting me in taking on the sometimes
emotional work of putting together this book.

Thank you to all the spouses for their support
of our mom and this project.

Cover Art:
The background for the cover of this book is from a watercolor painting by Louis

TABLE OF CONTENTS

LOUISE TELLS US HER STORY
By Daughter Ann

As Louise's oldest child, living in California for 50 years now, there has been little way for me to provide personal care and comfort for her in her last years. When she and I were younger, we were avid letter-writers and phone-callers; we may have kept an eye on the clock back then—because long-distance calls were costly!—but it was a priority for us to stay in touch. In her active years, Mom came to California to visit us and I traveled back to Ohio, too. Neither of us was an easy traveler, but it was always important to us to spend at least a little time in each other's home and surroundings, experiencing daily life and the opportunity for long conversations.

Then came the computer and iPad and Mom's foray into emailing. We had so many important long-distance conversations with one another that way, each of us feeling we were only fingertips-away on a keyboard. It was through my mother's eyes—and the way she swept into her embrace every detail—that I experienced the events, celebrations, funny stories, and times of trouble in my family's life back in Ohio. I was "there" and "saw" it all it by way of her words. But the time came when the computer and iPad were not easy for Mom anymore. And then even using the phone became a challenge. It was a huge loss.

In her last years, living all those thousands of miles away, I couldn't be of much practical help in doing the things so necessary to my mother's health and well-being. I couldn't drop in for frequent visits, take her to lunch, watch over her meds or the many aspects of her care, drive her to the doctor or church, eat breakfast with her, manage her finances or go to the bank and get her that little stash of "cash" she always liked to have in the dresser drawer. All of those aspects of her loving care fell to Molly, Tina and Bob. And what a marvelous, cherishing, thoughtful, creative job they did in helping Mom through her last years.

It was important to me to be with my mother at the time of her passing, and I always told Tina she was in charge of letting me know when the time came and I needed to come home. So when Tina called to say it was time, I went. I was there with the family for the last two days of Mom's life—a grieving time, but also a sacred time, a blessed time that glowed with love, hymns, prayers, scriptures, memories, stories, laughter and tears.

In the days just prior to her death, "Mom's White Binder" started to claim a prominent place in the family. It was a regular, white ring-binder of the office variety, but it was full of essays and remembrances Mom had written over many years. We passed the binder around during those last days, even reading some pieces aloud around her bed. I soon realized that in "Mom's White Binder" there was finally something I could do for my mother and the family. I could preserve her thoughts and her words; I could pull it all together and make a book for her.

In these pages, I have compiled material from the white binder, as well as some pieces found in family treasure boxes and Mom's desk. I also included a few pieces written *to* my mother—things she had saved—because they reveal something more about her life. I have placed them, for the most part, in chronological order, so we can see the arc of her life. Naturally, these written records couldn't capture her phone-call connections with people and family who lived nearby, so we are missing those links to important people in her life. I wish we had access to *all* the letters she wrote earlier in her life and the many, many emails that went out to us all. But the letters are ephemera by now and the aged-out iPad cannot yield her emails. Even in the limited materials we have, you will see her return again and again in her writing to things she is trying to make peace with, things she is trying to work out in her own mind, major themes in her life. Each piece—in her own words—reveals something about the person she was, what pleased and tickled her, what mattered to her, what she loved, what she believed, and the beautiful life of her soul.

When Mom would come to California to visit, she always exclaimed over how much she loved the weather, the temperatures in the low-70's, the soft breezes, the warm days that always cooled down into nights perfect for sleeping. Because of how much she loved it, we began referring to this as "Louise-y weather." In this book, in her words, may you find Louise-y wisdom and a way of being in the world that touches and deepens your life. My mother has passed on, but she remains vitally alive and present to us in her words.

Ann Keiffer

HER WORDS

My mother,
our mother,
died at 94,
leaving a fully-ripened,
meaningful life.
Oddly, I find my grief
isn't coming
in gouts of mourning
that she is missing...
I am grieving, more,
over Life's losing
such a sensitive observer,
one who truly saw Life
and held it all dear.

I am grieving, too,
that I have lived so far away
from home so many years
I may not have treasured
or perceived full-measure
what I might have shared
with my mother had I been near.
And strangely, now that she is gone
I find her amazingly close,
entirely present with me
in the words she left
on computer and paper,
as I gather them to make a book.

...Letters and notes of concern,
encouragement and congratulations
to friends and siblings,
children and grandchildren;

...Pieces she wrote for herself about
barefoot summers on the farm,
driving the blind team of horses,
milking cows in the barn—
finishing her milking
then helping her brother catch up,
falling in love with my dad,
such sadness in his early death;

...Her words about loving the busy years
when we kids were growing up,
boosters club and banquets,
carpools for football games
and cheerleading practice,
cooking, cleaning, baking,
sewing prom dresses
and wedding dresses for her girls;

...Her words about
growing old, giving up driving,
needing a walker, feeling "invisible;"

...Her words about
family reunions on the homeplace,
the hay rides, contests and races,
the picnic tent and porta-potty,
little kids' happy screaming
and games in the yard;

...Her words about
regret—no heavy self-condemnation,
only wondering how things
might have been different;

...Her words about
her joys, her abiding faith,
her thoughts on adversity,
how it can make you strong.

In her words,
she is still so present
maybe especially to her word-girl,
the one she knew me to be.

My mother and I lived
so many miles apart for so long,
still, she was always "there,"
back in Ohio,
my lifetime point of reference,
my mom.

In the weeks following her death,
I felt a little like a blind person
tap-tap-tapping with my very-long cane,
trying to find that reference point
that will tell me where I am.
I am tap-tap-tapping with my cane,
but my reference point is gone.
Except for her words.
Such a perceptive observer,
someone who painted with words,
a poet who rarely wrote poetry.

I marvel at what I had not known before:
my mother was a word-girl, too.

Ann Keiffer
April, 2019

IN MY OWN WORDS
Why Write about My Life?
Written in 1998

This morning as I looked in the mirror I saw an old lady looking back at me, her cheeks a bit round, in spite of wrinkles. My daughter-in-law, Kathy, has often described me to others as resembling Mrs. Santa Claus. Somehow that always seemed so endearing to me. My long hair drawn back in a bun, added to my round cheeks—all I needed was my red Santa's-helpmate dress.

I realize that I am in the "winter" of my life, headed very probably into my last decade. I had been suspecting the verdict of aging for some time; however, recent events in my life, including back surgery for the second time, required that I take a closer look at my life.

I come from a family of longevity. My maternal Grandmother, Rhuy Hanna Wilson Swan, died in 1952 at the age of 86, after a full life as a Presbyterian minister's wife and a medical missionary in China prior to 1900. My father, Eugene Perry Fluke, a life-long successful farmer in Ashland County, farmed into his 80th year and died in 1981 at age 83. My mother, Mary Johnston Swan Fluke, mother of the five of us, a hard-working, good mother, lived into her 96th year. She was born in 1900, and I always marveled at how easy that made it to remember her age. More about these loved ones later, but for now, I'm in awe of the fact they gave me life and continued on to shape my life as I have lived out my now 74-plus years. I owe so much to my heritage.

As I find myself in this stage of life, I wonder about the whole of my life—what it has meant—to whom and why. Have I added to the quality of life for any who have surrounded me on the journey? Have I been a mentor to family and friends? Have I lived the life God had planned for me? Is there a story here worth recording?

There are and have been millions of life stories in the world—each life, a story. Only a few stories will be preserved and recorded. Important stories will be lost, unrecorded, totally lost in three or four generations. Millions of souls have died, their life experiences forever lost with no mention of how they lived their lives, what was in their hearts, their goals and their dreams

Whether or not my decision to jot down my thoughts regarding my life is valid or important, I do feel a need, a desire, to do just that.

My Grandmother Swan wrote her story in 1948, four years before her death. I treasure that grey book with its wealth of information. My mother wrote her story over a period of time from 1968 through 1987. Neither of these dear ladies who were so important in my life recorded much about how they *felt* about life.

My paternal Grandmother Mollie Welch Fluke died January 2, 1909 when my father, her third-born, was just twelve years old. I always wished that more had been recorded about her life—that I could have known more about how she lived her life, her joys, her fears and disappointments. She came from the stiff-upper-lip time in life—she may not have wanted to share her deepest thoughts with those of us to follow.

I know Grandma Mollie was a good mother, evidenced by the fact that she raised seven wonderful children without any modern conveniences. She was the good and beloved wife of James Fluke. Together they owned a 170-acre farm in Orange Township in Ashland County, 100 acres tillable, on rather thin soil. It had to be a difficult life. I know she painted in oil, as I have a painting she did early in her life, probably in her youth.

This good lady died in the Nankin Methodist Church while attending some sort of elocution event in which her daughter, Opal, was giving an oration. It was probably some sort of stroke, leaving behind a struggling family, the youngest being only three years old. I've wondered about her life. Will my grandchildren or great-grandchildren wonder about her life—or even mine?

And so I have decided to record some events from my life that just might be of interest, trying to honestly account for my younger years, growing up on a farm, my adult life and my thoughts as I near my 75th year. Have I a story to tell? I have done nothing spectacular. Never a world leader or even a small-town leader. Never made a million and in the crazy vernacular of today, never became a "rocket scientist."

Did I leave some mark on contemporary society, in the lives of my offspring?

Louise

Let's see if her writing answers that question! A.K.

A BRIEF HISTORY OF MY LIFE
Written 1983-1985

Growing Up

I arrived into the world on May 26, 1924, the third child of Eugene and Mary Fluke—weighing in at 7 3/4 pounds, 21 inches in length. My mother noted in my baby book that I appeared to be darker in complexion than my sister and brother and that I was a "good" baby. I assume by that she meant I did not cry much, which was fortunate as I'm told it was difficult spring. Wet and cold. At the time of arrival the spring plowing had not yet begun—held up due to an over-abundance of rain. Even the lilacs were late. Dad picked a bouquet for Mom while she was confined to bed after my birth.

Babies came quite steadily in those days. I was to be followed by two more sisters in the next four years. I often wondered if my parents worried as to how they would care or provide for us all. And yet I realize that each generation, no doubt, wonders the same thing. Or perhaps more correctly, each generation worries about this for the next younger generation, their offspring.

Being born into a farm family was my destiny. I'm proud of my farm-raising, for it was there I learned to work, to organize and sort out priorities, to appreciate the land and all of the efforts of my father and forefathers to clear the land and homestead their acreage, to nurture it to productive yields. Land is our most valuable material possession. I consider myself fortunate now, having acreage of my own, even though it's a total of 21 acres only. The peace and quiet of the fields and woods is so very valuable to me. I need this to give me the peace I need after a busy day with people.

I worked hard as a girl growing up on the farm. I'm sure some might consider it too hard, but I'm certain it became my pattern for life—which helped me to physically cope with the raising of five children. Pride in a job well done motivated me greatly. One word of praise from my Dad made it all worthwhile. He wasn't lavish with praise, but I could tell when I did it "right," whether it be turning the cream in the separator at the right speed, setting the hayfork correctly, or stripping the last milk from a jersey cow.

I learned to milk cows when I was 10 years old and from then on until I was 19, I milked at least two cows morning and evening. Jersey cows aren't noted for being extremely easy to milk, being a little short in the faucet! I'd often have to remind my brother Donald that he hadn't milked his cows in the proper order. Academically, he was top-drawer. I'm sure his heart wasn't really into cow-milking and field-work, though he never complained.

We all had specific chores to do. I recall being assigned to lead out the horses to water at the concrete trough was a heady job. Our milking herd seldom numbered more than 10 or 11, quite small by today's standards. But it required much time and effort to hand-milk. On one occasion when Dad was detained at some neighbor's farm, helping with threshing, I decided to surprise him by doing the milking all by myself. I recall that my arms ached badly, but I was so proud of myself. Dad was surprised, and though I'm sure I didn't do the best job, he did not find fault. I'm also sure the quantity of milk was up the next morning.

Getting the cows from the 40-pasture—so designated because it was 40-acres in size—was a job we all took turns in doing. It was a long hike, especially when we would have to go to the very back-line fence. We amused ourselves by pretending we were mounting on "shiny, high-stepping steads" or driving new cars. You could choose the color of your horse when you started out from the barn. Your spirited horse would gallop off, side-stepping coiled snakes, leaping fences. As for the cars, we usually felt the best make of car in those days was what we called a "Zim-Zim" Plymouth. This was inspired by the fact that Uncle Alfred did, indeed, have a new Plymouth, the year being 1931.

Our imaginations ran wild, inspired, no doubt, by Donald's fantastic vocabulary. We played many of our games in the "third-person"—a type of game classed as a bit weird by husband Bob when he learned of the Fluke kids' childhood pretend games. In one of our favorite games we thought of ourselves as a wandering band of nomads tramping across the land, rugged miles, day after day. The south pasture, the horse pasture, was a favorite location. When I refer to these as third-person conversations, it was really more like a story we were acting out. "So they walked across this barren field and finally reached a river." (In reality it was the little creek that wandered through the pasture.) "And they decided to camp for the night." We took turns speaking the lines like that. I'm not sure of our ages—maybe Donald was 10, I was 9, Emeline 7, and Helen 5. Elinor never played these games—at 12 or 13 years old, she seemed too old. We can could have all been a little older. It was great fun, those times. We could generate much excitement and feeling for these story-book adventures.

Our toys were few, but our games many. Rainy days were often spent in the attic, staging dramatic productions behind curtains rather precariously opened and closed over Mom's clothes line. Out of comforts and quilts we fashioned the most unusual costumes. Emeline became famous because she was really good at making nifty "fronts" to her dresses, the devil take the hind side, where I'm sure the black sateen bloomers were in full view. We wrote our play—not really on paper—and used many stilted lines, such as "Shall we go to the ball now?" The answer was "Let us go ahead." At this point we got the giggles, because we all pictured a head of lettuce! These productions were usually just me with "the little girls," Em and Helen. How they hated always being referred to as "the little girls"—it went on for years.

We three often played another attic game known as "Hog Cholera." This was inspired by an epidemic of the real disease in our hogs all around the county. As I recall, we were awed by the seriousness of all the adult discussions of it. In those days a farmer had only a few pigs, maybe a couple of sows whose offspring we considered not only food for the table, ham and bacon in the smoke house, pork tenderloin sausage, canned; but also somewhat of a "cash crop." A hog-check coming back from Cleveland every time Uncle John Fluke took the hogs to market was a welcome event.

Thus, the Hog Cholera game was invented. However, in our game in the attic, humans got the dreaded disease. The victims "died" a most agonizing death. Game rules required that we took turns dying. There was much competition as to who really was the most contorted, most anguished. As each died, the "body" was loaded into our play wagon and hauled to the other end of the attic. The "body" was unloaded and "buried." Then the scene moved back to the original site and victim #2 died and was hauled away. The last remaining one must not be stricken until after she had buried victim #2, and then and only then might victim#3 meet her demise in the graveyard. Weird, yes, but fun. Imagination was whetted, vocabularies enlarged and childhood memories recorded in our minds. Mom was always very tolerant of it all and seldom interfered with our games unless we became too rowdy or fought. I can't recall much fighting, though I'm afraid I was quite guilty of being very bossy with "the little girls."

All through my life my sense of smell as been most acute. Much of my memories are imprinted with a sense of smell. The smell of cows from the pasture 200 ft. away. Fly spray in the cow stalls, oil in the lamps, new-mown hay, oats being chewed by dear old friend Fanny (our part-Morgan work horse,) the distinct odor of puppies and kittens (each so different,) the smell of the sow chewing corn. All these I liked. One I recall that I detested—that brought on nausea—was potato bugs. In the days before spray, the method of debugging the potatoes vines was to rap the potato vines smartly with a stick, causing the bugs to fall into a round bushel basket you carried. The bugs were dumped at the end of the of the row and, as I recall, burned by my Dad. The bugs gave off a hideous odor. I always wondered if it was because

10

we hit them. Guess I always thought we knocked the "juice" out of them, never really knew, just knew I hated that one job especially.

Winter mornings when it was cold, with ice and snow on the ground, did not make for especially fun memories. It was so dark; the lanterns gave off so little light. But the cows had to be milked and you must hurry to get the cow-smell off your hands and body, change your clothes completely and still make the kid-wagon, (At first that conveyance, our "school bus," was a coach-like wagon, later a converted bread truck.) I always hurried, didn't want to miss the buckwheat cakes or fried mush that Mom always had ready. If we didn't dilly-dally on any phase of chores and getting cleaned up, I'd have time to eat. More than one time, I fell down on the ice carrying a pail of milk and the lantern—not the best mixture, not a good way to start the day.

Schooling

I was never the best of students. I worked hard. I wanted to achieve, but I always felt sort of second-rate some way—all through school. The Nankin Grade School was a relatively new building when I started in 1930. Two elementary grade rooms plus a three-year high school were packed into the 3-room school. Because Donald and I were only 15 months apart in age, it meant we were often in the same room, a grade apart. Donald was a pure delight to all his teachers, an eager-to-learn student who excelled in all his studies and was never a discipline problem. He read far ahead of his age, all on his own. In those days, schools were not prepared to challenge the gifted. Libraries were very limited, maybe one shelf of books in the back of the room provided by concerned teachers. He actually read the dictionary—and enjoyed it.

Our teacher that first year was Miss Shuck, who delighted in Donald and marveled at his ability to read. Along came Louise—Louise didn't take to reading quite as well. I recall, vividly, my bad stomach-aches at reading-circle time. My mind blanked. I had difficulty spelling, was so poor at "sounding out" words. I **dreaded** to go up front to reading group. I recall inventing little games of dragging the buttons on my dress sleeves along the chair backs to distract myself or bribe myself to get to my dreaded seat in the reading group. My teacher couldn't have been too well-versed in Educational Psychology or she would never have ridiculed me because I wasn't measuring up to Donald. I didn't hate her. I just felt so sad, so lonely and so dumb. Never once did Donald ever make me feel that way. Nor did my parents. Only teachers—and there were several down through the years. Even my World History teacher at Ashland High School, who had Donald in her class the year before, asked me in front of the whole classroom why I didn't get good grades like my brother Donald.

I was good at jumping rope, fair at softball. I always liked active games. Even now I'd enjoy volleyball if the older shoulder joint could take it. Sled-riding at Ford's hill, Fox and Geese in the snow on the school grounds were great fun.

I graduated from the 8th grade at Nankin in a class of fourteen. I don't know any of the number well anymore. Always a bit of a loner, I didn't have a close girlfriend—always seemed I couldn't trust them. Wonder what that says about me? There was one girl, Grace, who was in my grade school and high school. She, too, was quiet. We certainly didn't attract boys or set the world on fire, but she was "safe" and trustworthy. Until I met Bob I can't recall that school was very much fun. I lacked confidence—such a wall flower.

Homesickness

Homesickness plagued me every time I was away from home for any length of time. When I was 10, Aunt Edna, my dad's oldest sister, who lived in Cleveland, asked Elinor and me to come up for a week's visit during Christmas vacation. It was a very *long* week. I was so homesick. Home looked so good when I got back. I was delighted to see Mom and Dad; it was almost like a holiday when I got home, because the day I arrived home just happened to be butchering day. I recall that butchering day was a somewhat dreaded day for my parents because of all the work involved. However, for me on that particular day, it was a joyous occasion. I remember racing up and down the stairs. I think I was loud and boisterous, for me. But it was pure joy to be where I felt secure and loved. Always blessed (or cursed) with a good appetite, I discovered I just couldn't eat when I was homesick. Smells or memories of smells remain with me even today as an association with Aunt Edna's home or Aunt Eva's kitchen in Wisconsin—another homesick session when I visited there at 13.

To this day, I'm a poor traveler. I think I want to take a trip, but when it comes down to the day ahead of a trip, I feel slight panic build as I make all sorts of mental excuses as to why I should *not* go. My home down through all the years meant security and stability. To leave home brings out many uneasy feelings. I question whether I will be a good guest. Will I be boring, too silent? It's so much more fun to be anywhere *with* someone.

Fun Times

Fun times in my childhood were family reunions. I especially remember a Fluke family get-together in 1937. Aunt Betty Quackenbas, Dad's sister, came with her family from San Diego. The house was filled with guests, fun and laughter, and good food. It was the only time Uncle Bill and their two children were ever to visit in Ohio. It was also the last time Aunt Betty ever saw her ad, Grandpa Jim Fluke, and I recall that at 13 I didn't quite understand the heart-to-heart talks by various members of the older generation in the pump house and the many misty eyes. That generation didn't cross the country like we do today.

For the reunion, we borrowed a pony from the neighbors for the duration of the visit. Oh, we were heady with excitement. Uncle John, Dad's brother, even rode the pony into the *house*. I recall that cold cuts, olives and potato chips abounded. I was in my glory! Dad's family all had a great sense of humor. Grandpa Jim was a joy to us kids. He was a great kidder. Mom and Dad were renting the farm from Grandpa Jim in this period of time. Because of our vivid imaginations we kids were always afraid Grandpa Jim might "foreclose." "Foreclose" was a household word in the depression era. Grandpa Jim used to tell us," Now don't worry. When I drive up someday and my hair is red, I'm going to foreclose." Grandpa was bald, had been for years! This would bring peals of laughter, and we would feel reassured once again. (Later, in 1937 Mom and Dad bought the farm for $5000–180 acres!) Grandpa drove a Model A. I loved the perky sound it made and the sound of the "oogha" horn as he drove up the hill. We would all race out to meet him.

My Life with Bob

In the winter of 1939 Bob Brownson came into my life. How proud I was that he took a fancy to me and sought me out. He would walk with me to the bus after school. I was so excited. Bob played guard on the basketball team at Ashland High School. He was a good student, active in school activities and was liked by his teachers and peers. I was 15 1/2, a girl from the farm, not in the swim of anything. Bob always said he picked me out at the Farm Bureau when I was there with my family two years before we started dating. He knew my brother Donald and sized up the situation—that I was Donald's sister. Bob had a bicycle-route selling ice cream and saw me as he rode by. He used to say that when he saw me at the Farm Bureau that summer he wanted to stop and give me an ice cream bar—but would have had to treat the whole family, and there would go his profits. I never knew if that was really true. Our first date was going to an AHS basketball game. Bob's Dad let him take their *new* De Soto for the occasion. Shortly, Bob and I were going steady, and we never dated anyone else. Life became decidedly more fun.

When I started high school I thought I wanted to be a nurse, but the thought of Chemistry and Physics scared me out. I wish now I had pursued the training, for even though nursing is hard work, it would have provided me with a better-paying job when I needed it badly in later years. By the time I was a senior in high school, Bob and I were engaged to be married and that put any training further into the back of my mind. Bob gave me my ring at graduation time, but we really had no wedding date in mind.

Bob was a top student and won a scholarship to Heidelberg College. Because it was only partial financial help, Bob's folks felt it would be better for him to get a job. Through his mother's relatives in Chicago, he was steered into a job with Western Electric in Cleveland, where he did installation for Bell Telephone. He hated the job, hated the city and was homesick for Ashland...and me, I think. He would hitch a ride home the first chance he could after work on Friday and would take the last bus back to Cleveland on Sunday nights.

I finished high school in June of 1942. Mrs. B, my Home Ec teacher, asked me if I would consider helping her husband Dr. B with office work in his medical practice. I jumped at the chance of a job. Later I would find out I was to assist with minor surgery, tonsillectomies, and give allergy shots when the doctor went away—all without any training and for $9.00 a week. The doctor was a difficult man to work for. He was a diabetic, on insulin, who ate candy bars on the side. His life span was not long; he paid for his ways.

I lived at the Business and Professional Women's Club during this time. I paid $2.25 a week for my room and $5.00 a week for groceries. The remaining $1.75 I could blow! Elinor lived there, too, for a time. While she was there, I had company and it was fun. We would walk up the street on a warm summer evening in our huaraches and get a pineapple sherbet cone. Then Elinor went to Cleveland to work as a secretary. I missed her so much, and I'm sure it was difficult for her to leave Ashland, family and friends.

By fall I realized I could in no way live on $9.00 a week. I applied for factory work at the Faultless Rubber Company in Ashland and was hired at 43 cents per hour to cement lifebelts for the Army. I'm glad I had the "shop-work" experience. I believe I understand more fully a "shop woman" and why she acts as she does and is the way she is.

One day in the spring, my boss had been "on us" all day about working harder and my co-workers were critical of me because I cemented too many lifebelts. (They were afraid we would be put on piece-work; my output was too much higher than theirs.) I picked up my boots right then and walked out. I never went back except to pick up my final paycheck. I'm sure that Dad welcomed my help back at home. I helped him on the farm for a year. We now had electricity and a milking machine. As I recall, I did quite a bit of the milking. Dad and I together made 72 loads of hay and cut and shocked 27 acres of oats. No small job. I worked really hard, but took great pride in it all.

Bob had finally left Cleveland and was working at Myers Pump in Ashland testing a new line of submersible pumps—and liking it only a trifle better than the work in Cleveland.
At the end of the summer Bob suggested that I apply for work at Myers Pump, where he was still working. I was hired in at 65 cents per hour in the nozzle-testing department.

Early in the fall Bob's Aunt Hazel died suddenly and her widower was anxious to sell their household furniture outright to someone. It was suggested that we could benefit from this deal. So we bought everything for $500 and set our wedding date for October. The furniture remained in the house, in place, as we rented the house from the owner. It was difficult to really like any of that furniture until we moved away.

We were married in the house at 827 College Blvd, close to Ashland College on October 16, 1943. The guest list was family and close friends, totaling around 40 people. Mom and Bob's Mom planned a nice reception there at the house. Elinor was my Maid of Honor, John Brown, Bob's Best Man. My Dad "gave me away," though he hated that kind of front-and-center position. It snowed and the roads were slippery. Both moms were most uneasy over our going away, because Bob's car was so untrustworthy. It was a 1934 Chrysler and left much to be desired. The moms were assured that we were only going to Mansfield. So our honeymoon was an overnight trip to the Leland Hotel (razed in the 1970's.)

My girls picked up their Dad's story that I "put up my hair" on our wedding night, and they never let me forget it. My corsage was of gardenias. The smell of gardenias brings back a flood of memories of a very unsophisticated bride and groom. How much we had to learn. How much we would have to grow.

I became pregnant in January. It was an ill-fated pregnancy from the start. The doctor suggested I quit work in February. I recall I was so nauseated, just couldn't seem to get to feeling any better. And in July I miscarried. Fortunately, God knew what was best. The baby was a boy, but never to be.

In April we moved to an 8-acre farm on St Rt 250 east of Ashland with Bob's folks. It was war time. Many people experienced the urge to "move to the farm," sort of survival instinct. Grandma Ruthie (Bob's mother) didn't really want to go, but said she would if Bob and I would go, too. Many people cast gloomy predictions at our going, but I can honestly say I didn't mind going along. And even though many hardships were to follow for all of us involved, there was still much fun and family spirit in being together, a large family.

That farm, known as the Swineford farm, was sold to the Brownsons with a couple of misrepresentations—namely, a shallow inadequate well and a non-existent sewage system—both *most* important for rural living. Mr. Swineford told us grain crops would grow "butt high," but he neglected to say you could hand-pump the well dry in 2 minutes and the "sewage system" involved large, gravel-filled tiles, which would never be classed as a sewage system.

So the first problem was to get water. Numerous holes here drilled by the drilling rig. All were dry holes. The only thing we ever got was a light-gray quick-sand. Then a well was dug by hand. Some water was produced, as hard as I've ever seen, but it could be used for toilets, etc. Modern- day water softeners might have helped, but we didn't have those in 1944. All washing, except for baby things, was taken to Ashland to a relative's to wash or to the Soap Bubble, Ashland's first laundromat. The baby things were washed in cistern water carried a distance. A sewage system was installed, but it never seemed to function correctly. Thus, we named the farm "Cesspool Flats." The house was in a very low area and in the spring the Jerome Fork Creek always flooded and came up to the house, causing more problems with the septic tank.

We lived there with the folks for four years. The first year we lived right with them, cooking and eating together. At the end of the year, Grandpa built on a kitchen for us and gave us two more rooms in the house, so we had an apartment of sorts. The house was difficult to heat. High ceilings and no insulation made for a really chilly existence. Bob went to a farm sale and bought me a small wood-coal range for our kitchen. I've always said it saved my life—and it provided us all with a cozy place on winter days and nights for popcorn and card games for all the clan.

October of 1944 finds me pregnant with Ann, who arrived on July 21, 1945. This time I had better medical care and was monitored regularly by Dr. Martin. All went well and Ann arrived, 8 ¼ pounds on a hot July afternoon.

Bob was by now working at the Flexible Company in Loudonville, as a "time-study" man. I have no idea now how he got this job. He still wasn't happy with his employment and yearned to go to college. I recall that one day in the late summer of 1945 we were sitting on the front porch, and he was voicing his desire to be a teacher and coach. After listening to him, his sister, Betty, urged him to go ahead and give it a try. (She may have provided some financial help.) I've always been grateful to her for her urging. So Bob enrolled as a freshman at Ashland College in September of 1945. Because of the desperate shortage of teachers, he was hired at Jeromesville High School to teach math and history and coach basketball while he was still in school. He attended classes at the college in the morning, then drove to Jeromesville at noon to teach, and finished out the day after basketball practice or games. I can't recall how he ever got it all done! I really can't remember how or when he studied. I just know he was in his glory, doing what he wanted to do. He graduated from AC in 3 ½ years by going winter, summer, evenings, whenever he could. He was an honor student and graduated magna cum laude.

I'm grateful to Grandpa and Grandma Brownson who made it possible for Bob to do this. I'm sure it was a sacrifice to them. Money was a scarce item. Tuition was only $120 per semester. However, half-time pay at Jeromesville was only $70 per month the first year and $90 the second. I milked the cows at the farm and we both did some chores in order to get milk and eggs. I made all our clothes and curtains etc. out of colored, printed feed sacks—even Bob's underwear. He made many jokes about this later in his speaking engagements—as to how his athletic teams never knew when he got dressed after the game if he would be wearing Ashland Equity or Farm Bureau. Actually, his underwear was always gaily flowered—no words or printing—but the joke would get a big laugh.

We survived with the generous help of family. They were rough times, but also fun. In the farm years I can never remember having any "words" with Grandma Ruthie. We had quite a system. When I was pregnant, I did much of the cooking and she the outside work. It was there that I learned to do "versatile" cooking—to create and oh, yes to cook in volume. I would bake eight loaves of bread at a time. Mickey (Walter now) who was 14 or 15 years old would keep a watchful eye on how the bread was lasting and when Bobby was born, Mickey lucked out. I had just baked eight loaves before going into labor. Mickey made sure those eight loaves lasted until I got home after two weeks at my folks' following the birth. For the next baking, Mickey offered to knead the dough for me—and he did.

Bobby was born August 20, 1947. He was our largest baby, 9 ¼ pounds, also the easiest delivery. The day before he was born I had processed three canners full of green beans, a total of nine hours of cooking. It was a hot, long day. At 11PM a backache told me this was the time. He arrived at 5AM. He grew fast and was a good baby.

Indeed, it seemed as though I was pregnant all the time I was on the farm—and I was, almost. Ruth (Tina) was on the way before we moved to New London to take the high school football coaching job in summer of 1948.

In New London we first rented a house one mile east of town on Route 162. It wasn't a bad house, but again it wouldn't heat and had an inadequate water system. We moved into town on Coleman Court in 1949 and bought our first home through the help of Forrest and Ruth Matter, who helped us with a down payment. New London was a great town. They learned to love Bob. His name is still legend there all these years later. Bob was successful everywhere he went. He had winning teams in basketball at Jeromesville and the town took him into their hearts. I never got acquainted while there—must have been because of too many little ones. In New London, I had some good friends, especially after we moved into town. We attended the Methodist Church there, though not regularly—again, I was so swamped.

Ann started first grade in New London with a wonderful teacher, Mrs. Hyatt. Ann was *most* apprehensive. Bob wanted to hold her back one year, but Mrs. Hyatt said, "Get back to your classes and let me handle Ann; she's just having trouble cutting the apron strings." I hadn't realized that she was so dependent on me. Of course, when you seldom have babysitters, children are pretty tied to mom, the constant companion.

Tina arrived April 4, 1949, a 9-pounder. She was so good. I truly felt she was deaf, because Ann and Bobby played under her bed, ran up and down the stairs and she never opened an eye.

In the summer of 1952, Bob got a call from the Board of Education in Portsmouth, Ohio, inviting him to come down for an interview for the head football coaching job. We were so *excited*. Bob had acquired an excellent record at New London; in fact, he received the Ohio Coach of the Year Award for AA schools in his 1951 season. He was making about $2600 at New London and by his working Saturdays at a grocery, he made $10 extra per week and this paid for the bulk of our groceries. He was asked by the Portsmouth Board of Education to state what salary he would come for. After spending several hours deliberating this, he decided he wanted $4000. When his contract came, it was for $4400. We were on top of the world.

Portsmouth was normally a town of 30,000 people, but because the government was building a big atomic energy plant north of the city at the time, the census had swelled considerably and housing was a most critical problem. We spent our first six weeks there in a summer camp on the Ohio River owned by Ott Sands, a local sporting goods dealer. We were finally able to rent a house at 1549 Fourth Street, just four streets up from the Ohio River. It was said in the 1937 flood, the water rose so high it was in the second floor of our house. Of course, the levee was built shortly after, with flood gates, etc. But somehow I never felt completely secure. We paid $75 per month—a rent considered really high—because of the A-plant.

We stayed in Portsmouth only two years. Bob, again, was very successful. The year before he was hired, Portsmouth had experienced 10 losses within two years. Bob had a wonderful undefeated season and again won the Ohio Coach of the Year Award, this time for A-level ball. For his efforts, he was presented with a trophy topped by a large gold football at the Coach of the Year ceremony in Columbus.

Although Bob was very successful, I never really cared for Portsmouth—don't think I care for river towns or maybe I just had too much on my hands to get to know the town. Also I was labeled a "non-partyer" right at the start. The fact that we moved into the Fourth Street home in the fall and Frank was born November 19, 1952—five weeks premature, at only 5 lbs and 2 oz—didn't make party life look too attractive to me. My days were filled! I was so busy. I couldn't have cared less that the staff wives said I was a wet blanket because I didn't drink and went home too early (midnight.) I was only afraid this would backfire on Bob.

The Gardners, Radio and Helen, became our good friends. Jim Gardner, their older son, played tackle and John, the younger son, a guard position. Later, after high school, in the early 60's, Bob was killed in an auto accident the night of his bachelor party, three days before his wedding. We drove down to Portsmouth for his funeral. The Gardners are the only people I remained in touch with over the years. The town of Portsmouth died down after the construction personnel left the A-plant site.

May Day at Ashland College in 1954 brought Bob back to the college for the day, and he was approached by the Board of Trustees to consider the Football/Basketball coaching position. I felt it could be a dreadful mistake to come back to Ashland, his alma mater, but Bob really wanted to take the job. Time proved it was a good move, but at the time I really wondered if it was wise.

In June we found ourselves on the move again. Another baby was due in August. We decided to buy the old Methodist Church parsonage in Nankin since we couldn't find anything suitable to rent. The morning the moving van arrived in Portsmouth, the birth process started for Molly, our fifth child. The water broke at 6:00AM. We started the movers on the loading, then headed for Ashland, a four-hour drive away. Actually, I waited around for a week after we got to Ashland, wondering when she would appear. When I developed the traditional backache and labor was established, we went to the hospital where the doctors and nurses told me I must prepare for a still-birth, as they could detect no heartbeat. Imagine my joy to awake from the brief anesthetic to hear my baby crying. Molly was born June 23, 1954, weighing 4 lbs 3 oz, 7 weeks premature. She remained in the hospital for one month in the isolette and, later, the incubator, until her weight reached 5 pounds and she was able to maintain normal body temperature. It was a strange summer. I was glad to be settled into the Nankin house where we were to live for the next eighteen years. It was the home where the children all had their childhood memories. It was good to be back with our families and back with college friends.

Bob became quite involved with building an athletic program at Ashland College and teaching in the Education Department. He was finally doing what he really wanted to do. To back up a bit, Bob had decided to start work on his Masters Degree at the University of Wisconsin. The first summer of his program saw us on our way to Madison. We rented, along with four other families, a huge fraternity house, a most unusual house said to be of Frank Lloyd Wright design. It was a long summer. We got pretty homesick, glad to see Ohio again in August.

In 1953 we made our second trip to Madison and rented a home a few miles west of the city. And in 1955, our third summer was spent in a rented English Tudor, the parsonage for a most unusual Unitarian Church that was quite a sightseers' attraction. This year we took a babysitter along, but Bob was so busy with his classes and it was so beastly hot, it wasn't a good summer (for me, anyway.) We were there for eight weeks. We had company from Ohio for seven of those weekends. Molly cried all summer. We finally learned she was quite anemic. I felt like such a bad mother. She was a year old, not walking. And Frank was two, not potty-trained and into everything. I recall it was a summer with many thunderstorms and much tension. I marvel that Bob could turn out all the excellent work he did. Guess it showed what a great student he was.

Our fourth—and last—summer session for the Master's program we rented a home in Oregon, Wisconsin, ten miles south of Madison. I had finally gotten my driver's license and recall that I was feeling some degree of independence. Oregon had a swimming pool and the older children learned to swim there. Bob's Masters Degree was in School Administration. And oddly enough, he never used it. He continued teaching and coaching.

While in New London in the fall of 1949 an epidemic of Hepatitis struck the town. Several were hospitalized. Bob should have been, but he wouldn't give up on football practice. He was miserable. Years later we were told that as a result of this illness, he gradually developed a block in the splenic vein. And ten years later, after some episodes of vomiting blood, he was sent to Ohio State University Hospital in Columbus to be checked out. March 23, 1959, he was in surgery for nine-and-a-half hours. His spleen was removed and his splenic vein grafted to the kidney vein in order to bypass the obstruction. The technical name for the surgery was a Splenectomy and Renal Shunt. Bob remained in the hospital for eight weeks— three weeks on the critical list. And he had to undergo surgery three more times while there. He developed a staph infection, abscesses formed, thus the additional surgeries.

It was a terrible time in our lives. I stayed in Columbus for seven weeks, never coming home. Much of the time was blank for Bob—due to medication. I was glad he couldn't recall all that happened. The three older children stayed with Ward and Virginia Pfeiffer in Nankin, good friends of ours through the years. The younger two—Frank, 5 years, and Molly, 4, stayed with my folks, Grandma and Grandpa Fluke. My mother felt it best not to discuss our being gone so long; however, one day Molly announced, "I guess my mom doesn't love us. She never came back." Mother felt so bad and hastened to explain and reassure both Frank and Molly.

Bob did get home in late April by ambulance. He was sent home with tubes in the surgery site and instructions on how to irrigate through the tubes. Being in Columbus all those weeks, was such a frightening time. I felt so lost, so scared. Every night I telephoned my folks, collect, and by hearing my mother's reassuring words I could make it through another day. Once I had to have her come down to stay overnight. I don't know what I would have done without her, without family and friends. Rev. Zavitz came down to see Bob. I know his visit was appreciated greatly, but in those days I didn't really experience deep-down faith in God. I just drifted from day to day, scared. Scared for Bob, scared for the time to come. It was to be 13 years later that I finally had the real feeling of what it means to be a Christian. It would have helped during that time surrounding Bob's surgery if I could have felt that God was right there with us. Now I know that He was there. I needed to grow, to know and to feel. I was 35 years old then. Bob was 37. It was a most difficult time in our lives...to be followed by many more.

Bob did recover, at least to a degree, but he was never really in good health again. He had to undergo surgery six or seven more times as the years went by, the most serious being the muscle repair in 1960, one year after the shunt was done in Columbus. Because of the various surgeries while there and the staph infection, his wound was left open with those irrigation tubes, so he later needed the repair. During all those various sessions in surgery he was given large amounts of drugs, pain-killers, necessary, I'm sure. But the sum total was too much, leaving him with a tendency for dependency on something to ease the pain and tension of his life. It was so very sad to watch. How devastating for Bob. He had achieved much success in a relatively short few years and suddenly life became very hard. He became very quiet, communicated with us less and less, and spent much time in Mansfield General Hospital under the care of a psychiatrist. He retired from coaching, then the Athletic Directorship and finally, in 1972, from teaching. Life became empty for him, I'm sure. I felt so inadequate to help him. One does not watch an active, successful, gregarious man retreat without great sadness.

In the spring of 1972 we bought 40 acres 2 ½ miles north of Nankin and during the summer built a house in the woods. I'm sure I enjoyed the building process and the move to the country far more than did Bob. I really believe he didn't want to leave Nankin, his various gardens and truck patches. I designed the all-electric house. LaRue Builders built it from my plans. Shortly afterwards electric rates began to climb and we felt we had made a poor choice on electricity for fuel. So we bought a small wood stove. Later it was to be replaced by a larger, more efficient stove that would heat the entire house. Because of the 20 acres of woods we owned, it was no problem to find wood to fire the stove. Trees were cut during the summer and in early October we would have a wood-splitting day with the family. On October 6, 1975 we were having the annual event. Bob seemed to enjoy the day. However, that evening he complained of not feeling well and he went to bed early. About 10:00PM he was up and vomited blood. As our eyes met we both knew this was something serious—so like the earlier time. Molly's boyfriend Glenn Smith was at the house and the four of us hurried in to Ashland Samaritan Hospital. Bob's doctor was summoned. He tried to stop the bleeding in the ER without success and Bob was admitted into the acute medical unit. After an extremely restless night, the bleeding continued and by mid-morning he was on his way to Cleveland Clinic by squad. Dr. Huggins rode with him. The doctor told me that Bob was aware of where he was and where he was going, but Bob lost consciousness by the time he got to the ER at the Clinic.

Twelve days. Everything that could be done was done, more surgery. It was the same problem again. This time it could not be corrected. How helpless we felt standing around his bed, all the tubes, the respirator, the monitors. No improvement. Finally only the life support systems kept him alive. October 17, 1975 Bobby went with me to the Clinic—just us two. We were informed of Bob's hopeless condition and told that I could sign to have the life support discontinued. The day before I had seen an elderly man faced with the same decision regarding his wife. Through tears, he signed the necessary papers. With Bobby's support, I likewise made the same decision. Bobby made a request that we be allowed to see Bob once again, without all the medical equipment. The request was granted and we got to say our goodbyes. He was at peace, unencumbered by all the medical devices. I'll always be grateful to Bobby for making the request. Actually, medical units don't have much time, but they graciously granted Bobby's request. Bless them.

On the way home from Cleveland, Bobby told me he thought I should trade cars. He said Bob didn't like my car—a Pinto wagon—and urged me to get another car. The girls and the little ones were sleeping on the living floor when we came in. In shocked silence they heard the word. Though expected, it was still such a shock. Later they told us that at the time Bob died they had been at Gerwigs White Barn Market in Bob's old Valiant wagon and it stalled out in the parking lot. Someone brought them home. Bob wanted to play a new tape he had of Christian singer, Len Mink—a song about being raised up and healed in the name of Jesus that he thought would be helpful to us. I didn't want to say no, but I could barely bear to listen. I wanted to go and scream in my bedroom, but my training had been to keep coping and I did. Whenever I hear Len Mink, though, a wave of sadness closes over me and I remember that day.

Two churches supported us through these sad days. Bob and I had been attending the Ashland Assembly of God with Bobby's, Tina's and Molly's families. Pastor Norman Lance was a great help. Cremation was followed by private funerals at the Assembly of God Church and a few days later at the Ashland College Chapel. Our old friends at the Nankin Federated Church also responded to our needs. The following May I returned to the Nankin church, back among old friends. I had learned to enjoy much in the Assembly of God church, especially their open, expressive way of showing their love for the Lord, but it was also good to be "home" at the Nankin church again.

And so I find myself alone in life. Because of Bob's failing health over all those years, I'm sure I was gradually preparing for a life alone. In a Death and Dying class I took at Ashland College in the summer of 1979, I learned that I had probably gone through an "anticipatory" type of grief, gradually adjusting and sorting it all out. I was glad I was already employed. That adjustment had already been made. In August of 1978 I decided to sell my house to Molly and Glenn and build another house, a smaller one, next door. Again, I designed the house, and this time builder Bob Simonson built it from my plans. The house is just right for me. The Warm Morning stove keeps me very cozy. The family cuts the firewood. Glenn plows the snow on my driveway.

Employment

I worked for Dr. Huggins from August, 1972 to February, 1978. He was a good man to work for. He never lost his temper and he had such a good sense of humor. I was never sure if he really, truly liked "medicine," as he seemed to lean more toward the computer approach to everything. When I had a hysterectomy in 1975 and was off work for five weeks, he paid me my full pay every week. Earlier, during one of the times Bob was hospitalized and Molly was working at Riverside Christian Training School, the doctor asked me if I wouldn't like to have Molly home. I *did* need her. He flew his plane down to Hazard, Kentucky and brought Molly home. These were the extras he provided. In the winter of 1978 Dr. Huggins went half-days-only with his practice. At the same time, I was having back problems which required removal of a ruptured disc. Because the practice had gone to half-days, I did not go back to work there after my surgery.

A couple of unsatisfactory jobs followed in the spring and summer of 1978. Later in the summer I got a call from Betty Woodbury at Ashland College asking if I would consider working in the Registrar's Office. I got the job and stayed for three years, leaving because I felt I had to have more money. I applied for the job of Office Manager with Dr. M, a new Ob-Gyn in town. I was hired, but it proved to be a most unsatisfactory job. I found him difficult to work for. In his own words about himself: "I'm hell to work for, and I know it." One day I could not stand it any longer. I gave two weeks' notice, but ended up leaving before the expected date. The doctor and I were miles apart on moral and ethical issues. I am sure it was his wife who had hired me. I really was not his choice. His wife didn't want me to leave, but she understood my feelings.

As Dana Knapp, our minister at the time, said, "You took a real step in faith with no job in sight." But I'm sure the good Lord knew what was best for me. I called Dick Obrecht, my former boss at the college, to check to see if my old job at the Registrar's Office might be open. The girl who replaced me didn't like my job and wanted another position that had just become available. So I returned to the college and the making of transcripts. When I started at the college in 1978, the annual number of transcripts produced was 3000. In 1984 the total had jumped to 8000. I'm grateful they made room for me to come back.

In January of 1985 I applied for "widow benefits" and started to receive Social Security. By keeping my total hours per week down to 24 I could qualify. The three-day work week is great. The Tuesdays and Thursdays off are wonderful. I'll forever be grateful to Dick Obrecht, a great boss, such a good, moral Christian man.

Family

I have been blessed with wonderful in-laws all the way. Grandma Ruthie and Grandpa Frank were always very good to me. Bob used to say they always took my side in every difference. I couldn't have asked for better in-laws. I treasure the years and memories with them. Not all of the grandchildren will remember them personally, but their influence lives on.

My sons-in-law and daughters-in-law are a blessing. Not many can say that! How could I have been so fortunate?

As life goes on my relationship with offspring and their families is one of the most important aspects of my life. Friends are nice, but it's the day-to-day thoughts and feelings of family that really count. Picnics at the pond, birthday get-togethers, holiday meals with the big gang gathered around, breakfasts at Hart of Savannah or Perkins are so much fun. So nice to included.

I've always felt that family fellowship around the table—for all the holidays, especially—just could not be topped. I've always hoped that all the little ones will have some nice memories of Grandma's house. They are growing up so fast. Sometimes I wish I could slow down the whirl of time and have more time to enjoy them.

Would I like to do any part of my life over? No, not really, but I can tell you that the best part was when the kids were "home" in Nankin, and Bob was well and felt successful. They were all so on-the-go, the boys in athletics, the girls in cheerleading and the various busy things kids are now involved in. I was *really* busy, not much time for myself, but it was by far our best time as a family. I just didn't realize it at the time.

Louise

REFLECTIONS ON BUSYNESS
AND QUIET TIMES
Written in 1989

In my younger years I was so busy raising my family that I really never took time to try to figure out what I should strive for, what my goal in life should be. There wasn't time to think about why I was here (born) and what my purpose and objective for life was to be. I was just too busy.

In fact, in Ann's book in 1989—writing about her life, growing up and her physical [and mental health] difficulties as an adult—she also wrote about me, her mom. She was uneasy about how I would react to her observations and memories of me in the days when 24 hours was all I had to work with and it wasn't enough. I wasn't upset when I read her recollections, though; I know, in all honesty, that I did portray a "work horse" image—not her words, mine. Wistfully, I somehow wish it had been different.

I didn't take enough time to smell the roses, nor did I take enough time for me. How I treasured the brief time at the end of a hot, work-filled summer day when all the little bodies had been bathed and all were tucked into their beds, and I could grab a bath with Dove soap, in twice- or thrice-used bathwater (seemed water was always so precious,) And, in my robe, I would retreat to the backyard, breathe in the fresh night air, glimpse the stars as they winked through the apple tree, listen to the corn leaves rustle in the garden and hear the dog chains jangle in the kennel.

But I didn't question why I am here, what's for me in life as the years go by. If asked, I would have felt I lacked the intellect to try for an educated answer. Just to be able to cope with picking and freezing the peas the next day and still wash and hang outside three loads of Maytag-washed laundry before taking on a dozen fourth-graders at Vacation Bible School at the church the following morning was all I asked.

Powerful Katrinka—an old cartoon character—that was me! With tongue latched firmly between my teeth, I tackled all the tasks that awaited me. I was certain that I could do what was required and pride and years of training allowed me to see it through.

Workaholic? No, I don't think so, really, just a firmly embedded will to complete in an orderly fashion anything that I considered my responsibility.

Now, since I've been retired and been remarried for three years, I notice that I'm much more sensitive to thinking about the future, the quality of life, and listening for the hurts and pains of people—family, friends and contemporaries. I sometimes take on more than I should do...then I feel I've cheated those whom I wanted to help. I still find solitude in the evening—outside, with my feet propped up on a redwood bench on the patio, reading, thinking, praying. I've so much to be thankful for. It is a different time in life, different spouse, children grown and away, but I still treasure the quiet moments at dusk when it seems as though the world slows down a bit and the finches grab the final thistle seeds of the day from the nearby feeder, the chipmunks dart back and forth under my feet and the geraniums bloom in the tubs that border my sanctuary.

One of the nice things about retirement is being able to read or write when I want to. To get to take my 2-mile walk and be aware that today there are no real demands is a luxury for me.

I'm 65, now on Medicare. And it's not bad. Good health is sure a blessing.

Louise

CHARLIE IS HOME
May 31, 1990

He left us today,
No time to say goodbye.
Just an ordinary day.
Little did we know
It would be Charlie's last.

We remember—
His many contributions
To his church and community,
Baseball, softball, behind the plate.
Wherever, whenever,
He gave his best,
Always fair and firm.

He could make a point,
Give his view—
Question a decision,
In all church affairs,
Large or small.
He was always heard
—Mostly heeded—
And never taken for granted.

Small, mischievous boys,
Knew his wrath
As he faithfully guarded
Church properties.
To have to "ask Charlie"
Required "super" courage
From these same small boys
Who often performed
Daring, pesky acts.

Who will count
Our Sunday numbers,
Open the doors, ring the bell
And check the garbage?
I can just hear him say,
"You people—carry on!"
And our good Lord said,
"Charlie is home—
Play ball!"

CONTENTED YEARS WITH JIM CONERY
Written in 1990

A new era in my life. I fully expected to live out my life single, as are so many of my friends. It seemed there were so few eligible, good men available.

I'd known Jim Conery for about 45 years. Betty Brownson, Bob's sister, was babysitter for Jim and his first wife Freda, when they moved here from California. Jim was born and raised in Chico, California. He was sought out by Myers Pump to come to Ohio and bring the submersible pump—or was it the jet pump?—he had designed. So Jim, Freda, and sons Leonard and Billy rented a house on Grant Street, two doors down from Bob's family, the Brownsons. The Conerys came in January. It snowed and being unused to snow, Jim got stuck in his driveway. Mick (Grandpa Brownson) came to his rescue. The Conerys and the Brownsons became close friends and remained so down through the years.

Freda died of cancer, spending the last months of her life with the Brownsons in their home on Broad Street. Jim married Anne Kiner from Mississippi, a cousin of Eslie Jones', the year after Freda's death. (Eslie was the husband of Betty Brownson.) Anne was an R.N., but she never worked as a nurse after she married Jim and came to Ohio. Jim built a home for them at 1542 60 South in 1953. Anne and Jim's daughter Barbara was born in 1954 and son John in 1956.

Jim "retired" from Myers Pumps in 1985, though he then worked at home for them for ten years, doing drafting, design and much computer work. At the time of this writing—1990–Jim is still under partial contract with Myers. This contract is scheduled to end in September of this year. This spring he was asked to design eight new pumps for Myers. He worked many long hours and completed the assignment. How wonderful to have this great talent and to be successful all these years. Jim at 81 years old could put most men to shame in engineering. How great for his self-esteem. I know he is considered an expert in the field of sewer/pump systems. Sometimes he gets up in the middle of the night to work out solutions to a problem that have just come to him.

Jim's wife, Anne, died in December of 1985 after several years of heart problems, heart surgery and poor health. Jim missed her very much. Not one to like to be alone—he especially hated to cook and eat alone— he started to look around and see who might be willing to share his life. He thought of Mabel (Grandma Ruthie's sister) but she didn't seem interested. Then he asked Betty if she thought I might be interested in going out. I wasn't too anxious to change my lifestyle. I was used to being my own person, had my good friends Betty, Marilyn and Marie and we went out a lot on weekends. I wasn't sure I really wanted a man in my life.

Jim and I did start to date. Our first date was with Pete and Betty Smith. We went to Chi-Chi's in Lorain. It felt really strange. I really had seen very little of Jim or Anne in recent years—didn't feel at all acquainted, so had to start over.

Jim let me know early that he did hope our relationship might grow and lead to marriage. We went to a couple of plays in Cleveland, one was "Do Black Patent Leather Shoes Really Reflect Up?" It was winter— cold, snow, and not too nice. I'm sure it was a strain for Jim to go through courtship. And he minded the cold weather and driving too many miles. I found it difficult to get acquainted, couldn't make myself take hold of his arm on icy sidewalks. It just seemed too foreign.

At Easter I told him I didn't think it would work. I had asked him to come to dinner on Easter Sunday with all the clan, but cancelled him out. He felt really bad. He said, "I would have fought for you, except for our age difference." I was 61 and he 77. He felt it would be wrong to urge me to stay in the relationship. Jim had all the qualities I liked and needed. I felt that I needed to bend, to be able to give some, and to allow someone to share in my life. And so we resumed dating. Once I got over my reserve, all went well.

We were married August 2, 1986 on Jim's birthday in the Nankin Church by Rev. Ed Tolley. A dinner reception was held at the Accent Room at Ashland College, following the afternoon ceremony. We went to Atwood Lodge down near Dover and New Philadelphia for a 2-day wedding trip. We should go down again—maybe this year after our fourth anniversary.

Jim is a good man. I'm happy. We are happy. Our lives have grown ever closer together as time goes by.

Jim built his own home when he and Anne were married, as I've written. It was a year in the building. He had only minimal outside help. Grandpa Brownson helped some and also Fred Covert. It is a well-built house, good detail and finishes, cedar closets, many good shelves in the den and living room. But after much struggle for both of us with the sewer system and lawn, especially the big bank out in front, we wondered how long we could give proper care to the sizable lot.

I checked out the new condos on Avalon Drive in Ashland behind the stadium and fell for one. Beautiful! I knew I could be happy there, but could Jim? Jim agreed to take a look, and he liked what he saw. We signed a purchase agreement in May. Our plan was to rent out the condo for three or four years, then move in. After another struggle with the steep bank in front of Jim's house—finally hired the work done— Jim contacted a real estate agent and signed a contract to sell his house. The condo is being purchased jointly by the both of us. It will be "ours." I feel good about it and so does Jim. Because we needed to take one of the two condo bedrooms for Jim's work area—computer, desk and drafting table—it cuts down on bedroom guest-space. However, we think we can squeeze in a sofa-sleeper in the same room and still be able to have folks stay over.

So this summer will be my last to plant flowers and tomato plants, dig up flower beds (and hurt my back.) I like to mow with the riding mower, but there is a lot of trim that has to be done by hand-push mower.

Once again, we combine possessions, sort out and trash, burn, give to Goodwill and make sale. Can I tolerate a big yard sale? Guess it is the only way to go, though I find it difficult to think about. I don't want possessions to rule our lives. So often the elderly continue to live in the clutter and accumulation of a long life, and therefore find it nearly impossible to make a major change when they are no longer able to cope with the proper upkeep of a home and all it entails. We want to make this move, sort out and cull all unneeded "stuff" now. I asked Tom Rowe, builder of the new condos, why he did not put in basements. I thought there should be a basement area for storage. He answered by saying, "What do you want a basement for? Basements are a place to store the junk you no longer want...and the kids don't want it either." How true!

During this time in my life I have done quite a lot of volunteering. I have a need to be busy, just can't sit around (unless I have a good book.) So I decided to check out the possibility of volunteering at Samaritan Hospital.

In the fall of 1986 I signed up to work at the reception desk, four hours a day, every other Tuesday morning. I did this for a couple years. Then I was asked to consider being Vice-President of the Samaritan Auxiliary, a job that had me taking all prospective volunteers on a tour of the hospital and then helping them decide where they would best be suited as a volunteer. This VP position never lasts more than one year. I did enjoy the position and felt I was good at it. I was then asked to be President of the Auxiliary. I declined. Not my cup of tea. Because I knew that clerical help was needed in the business office of the hospital, I signed on there. I've found the computer—quite mundane—to be quite enjoyable. Some typing and filing is required. Because of my vulnerable back, I asked to be relieved of constant filing, stooping, etc. The office manager has been flexible on my behalf.

I've also considered Hospice or teaching adults to read as possible additional volunteer areas, but so far I've not pursued either one. I'm not at all sure I could handle patient/family contact in Hospice work, but there is office help needed there.

Volunteering is a very worthwhile occupation—very much needed and greatly appreciated. It feels good to know that your efforts, though small, are needed in a large operation. Personal time, donated, is a true gift.

Louise

FINAL DAYS

Death comes to us all.
It is inevitable.
Sometimes it snuffs out
A tiny new life,
Sometimes it comes
In the prime of life.
But most often it creeps up
On us when we are old
With faltering steps
And weary hearts
Worn out by decades
Of living and struggle.

Pain rears its ugly head
Making jeering faces at us,
It tortures our hearts
And saps our strength.
It twists our emotions
And weakens our reasoning.
The focus of our lives
Is dark and bleak and hopeless
And we feel trapped in
Its binding, strangling clutch.
We cry out for help,
For love, for understanding
For freedom from
The vise-like grip of death.
We are surrounded
By family who love us
But they have little knowledge
Of what to do.
They try all the home remedies,
Including loving, soft-cooked foods,
Foods we can't even force down.

We pray to the good Lord
For release, For healing,
For freedom from
The nagging, constant pain.
And the days drag by, slowly
Painfully, down into darkness.
No one sleeps—
The family huddles around

Anxious days—
Dark, pain-filled nights.
And the clock ticks off
The days, hours, and minutes.

Only our God knows
The time for our final breath.
Only He can close
The tired and weary eyes
And allow yet another
Dear soul to slip through
To experience
The land of life eternal—pain-free,
Face to face with our Maker.
The battle is over—
The victory won.
Hallelujah!!

Another child of God
Has come Home.

Louise

COMFY SHOES
Written in 1990

It has just occurred to me that Reeboks are a very important part of my life. They have given me courage to do what heretofore seemed impossible. They make me feel young, capable and agile. At an age when so many of my contemporaries are moaning around about their feet, I'm feeling good about mine.

Whoever dreamed up the modern-day walking shoe/jogging shoe should be knighted or at least have bestowed upon them the Nobel Prize for Podiatry. I can't imagine how I existed before their inception.

Shoes—all our lives we are so aware of what we will wear on our feet. We want pretty, smart-looking shoes—and in our youth, often nearly ruin our feet because we allow ourselves to be talked into wearing potentially-crippling shoes. Then in our 60's the bunion joints cry out in their torture and pain.

Gone are the barefoot days of my youth, when the hot sand of summer felt so good underfoot and the cool evening dew on the grass so soothing to the calloused feet of this farmer's daughter. Grade school days brought brown leather oxfords, serviceable, neat and ugly. I longed for Mary Janes in black patent, maybe even with the ankle strap!

In high school huaraches became the thing. I endured their overwhelming odor in an attempt to be in style. They squeaked when I walked. Yet I was intrigued by their style.

At 18, after high school graduation, I worked for a physician and purchased my first pair of "nurses" shoes. They were comfortable, but how un-fun to apply the white polish daily. It caked and dried, so the shoes cracked. They looked so ugly.

Then it was "war time," the reason for so many things I found less than grand. Like leg makeup. No nylons available—we did without and applied Bonnie Bell suntan lotion in an attempt to give the impression we had tanned, lean and silky legs. However, leg makeup is messy; the slightest moisture on a hot day caused distressing runs, spots and blotches. The bedsheets took on a golden glow and the washcloths an odd rusty hue.

As a young working woman in the 1940's I had a bit more freedom; I'm afraid my shoe choices were not always good. I once bought what I considered to be a stylish pair of brown pumps and wore them to Cleveland to visit my sister, Elinor, who was living and working there. I felt so smart walking up the streets in Cleveland, riding the street cars—but by early evening my feet were burning up with pain and I couldn't wait to get back to Elinor's apartment to remove the offending shoes.

I can't recall when I got my first pair of sneakers. Their lack of support was hard on the arches of my narrow feet, but the freedom-feeling was there. The canvas construction didn't wear long and, again, damp sneakers/tennis shoes have a most unpleasant odor.

Then came the early 1980's, and I found Trax shoes at K-Mart. For $9.95. I could buy what seemed quite comfortable. They didn't wear well, nor did they have much arch support. Then in 1986, I discovered Reeboks and I delighted in their comfort. During an episode of "painful heel," I found a special padded insole for my Reeboks. These made me feel like I was walking on air. How I could have used these in my childbearing and child-raising years!

My Reeboks have taken me miles and miles, indoors and out, to the grocery store and to the mall. Oh, I know they don't look that smart and stylish. But now, at my age, I've sacrificed a stylish image for comfort. My Reeboks are better than boots in a medium snowfall, safer to walk in and fairly waterproof. At age 65 I should be into fancy boots and higher heels, but who cares! I'm comfortable! I'm me! Thank God for Reeboks!

Louise

BABY MAGIC TO WHEELCHAIRS
Written in 1991

Today as I held my four-day-old grandchild, I found myself contemplating the riddle of life, the cycle of life that takes us from birth to the grave. At either end of the life cycle we are totally helpless, ever dependent on loving hands to administer to us, to watch over us. We have virtually no control over our lives at either end. We are so vulnerable.

The tears of the newborn command prompt action from another generation, usually mother, but often whomever is nearby. Young fathers, grandmothers, all are quick to see that our new little being is dry, warm and fed. We check for drafts, cold little feet and hands, gently patting and reassuring that all is well, they are loved and should have nothing to fear.

The tears of the elderly come from their loneliness, their dependency, coupled with depression, deteriorating health, diminishing abilities and lack of control over their lives. And again, another generation is in charge, usually a middle-aged (or older) daughter. Does it seem the younger generation, as caregivers for the elderly, aren't quite as quick to jump into action to hug, pat and reassure these older vulnerable ones as they are with the babies?

In the years that bridge infancy and old age, we grow in stature, obtain knowledge and form our attitudes for life. But have we learned? Have we learned compassion and caring or have we settled into a "me-first" posture in life?

All of us will experience these opposite ends of the cycle. We will not remember our time as a newborn, and often we will not be aware of our final days...one generation caring for another.

Young women are waiting longer to start a family. These same women seem often struggle with fertility problems. Disappointments and failure with attempts to start a family often plague their lives. What is God telling us?" Very young mothers, teenagers who become mothers—of which there are so many—lack experience and will struggle desperately to raise a child. Who is in charge? Who will suffer? Our society is changing. We are living longer. Caregivers of the elderly are becoming older themselves, less able to cope with the time-consuming, physically-demanding care of aging parents.

This morning I held my newborn grandson, my fifteenth grandchild, my younger son's child from his second marriage (his wife's second marriage also.) Extended families, older children, former mates, financial sorting-out, custody, these are the norm for today—all creating pressure and tension. But this second marriage for both of them, contains love, real respect for each other and a wonderful desire to make the marriage work, to interweave into the fabric of life four other children, his and hers, to make it work for the benefit of all involved.

As I held this little boy in my arms and looked into those beautiful eyes, I had prayed for his life, that he might enjoy good health, grow strong, be educated, and most of all that he will be a caring person, a positive force, a servant to his fellow man and to God.

I bathed him. It was my privilege. I enjoyed every moment of the experience. I washed his little head and noted that the reddish-blonde hair was much like his father's, my fourth-born, with a strong promise of curls. I toweled his hair dry and felt the satin smoothness of his newborn skin. I smoothed Baby Magic into his fingers and toes and over his little tummy, ever mindful of the stump of the cord, a reminder of his 9-month lifeline to his mother. He cried but little and I thought, "Well, Grandma, you haven't completely lost your touch." I dressed him in his dear little clothes, quite different from my experience of 30 years ago with my own children. Gone are the tummy bands, diaper pins, and plastic pants. I am so glad to know that receiving blankets are still in vogue and I loved the sensation of laying him on the flannel square, corner-wise, and then bringing the three corners over him, one by one. The next motion of cupping his head in my left hand, his tiny bottom in my right and raising him to my left shoulder nearly brought tears to my eyes as I recalled all the times I'd done this with my five children. He felt so vulnerable, but so warm and cuddly. The start of a new life, full of promise, full of surprises to come as I watch him grow.

This afternoon I drove 10 miles to see my 90-year-old mother in a nursing home. I felt her pain keenly as I watched her struggle with confusion versus reality. She was sleeping soundly on her bed when I came in and looked comfortable. I hated to wake her, but knew I would be a bright spot for the day, even if she does get a little angry with me sometimes. I looked down at her lined face, at eyes that don't see well, that can no longer read, at her lips that don't smile very much, and hated to disturb her.

"Mom," I call quietly. Her eyes pop open. She knows and recognizes me. And she does smile. I suggest that she remain lying down. I'll pull up a chair. "No." She insists on getting up and into her avocado green swivel-rocker. Our conversation starts. As usual, it is entirely focused on her and her existence in the nursing home. Today she was totally consumed with her blood pressure. Some nurse's aide had told her of a high reading at the early-morning, pill-time reading. Mom had asked the aide (as always) what the reading was. Then she frets all day. I've suggested to the staff that maybe they all might low-key it by saying, "Oh, it's a bit high today," but then reassure her that blood pressure fluctuates a bit. She had tried to get me by phone all morning, but was unable to remember how to complete the dial and was most disturbed by a recording that indicated my number "was no longer a working number." She asked if my number had been changed. Poor dear, each unsuccessful experience is so shattering.

My mother can't recall the bath schedule or the day of the week when she gets her hair set. Each day is a jumble. She hallucinates, sees "bugs," spots, tracings and borders. The professional medical people tell me to remain supportive with realism and to gently reassure her the "bugs," the mounds of their "carcasses," are not there. The floral patterns on the walls, borders around the doorways, the green patches of grass on the floor really aren't there. All this bring anger. She can tolerate, just barely, that the staff cannot see these things, but from me she expects more agreement. Then I feel so torn, guilty that I've let her down.

Many falls and much weakness have undermined her confidence and she asks repeatedly, "When will I get well?" I can't say she will get well. It seems best to try to assure her that she is doing the very best she can and to encourage her to believe that all of us (family and staff) have her utmost comfort in mind. Paranoia takes its toll. She feels the staff is laughing at her over the "bugs" and the fact she has difficulty telling time and heads for the dining hall for breakfast at 2:00AM.

She fights this gradual drifting into total dependency. She tries to remember the names of aides, and her doctor, who says she is building no new memory. In some ways she is so vital and this, no doubt, makes life more difficult for her than if she didn't care, wasn't aware. I bought her a wheelchair. She can't/won't say "wheelchair," but refers to it as a "buggy" or "cart." Her days are long with nothing to do, no desire for crafts or TV, and she naps most of her day.

My mother worked hard, a farmer's wife, the mother of five children, a widow of ten years now. Little money or material things curtailed her life dreams. Her good moral character has been an example to us all. It is sad to watch her decline, to see a very aware and curious lady try to fight life, to see her experience abnormal compulsions in an attempt to keep order, constantly "sorting" her closets and drawers. The burning need to organize seems misdirected and unnecessary to me, but it is somehow necessary to her. I care. I try to give her quality time, frequent visits and to be her liaison with the staff. It isn't enough. It never is.

Roles are reversed. Today I ate lunch with Mother at the nursing home. She told me that she now thinks of me as her mother and wonders if I think that is strange. Not at all. My mother has become the child dependent on me and her family. And I have become the parent.

The generations—the newborn grandchild and his aging great-grandmother—will never really know each other. Baby Frankie, too young, Great-Grandma with too little quality time left in her life to watch him grow.

Sometimes I hear my contemporaries lament that they have little left in life—retired from the work force and a bit lonely in their 60's, with the aches and pain of the aging. I have not experienced this "little left" feeling as yet. Perhaps it's because I can still provide a bridge among four generations and it feels good—a useful place in life, a nice place to be. As I pat on the Baby Magic and rock a tiny body or push a wheelchair down a long, carpeted hallway, I can understand my reason for being, my place in life at this moment. A good place to be.

And so soon I will be identified with the far-end of the spectrum of life.

Louise

ROBERT W. BROWNSON
FAMILY MEMORIAL SERVICE
Held in my woods, a commemoration of the
16th anniversary of Bob's death (October 17, 1975)
Written on October 13, 1991

Under overcast skies we walked back to a small clearing in the south section of my woods—22 of us in all. Bob's ashes had been scattered by son Bob in these woods. For this family service, a site was selected where it seemed just right to plant a tree in memory of Bob Brownson. The 6-foot pine tree selected by Frank, our youngest son, is a beautiful example of hardy stock, quite symmetrical and with branches full and round. The nursery man who dug and transported the tree to Frank, assured him that it would adapt well in the north Ashland County soil and would co-exist perfectly with the many oak and maple trees already there. It was further reported that it would probably grow to be at least 40 feet in height. I liked this idea of strength and durability.

The tree was transported back to the site by Frank in his Scout and unloaded beside the hole dug a bit earlier in the morning by Bob and Glenn. After the hole was enlarged a bit with several of the men taking turns with the shovel, the tree was carefully placed in its new and special home. When the hole was refilled, a joint effort again, 5 gallons of water were poured out around the roots in the very dry soil caused by an extremely dry summer. Without being told, all 22 formed a circle around the tree and our rather loosely formed service got under way.

Allow me to try to have you "feel" what we were all experiencing as we stood there with a constant sifting of falling leaves raining down on the assembled group. A gentle breeze caressed our faces—not cold—just a nice soft stirring of the leaves on the ground and in the air. Occasionally a few rain drops fell and the leaves dripped small drops on us. The air smelled fresh, nutty and oh! so good. I was experiencing the peaceful climate of the woods and the love and strength of the entire circle. I explained briefly that we were remembering a most special man, our father, our grandfather-to-some, father-in-law, and to me his wife of 32 years, by planting tree, a living memorial, commemorating the life of Bob Brownson in a place where we can all come in our own time to pause and reflect on his life—a place where we can whisper a quiet prayer, drop an acorn or some rose petals, or maybe even plant a flower.

I then related what the nursery man had said about the tree's projected growth and future life in the woods. This pine is the only one in the woods, truly an original, as Ann had used the word in her communication, for an original man who was himself wherever he went. The tree stands for life, ongoing life, a beacon for all to see who pass this way. A place to meditate by its sturdy boughs. Many in the circle today share in his blood and his genealogy.

Roses were always his favorite flowers. He gave them to others on special occasions. A dozen for the new mama and to each new baby he presented one red rose in a bud vase. He gave them to his mother and other mothers on their day and to me, his wife. After his death I have continued to carry on this tradition. And so roses seemed a most necessary part of the service. Pink roses were still blooming in my tiny garden. I picked them all and made up two small bouquets to be presented by the two youngest grandchildren—Frankie, 6 months old and Molly McFrederick, 6 years old. Frankie was assisted by his dad. Molly McFrederick carefully placed hers under the pine boughs. I had saved rose petals and had placed them in a basket along with strawberry-scented potpourri. Each grandchild was asked to take some and scatter them around the tree, which they did. The grandchildren totaled 17. Only Rodd can remember a bit about his grandfather—the rest are too young or not yet born at the time of his death. All the grandchildren attended the service except Megan who is in Wooster and of course John in California. Sherry's other two sons, Chad and Adam, are included in the 17, but were not with us today.

I then asked that all, individually, share their memories and thoughts, calling on the grands first. I was so proud of Matt who said, "I wish that I could have known Grandpa—I've heard so much about him." The others probably didn't feel comfortable enough to allow us a glimpse of their feelings. Glenn responded first for the adults. By this time the air was charged with emotion—hearts were filled with memories, emotions spilled out all around the circle. I do so wish that I could have savored the words spoken by all. Love, pride, tears and a wonderous feeling encompassed us all.

There is no way to describe the depth of what we were experiencing. I have never felt so much complete joy and pride in my family. Even as the tears flowed, I knew how truly blessed we all were and are. Loving tributes were given by all.

Tina read a letter, written by her dad in 1951, to his parents, in which he so wonderfully well expressed his love for them. He wrote so few letters. Grandma Ruthie had treasured this letter. I found it with her things—her treasures at the time of her death in 1982. I gave it to Tina to keep with her dad's various mementos, pictures, trophies, etc.

Molly spoke so warmly and lovingly about her dad—a beautiful tribute.

Bobby expressed himself so well—-from a deep loving spot in his heart. Frank related his treasured memories spent with his dad tramping this same woods, coon hunting and fishing at various ponds together.

Ann, bless her heart, had wanted so very much to be with us on this occasion—she almost bought a plane ticket home—had written a beautiful tribute to her dad full of memories that the rest said she put them all to shame by remembering so vividly events from their growing-up years. As her communication was read by Frank—her request—smiles and chuckles were seen and heard all around the circle there among the trees. Only she can weave a word picture and tug at our heart strings the way she does. Her written tribute was in California the night before, no time to "fax" it to us. I knew how much we were excited to hear from Ann. I called her early in the evening and "long-handed," via phone, her writing and typed it up before going to bed. Our service would not have been complete without her loving thoughts.

Now it is "Mom's" turn. I recalled how proud I was as a 15-year-old farm girl to be walked to the school bus after school by Bob Brownson, age 17—a ring leader in his class, a top scholar, athlete-playing both football and basketball as well as tennis. He asked me to go to his basketball game at Ashland High School. We had many great years together though his last years were a great sorrow to me, watching his health decline. I included Jim Conery in my thoughts. Jim, whom we have included in our circle and who means so much to us all.

I had made some copies of the hymn "Sweet, Sweet Spirit" which we sang followed by forming a tighter circle with all joining hands for the closing prayer. A candle was lit by Tina and Rodd (as the oldest grandchild present.) Rodd held the pewter hurricane lamp through the remaining moments of the service. Bob lead us in prayer. I wish I could remember his words, the remarks he made to preface his prayer. I was so moved.

My heart was filled with pride for all my family and memories of Bob. As the saying goes, "there wasn't a dry eye in the house"—in this case it was in the woods. As I looked at the circle, I realized just how much these wonderful, handsome and sensitive young folks were truly "feeling" as they—the adults, their parents—expressed their love and pride in their father, family and each one of them, their children. The circle let go. The hugging started. Around and around—all ages—brothers with sisters, spouses, grands and with me. I hugged every single one and felt the deep love and emotion within my arms. It was a day when it was okay to cry and to allow our feelings to show.

No one seemed quite ready to leave this awesome spot in the woods. We had been there for over 1 hour and it seemed like minutes only. Time just sort of stood still for us. It is a day we can never duplicate—it would never be the same. Bob said in his heartfelt thoughts preceding the closing prayer, "We cannot be assured that we will all be here tomorrow night." Life is precious, life is so fragile and so uncertain. We each took our portion of love and caring out of the woods with us to use as we choose in time to come. Our lives were enriched—all generations were one. We honored a good man and we felt his very presence among us as the sun came out and shone brightly on our circle. May the good Lord bless thee and keep thee while we are apart from one another. Our circle in heaven will be complete--just as He has promised.

Louise

AND FINALLY EVEN THE WHISPER FADED AWAY
For Death and Dying Class/Religion 350
Written in July, 1980

Twelve days was all he had. Such a short time to wage the battle for life. This was to be the final bout—we just didn't know it.

His career had been filled with much success, winning football teams, students waiting in line to register for the classes he taught. However, at 36, a cloud of gloom settled over his mental and physical being. Serious physical problems culminated in a 9 1/2 hour session in surgery, followed by two more trips to surgery within an 8-week hospital confinement. During those 8 weeks utter panic descended on me, a young mother of five, untrained, with no particular skills. Those 8 weeks that I remained with him, 80 miles from the children, parents and friends, remain agonizingly clear in my memory, years later.

The Lord spared him. He gave him 16 more years—years to teach, coach and to see his children grow up. However, a shroud of depression and gradually waning health caused him to slowly but surely give it all up, item by item. I am firmly convinced that there is very little more heartbreaking than to watch a successful, gregarious and talented man give up. And, yes, now I realize he died a personal death somewhere in those last 5 or 6 years of his life.

My heart and mind cried out for a way to deal with all this suffering and decline. How ironic that I, untrained, was forced into the role of trying to deal with this complicated demise of an extremely sensitive man. And, oh, how I erred! I truly grieved as the years went by. Now I realize that I denied his decline by attempting to hide the actual inward progression. I also became extremely angry. I felt put-upon, all the decisions to make, all the work to do and all the hospital visits. I tried to "keep a lid on it." I even developed an ulcer at one point, which I blamed on other causes, not on, perhaps, the real cause. Gradually it became a way of life.

October 5, 1975, a grand, fun-filled day with all the family home for what was to be his last conscious day. In the evening he suddenly complained of extreme nausea and fatigue. An internal hemorrhage had occurred. When he turned his ashen face to me, I sensed that this was an extremely serious situation.

Twenty-four hours in our local hospital could not halt the loss of blood. Alarmingly restless and agitated from the blood-loss, his last words to me were a command. "You get me over to the doctor's office and get me some help." How I wished that with his last words he would have told me that he loved me, instead. Maybe it is only in novels that such endearing last words are murmured. I did get help—action in the help of a transfer to the Cleveland Clinic. He never regained consciousness.

Twelve days was all the time he had left. Monitors, needles, tubes and dials—a nightmare of sounds, sensations and heartache. Everything was done that could be done, to no avail. His body could take no more. He was kept alive only by the pulsating machines. His will to live was gone.

During those twelve days it was our habit to gather as a family every evening for prayers—to pray for healing. On the eleventh day, I suddenly felt our prayers should be for release, instead. Not all the family agreed. We made our own pleas to The Almighty Father. Death the next day at noon— the day of our 32nd wedding anniversary. Bob was gone—only a worn-out earthly body remained, his soul free, home at last.

Indeed, he was given those 12 more years after his surgery. Was it to teach, to coach, to raise his family, or was it, perhaps, two years before his death, to dedicate his life to Christ? Victory, as well as death came that day.

Life goes on, memories fade, especially the painful ones. A little of this man lives on in everyone who knew and loved him well. With deep sadness I regret that I can no longer hear his voice. A powerful voice was stilled, little by little, until even the whisper faded away.

Louise

MY PHILOSOPHY OF DEATH
For Death and Dying Class/Religion 350
Written in July, 1980

As individuals, we are born to die. Between birth and death much takes place and what takes place is a preparation for that which is going to come after death. The quality of that preparation is what really counts.

My body counts for little, merely an assortment of chemicals of little value—but my soul, that which gives me life, represents the value of my life, my reason for being. My soul, when released from my earthly body by death, will be free to join eternity. And even though I would hope to be allowed more time for living, I won't dread the day death comes, because I do believe it will be a joyous occasion. With the right perspective on death and the right relationship with God, I am going to view death as a passageway to glory—a reunion with many loved ones who have already made the transition. My mind provides me with some great mental pictures.

Preparation for death is really a preparation for life—a never-ending process of learning to create a higher quality of life in the length of time given. I really liked the [class] discussion of the two kinds of time—Kronos and Kairos. We are all given twenty-four hours a day to live, but how we use that time is what is important. Sometimes the years given are few or cut short of the usual expected span of time. Therefore, the quality of life becomes paramount.

My father's life exemplifies, to me, the proper attitude toward life and death. At age eighty-three he has this spring retired from a lifetime of farming. His waning strength had made it very difficult for him to till his 180 acres these past two or three years. As a family we worried about how he would come to the decision to finally give it all up. We need not have worried. He calmly announced last fall when the crops were all harvested that he would rent out his fields in the spring. No backward glance, no moaning about giving up—only acceptance. His years have been filled with hard work, but I feel he considered himself a shepherd of the soil and felt grateful and contented to be allowed to participate in its preparation, care and harvest. He is reticent to discuss his deep- down feelings, but his devotion to the guardianship of his acreage comes through. He truly understands the lifecycle of the seed, the stalk and the harvest. He has lived his entire life this way. His approach to living has played a big part in my deep feelings in regard to the quality of life...and also death.

As I mentioned in class one day, I am moved and reassured by that portion of [William Cullen] Bryant's Thanatopsos which reads:

> "...So live, that when thy summons comes to join
> The innumerable caravan, which moves
> To that mysterious realm, where each shall take
> His chamber in the silent halls of death,
> Thou go not, like the quarry-slave at night,
> Scourged to his dungeon, but, sustained and soothed
> By an unfaltering trust, approach thy grave,
> Like one who wraps the drapery of his couch

43

About him, and lies down to pleasant dreams."

In high school, in sophomore English, our teacher Arthur Gorsuch required us to memorize the above. I saw no point in it at the time—now it has taken on great meaning for me.

And so I believe that death is not final—it is not to be feared—it is the passageway from the old to the new life.

To die is GAIN! This I truly believe.

Louise

GLUTEUS MAXIMUS TENDONITIS
Written in 1992

There are backaches galore. I've experienced a few over the years. The kind that require that you roll out of bed and use the all-fours method of managing a trip to the bathroom. The kind that shoot the pain down your leg when that herniated disk pinches away at the leg nerve. The kind that keep you in a semi-bowing position all day and folks ask, "Does your back hurt?"

Oh, there are bursitis pains in the elbow and hip, sacroiliac inflammations that come and go, major and minor muscle spasms, and cervical problems that cause the likes of pain unspoken of. The kind that cause me to sit on the edge of the bed in the wee early hours and rock back and forth, wondering if I will ever see the light of day, as I try decide if it would make me look weak to try to pull on a sweatshirt and jeans and drive to the nearest ER. Tylenol with codeine does nothing. The tears are ready to flow and my mind pictures surgery on my neck! Well, it, too, shall pass. Finally, after several days, the pain lessens. Another bout with spinal problems overcome.

Seems as though I have a bout with some area of my back every year or two. It used to be that nearly every time I made a trip to California to see my daughter, Ann, I'd have an episode of back problems. Sometimes I wondered if I could actually get on the plane, let alone carry my luggage. Perhaps it was psychological. I'm a poor traveler, feel more secure at home, it would seem. Sometimes I've had a backache start after I got out to California, just sitting around. I haven't made a trip out for two years. However, I had another bout from "bad back-itis" anyway, while at home.

We live in a condo. The snow is plowed, but not until after the snow exceeds three inches. Sounds good. However, the peer pressure for the hand-shoveling of snow on sidewalks and driveways when the snow is less than three inches is terrifically high. All the retired men with reasonable health and years not too advanced are out at the crack of dawn with their trusty snow shovels. Wifey said they could sell the last shovel at the garage sale they had just before moving to the condo—the one where you sell the spade and rake, which you replace soon after you move into the condo. The shovels rasp across the concrete driveways. The man next door finishes his and starts on ours. This makes me extremely on edge. I can't have someone doing my work. Jim has a good excuse; he had a heart attack two weeks before this—and anyway, he is oblivious to what goes on outside the condo, outside his drawing board and computer area.

So at the next two-inch snowfall I grab my newly-purchased snow shovel, bought hastily at the Home Hardware, and I commence the snow removal. Gee, the fresh air felt good, and I tell myself this isn't too bad—until my back/hip start to ache.

Three months later I still have pain, and I finally make an appointment to see my orthopedic doctor. X-rays taken, to be compared with those of three years ago, indicate that the back spine actually looks pretty good. Back surgery of 1978 looks pretty good too. So the current pain isn't really coming from there. What is it? So aggravating after all these weeks. Diagnosis: Gluteus Maximus Tendonitis. I looked this up in my bookclub freebie medical book. An inflammation of the tendon in the Gluteus Maximus area. In other words, it's a pain in the butt. For sure.

But it, too, shall pass. A little cortisone or maybe some physical therapy should do wonders. I hope.

OLD AGE
Written in 1992

When did I stop running up and down the stairs? I can't recall the time. It escapes me completely. In my mind I think that I can/could still do this, but I'm afraid to give it a try. Did it come from living in this one-floor condo with no stairs? Makes it hard to test my ability to skip up and down steps. So I find myself clinging to the handrails when I go out, and I watch my peers do the same—especially, women. Men are much more macho and would not allow others to see their need for assistance.

No longer can I work all day without stopping. After 1 1/2hours of cleaning the condo, I need a break, a rest. What happened to the time when I could prepare meals and wash and clean for seven hours? And still be able to can three canners of green beans in one day and give birth at 5:30AM, the next day, all in the August heat.

When did my knees become sort of enlarged and bulbous, my legs lose their rather symmetrical look, and my heels jut out at the rear, leaving the shoe gapping behind my heel in my new black pumps? My husband Jim says, "Your shoes fit strangely."

We made a trip to California, leaving our car at the "Park-N-Fly." Upon returning to Cleveland, we were being transported by the little shuttle bus to our car, and a voice booms over the radio. The dispatcher says, "You say you have an elderly couple on board who may need help with suitcases?" And I realize our cute little female driver had anticipated that we might need assistance and had quietly voiced her concern to her headquarters via radio. By the embarrassed look on her face, I knew she meant to be discreet. So...we are elderly and need help. I made a valiant effort to retrieve the luggage myself and to attempt agility as I exited the bus.

As I look around most assembled groups, be it at committee meetings or even Sunday morning church services, I realize I am surely one of the older ones in attendance. Gives me a strange feeling. One has only to go to a restaurant to see the reversal of this. Not at fast-food restaurants, but rather at the meat-loaf-and-mashed-potato places filled with gray-haired couples and little three- or foursomes of white-haired ladies passing the evening, a break from a sometimes boring day...a chance to fellowship in the early evening and be home before dark.

As a young person I often thought that "old people"—probably anyone over 45—had no fun. They didn't go sledding or swimming, just watched Lawrence Welk and turned in early. It seemed that most dreaded the Christmas season and holidays and wished they were past—long before they actually arrived. They "no longer drove at night," couldn't eat pizza because it had adverse effects on their bowels, dwelt on death. And accounts of recent funerals seemed the number one topic of conversation. The other day I mailed out two sympathy cards in one day and listened to three stories about hospice home care, heard about cancer in a friend of a friend and wondered if I should "drive at night" that night.

Our conversations with contemporaries often become a litany of concern for the aged, the depressed and the dying. And I have to phone my daughters to hear the positive and fun things that make up a busy family's routine, to know that there is action out there, that the kids are still having fun with sledding and swimming.

You get up in the morning and check the calendar! Now, there is a must. Who, over 60, would trust to their memory all those messages and reminders? There is volunteering scheduled for the month, doctor appointments for both me and my husband, the day the income taxes need to be made out (for us or my mother.) And then there is that entry which says only "Sara," and I'm drawing a blank. Is 12-year-old granddaughter Sara "in" something I should attend or am I to pray for her or have I simply doodled her name? I phone her mother, but no light can be shed on my entry for the first Sunday in March and the carefully printed "Sara."

I keep all birthdays on this calendar—all those I've decided to keep remembering, friends and family. With 15 grands now and three step-grands, I'm hard-pressed to remember soon enough for the US Postal Service to deliver birthday remembrances on or before "the day."

I used to long for things. New clothes, dishes, bath towels and hot-pan holders. Now I can't think of anything I need. I overstock on soap, paper towels, toilet paper and cans of tuna—a hedge against running out, as I did in our 7-in-the-family days. Funny how our priorities change. I see my children struggle with "needs" and I feel guilty to have it so easy. I see their vans break down and their dental bills mount, their job pictures a bit precarious and in some cases actually dangerous, and in still others, boring, and I yearn to be of assistance. Then I try to recall in 1947 when I helped my husband tear down the motor of our old 1937 car to replace a 25-cent "freeze out" plug when we had no money to pay someone with mechanical skills to do this motor repair job that was virtually labor-only. We did it!

I then wonder if in the "someday" of time, these young folks will ever experience paid-for homes, vans, braces and college education for the grands. These are different times. Our generation has experienced a lot of "paid offs" and ended up with late model cars. But can this current generation? Is the USA losing the standard of living we've enjoyed? Have we already lost it?

Next time I find a really good, comfortable pair of Naturalizers on the sale rack for a really good price I'm going to sort of mash down the heels and hope my aging heels don't appear to be sliding too far forward.

My sisters and I used to say that we would probably be strange in our old age. I conceded that when we wore tennis shoes and a purple dress to church we would be classed as aged and a bit strange. Now I wonder? I wear my Reeboks lots of places and my purple dress doesn't seem strange. In fact, I kind of like the color. But does it help with "night driving?"

Louise

REMEMBERING

November, 1993

I was but fifteen
When I met my hero—my love.
He, just one year older,
With wide-set, brown eyes
And dark curly hair.
With friends galore
And the will to achieve,
He possessed the assurance
I had always longed for.

I was shy—quite unsophisticated.
He let me know that he chose me.
I loved the sun-tanned skin
On his back and arms with
Its faint scent of youthful sweat.
It was "puppy love,"
Romance, full of promise.
It was lilacs, athletics
And never to feel lonely again.
He made me feel important, loved.
He was gregarious and so outgoing
And I marveled at his abilities.

We married young—
Too young some said,
Raised a bright family—
3 girls and 2 boys.
And together we enjoyed
The joys of success.
Suddenly there was the sadness of
His premature decline in health
And all the feelings of fear and anxiety
Descended on our youthful lives.
Once focused on achieving success,
Security and happiness,
Our world took a dark turn.
We were never to know those
Heights of happiness again,
For suddenly his life was over.

Twelve days in a coma,
Never to have the opportunity

Of talking through
Worries and wonders.
No loving words of goodbye.
Only tears of sadness and
Numbness of mind and heart.
And so I allowed myself
To rewrite the script
And slip in new "snapshots."

I see myself rejoicing with him
Over yet another "win,"
Another success-filled
Mentor/student relationship,
A dark night's "catch"
With three raccoons belly-down
On the back porch in their early AM,
A twenty-dollar bill
Stuffed down the front of my bra
While he's doing his dippy dance
Round the kitchen
Amid the "gang"—
The room laughter-filled,
A string of real pearls
On Christmas morning
With a note enclosed,
"To my dearly beloved."

I will no longer brood over
"What might have been,"
For I know I shall see him again,
Reunited on that radiant shore,
With no pain, no dark, silent days.
For only then shall we both
Know the ultimate love
And the completion of our quest.
Peace and joy will surround us
And fill us for all eternity.

Louise [Brownson] Connery

VACATION BIBLE SCHOOL
Christ Community Evangelical Free Church
Written in 1993

It had been years since I'd helped in any way, except financial, with Vacation Bible School (VBS)—not since Nankin Federated Church days. Seemed all organized and handled best by the younger folks. But with an enrollment ratio of 100 kids/40 adults, there was a cry for help. I volunteered. Partially for selfish reasons, as I knew it would be a way to get to know people, husbands, wives and the children. In order to become a part of the church I needed to know the various age groups and families. I was assigned to crafts! No objection. I surely didn't want to teach VBS material nor music.

Such a sea of kids. Luckily "crafts" was assigned to the conference room in the air-conditioned area of the church. So I worked with glue, paint and overseeing of over-eager little folks from K-6 grades. One period—the one for 5th graders—had 20 kids. It was quite active, loud and sweaty.

I'm so impressed with the way the dads helped, in many capacities. Some came into the "crafts" room—to assist with nailing, mostly. But all through the program I saw dads being the best role models I've ever seen in church or school functions. One man spent several evenings, three hours per night, keeping track of a boy with Down Syndrome about 10 years old who is extremely active. Once I saw this man sitting with the boy on the floor in the hall playing popcorn games, trying to catch the kernels in their mouths, laughing and eating. Other men were comforting the lost and misplaced newcomers who didn't know their way around. All were trying to make the kids comfortable.

Oh yes, there were the usual challenging families to deal with. I mean the kind where all the kids in the family are most aggressive, eager and pushy. All schools have them and so do churches. The VBS leaders handle them well.

The theme for VBS was Noah's Ark. Mr. and Mrs. Noah were in costume and character all five nights. There were animals galore—a few actually live, plus animal puppets and toys. I really wish I knew more about the story line, but supervising the paint and glue for 100 kids doesn't allow checking out much else. All classrooms were decorated around the Ark theme. One was like outside the Ark, after it settled on firm ground. The neatest classroom was converted into the inside of the Ark. I was amazed. Even the window had clear plastic over it with little tiny fish glued on it to give the appearance of being in sea water. Bales of hay all around in a big circle, canvas on the floor. It was wonderful. These young mothers and dads had hauled in so much to make it believable for these kids.

I was glad to be a part of it all. I felt truly accepted. I was tired! I will admit it, but no more tired than the others. One dear new friend—Kim Powell (Matt Brownson's kindergarten teacher at Savannah, OH) has been so helpful to me, all of us new ones at church and Bible Study. At VBS one night, she said, "You look really tired." I said, "Not really. What you see is age." Later I looked in the restroom mirror; I did look tired and I looked my age, 69.

Thank goodness for my new friends in Christ. As Pastor Jerry said God would, God has made room for us here.
Louise

HOSPICE—MY FRIEND
Written in 1997

Our days on earth are numbered and we usually have no idea when our last day will come. We can hope for a long and healthy life but often the end is signaled by a steady downhill go and life gradually slips away.

Too often the final chapter of our life is filled with the pain of cancer or fighting for breath as the final diagnosis is given. The patient struggles to maintain a grip on life, at first denying the fact that death is near. The family surrounds this fragile life praying for a healing, feeling the pain of their loved one as only a "watcher and waiter" can, searching for meaning and asking all the age-old "whys?" and "what can we do?"

In time past there was virtually nothing that could be done and the patient, filled with pain, was supported through to death by a family totally unprepared to deal with this demise.

Today there is help, blessed help, in the form of Hospice—an organization geared to assist and support both the patient and the family, to allow those final days to be as nearly free of pain as possible. With appropriate medication, administered properly, the patient can be reasonably comfortable and be aware of their loved ones gathered around, together for the final chapter.

What is often a time of extreme anxiety for all concerned can be a time for the sharing of memories and of loving goodbyes because comfort can be given and all concerned can feel surrounded and supported by the entire Hospice staff.

My husband, Jim, needed help. I needed help. The diagnosis was congestive heart failure. Three months of extreme anxiety preceded a heart attack, his second in five years, and the downward spiral had begun. He qualified for Hospice care. I called and they came. For four months Hospice provided all that was needed to make the final journey less difficult. The day his nurse, Sarah, lovingly told me that it wouldn't be long, maybe hours, was a sad day. However, the honest and heartfelt way she had prepared me for the day made it bearable. I will always be forever grateful for her.

I can never say enough good about Hospice. I find that in volunteering for this wonderful organization I can repay, in a small way, the debt I owe for the loving manner they cared for my Jim.

Too many wait too long to call for the services of Hospice and have thereby denied themselves, the patient and the entire circle of family and friends, the gift of loving time shared together, an easing of pain as well as dignity in death for the loved one.

Louise Conery

LETTER FROM ELINOR
AFTER JIM CONERY'S DEATH
April 8, 1996

My Dear Sister,

I can't begin to tell you how often I think of Jim—and about you and Jim—and about his life and leaving. You must be enduring all kinds of emotions and I suppose it will take much more time to settle back into who and what you were and *will* be in time to come. You are blessed in knowing what paths you want and you're already taking steps toward acceptance and peace.

What an exceptional man Jim was—it's been a rare look at outstanding talents and qualities and we'll never forget him. I expect I felt a certain intimidation in who he was—in fact, I *know* I did—but he didn't invite that of anyone. I so wished I knew how to talk with him. Come to think of it, though, he didn't expect that most of us *could* speak on his level! So uniquely gifted in engineering skills, he was totally focused on that, and golf! Maybe he didn't even notice that most of us were just kind of stumbling along in his wake, wishing we could keep up! And typical of someone with rare knowledge and drive, he just *had* to let most of the mundane aspects of life fall by the wayside! We all knew that!

You two—added so much to each other's lives! He must have blessed the day he met you (again.) For you opened up on many avenues of life for him. *Dancing!*—wish I could have watched you. I thought that was just so *cool* that you two took lessons and got it perfected! And you never ragged on him about playing too much golf! And you appreciated his skills in engineering—which went on for all his life! And you created with him, a neat, handsome, comfortable home—and oh, how he appreciated your talents in cooking! Then, the travel and entertainment you helped factor into his life!

But, most importantly, you brought his family back into his life. Literally. There was a new recognition, respect and enjoyment in reviving all areas of his past. John, Barb, then, Leonard and a rekindling of responsibility for Bill, Donna, the spouses of all. And what a joy for him in any time spent with Ian and Kelly! And *you* made it all possible. Again, your gift for bringing people together.

And *then*—by the end of his life, you had helped bring him, this struggling Christian, to a new spiritual awareness, a long-sought faith, comfort and sense of peace.

The last weeks, days, had to be *so* hard for him. We hate to think what he had to endure. You attended to him beautifully, but the memory must linger. Please may it fade, replaced by the admiration we all feel. I know you will have happy memories to carry with you always.

Much love,

Elinor

SO, HOW DO I LOVE YOU, BOBBY?
On His 50th Birthday
Written in 1997

You were born on a hot and humid day—50 years ago! Can it be possible? Guess most days in August are hot and humid, though. You arrived about 6:00AM, just as the sun came up. You were ready to start the day. Dad was so happy to have a boy, as visions of a football and basketball player danced in his head. Yours was the "easiest" birth of the five, even though you were the largest at 9 lbs. 4 oz.

The day before your birth, in extreme heat, I had struggled up the hill to the garden—at Grandma and Grandpa Brownson's on the "good old place" to check out the garden. Ann was a sweaty little appendage on my hip as we looked at the green beans, ready to pick. I think Dad picked the beans—I don't remember doing that part. But I DO remember snapping them, probably with dear Grandma Ruthie's help. And I DO remember the canning of the beans that day, three canners full, each requiring THREE hours of actual cooking time. A HOT day's work. I finished up about 11:00PM and suddenly realized the symptoms of the onset of the birth process. So it was off to Samaritan Hospital. I think you may have arrived before Dr. Martin did, as I'm sure I was given ether in the hall on the way to the delivery room. All went well.

On your 5th birthday we moved to Portsmouth, Ohio, arriving at the "summer camp" where we were to live for six weeks. Your bike got banged up a bit between the little trailer and the car trunk during the move. I think I baked you a cake—the first time I ever used a "mix"—and it was a bit burned, but I do not recall that you complained. You enjoyed the "shower" from the tank on top of the cabin that held water heated by the sun. Woe to the bathers who were last in line...they got either cold water or no water.

Dad and I took great pride in all you did as you grew up—sports on all levels—and you did very well in school. Many a cake pan was relegated to the backyard in Nankin to become a home plate as Dad worked with you in finding the strike zone. And also a few grey shingles bit the dust...and a stained glass panel in the window in our church next door caved in from a hit or two. These were days I wish I could have slowed down a bit in order to have savored more the growing-up years—for all of you. I was too busy to take time for the finer things of life.

I'm always proud to say "my son Bob, who teaches science at the high school." You are a good teacher. There really isn't a more important job than teaching the youth, and today it is such a challenge and not appreciated enough by the very parents whose kids are sitting in those seats. You are a good dad, sometimes working through great adversity and always with worry and concern. There will be better days!

So it is happy birthday and all good wishes to a special son from a grateful mom on his 50th birthday.

Love, always and forever,
Mom

MY BIRTH AND FEELING LOVED
Written in 1998

I was born at home at the "Rudy" place, the farm next door to the Jim Fluke farm. Nearly all of my generation were born at home. Dad rented the farm, which was adjacent to the Fluke farm where my dad grew up.

The doctor was alerted and he made his way to the farm for the event. That was the way it happened in those days. Sometimes another doctor would come in place of the usual family doctor, and that was the case for me. Dr. Patton was our family doctor; however, he was out of town and Dr. Ensign came in his place.

I was the third child, being preceded in the birth order by Elinor in 1921 and Donald in 1922. Two more would follow me, Emeline in 1926 and Helen in 1928. Five children. I'm sure my father felt great responsibility for our care financially, his fast-growing family. Times were hard and money was very scarce.

The date of my birth was May 26, 1924. According to my mother's account, it was an easy birth. I was the smallest in size, 7 lbs. 3/4 oz. and 19 inches long. She reported in her book that I was "roly-poly," darker in coloring than Elinor and Donald—they were little blondes. She further indicated that I was a "good" baby, the desire of all parents, I guess. She also referred to me as "another darling little girl" and those words sort of wrap me in a wonderful, motherly hug.

I popped my thumb in my mouth within an hour—ever a good appetite. A practical nurse by the name of Grace Tedrow was hired to help. I wonder where my parents found the money for the added, paid help and later for the two local girls who helped out for a time. Grandma Swan was also there to give an assist with the other little ones, the cooking, washing and cleaning. Mother's book states that she (Grandma Swan) was worried about her (my mother.) I don't think my mother had any special health problems, but maybe it was that my mother was Grandma Swan's only daughter and she had great loving concern for my mother and her family, the ever-increasing burdens and responsibilities.

Today's disposable diapers and modern laundry facilities make it difficult to recall how much more there was in caring for newborns in that day. My mother nursed us all and that had many advantages in addition to wonderful nutritional value.

The spring of 1924 was notoriously wet. At the time of my birth on the 26th of May, no plowing had taken place. This was in the days when plowing was being done by one team of horses, pulling one single-bottom plow. It took a long time, many days of progression, to turn over the furrows. With the lines tied firmly around his waist, firmly gripping the handles of the plow, with a "cluck" to Fanny and Polly, Dad was off down the field. I still sense what a battle it was to keep ever in the right direction and the furrow at the right depth. I remember my joy as a small girl following Dad down the freshly-plowed furrows. I loved the smell of the damp, fresh earth being exposed to the air and watching the "fish worms" trying to slither back in their protective homes. We didn't actually fish much, not big-time anyway, just a bit of North-pasture creek fishing with bent pin and stick-pole, but I was intrigued by all that activity under the soil.

At the time of my birth Dad would have been plowing the Rudy place. I don't recall the tillable acreage, but the job must have loomed ahead as monumental. I've heard the story of the extremely wet spring many times, but I never learned about the actual harvest in the fall. Often, today, the farmers sweat out an either too-dry or too-wet planting season and usually their harvest yields are pretty good. I'm sure through valiant effort my dad made it in the year of 1924. I wish I knew, and now there is no one to ask. Mother would have remembered and somehow I never thought to find out about the harvest for that particular year.

My mother had a basket of fair size—maybe it was a big laundry basket—and for each baby she would make a new liner out of some pretty print fabric. I have a picture of me taken out in the yard as a fairly young baby, maybe a few months of age—at least I'm old enough to be actually grinning. I like that, because a smiling baby tells me the little one is happy to be here. Mother was such a good mother. She kept her babies clean, warm and well-fed.

In those days, with all the work to do, we didn't get to church much. It just seemed too much to get everybody ready and the chores done. Our cars at the time were poor, at best. Tires were always bad, and it was nothing to have a flat just on the way to Nankin on any given day. As a grade schooler I remember standing impatiently watching Dad shave—he was always neat and clean before he would leave the house—thinking that I was glad I wasn't a boy because I thought shaving was such a bore. If he would cut himself while shaving with his old straight razor, that would be even more time, and then we might also have a flat and be really late. I never did like to be late. Still don't.

One has no actual memories of one's first couple years. However, I have a picture in my mind and heart that I was loved...and that is treasure I hold dear.

Louise

EDITORIAL TO MY CHURCH
An Older Point of View
Written in 1998

As our church grows in number, I note that one of our fastest growing groups is the "Over-Fiftys" and rightly so. The young adults who have been with the church since its inception are adding up some years. Some have already reached that plateau and some are edging ever nearer.

With aging comes—hopefully—growth, wisdom and knowledge. You are the leaders of the church. With growth in numbers comes the problem of how to reach everyone and where to seat the overflow. Not a bad problem really. In fact, it would seem a very positive one.

How to reach the numbers for Christ should be our most urgent concern. However, I sense unrest at times—not enough unity—it is seemingly often difficult to find balance and harmony.

At last count I was told we now have at least 25 denominations represented within our congregation. That adds up to 25 different ways to worship—in the order of worship and the music we sing, to mention just a couple. We gather ever more talented people who have a need to be used, to be able to find their place of service in the church.

In this "me-first" world of today the tendency is for us all to want to be served and to serve "OUR WAY!" It just cannot be—how about all the 24 other backgrounds?

As one of the oldest in the church I need to say I have NEVER been offended by even one single worship service in the six years I have been at this church. All who participate have a message to bring. We absolutely must reach our youth in a message clear to them, even if it means another service. I am well aware that there are those who really do not want to hear about this. However, we must give this consideration with our heartfelt thoughts and fervent prayers.

Variety and change will not necessarily hurt us—we can only experience more. In fact, it is the order of the day. It is my challenge to all ages that we be FLEXIBLE—that we work together to use the God-given talents within this body of believers to reach more souls for Christ.

Louise Conery

THE OLD
Written in 1968

The old gym came down today.
Wrecking ball, dozer,
Mortar and bricks. Down in a heap—
Rubble, dust and memories.
Time has passed, sixty-two years,
Bittersweet, An era gone, finished.
Fond memories remain of riotous
County basketball tournaments.
Nervous, tense teenagers
Competing for the county crown.
Giddy, frenzied cheerleaders—
Hoarse from chants and cheers,
Parents bursting with pride.
An era gone, finished.
Gone are the old-time (AC) Eagles—
Many good years and some bad.
A trip to Kansas City—heady times—
Auger, Shine, Boze and Purtell.
Football at Redwood where Kilhefner
Now fills the yard markers.
The tarnished Purple and Golds
Fade away with the rising dust.
An era gone, finished.
May Day, indoors –
Queen Shirley Klink—Zody to be—
And her court, May Pole dances,
Little Molly "B," my Molly "B,"
Four years old, flower girl,
Awed and yet so brave,
Clutching her basket of flowers,
Calmly strolling down
The long, white aisle.
An era gone, finished.
The tiny cubicles,
The offices of the staff
Are the last to go,
Voices echo amid
The crumpled girders—
The warm banter
And, yes, voices raised,
Not always in total agreement,
Memories hang there

63

In the crisp March air.
An era gone, finished.
The "A.D.," my Bob,
Coached there and
Planned and dreamed there,
Hired, counseled and cheered there—
His boys—his love.
I thought of him today
With loving memories—
A happier time, bittersweet,
A parking lot to be.
An era gone, finished—
Now complete.

Louise Brownson Conery

MOTHER'S DAY POEM FOR MOLLY
May, 1998

To My Molly...

Who blesses my life today and has ever since
her arrival, my preemie, in 1954,
Who allows me freedom to do my thing and
be who I am,
Who encourages me all along the way
when I feel a bit down,
Who stood by me and with me all of
Dad's dark days—and nights,
Who listens to me go on about my aging
aches and pains, real or imagined,
Who allows me to feel needed and
worthwhile in the lives of others,
Who loves her children well and is their
role model for the years to come,
Who provides great love and strength in her
marriage to Glenn,
And who assures me that I will not become
homeless with no roof over my head,
Even as the sunset years become close for me.

From a grateful mom on Mother's Day

MY 75TH BIRTHDAY PARTY
1999

How does one say "thank you" for such a beautiful party?
My heart overflows with love for you all,
my wonderful family and my dear friends—
all who came to wish me a happy 75th birthday.
I'm still overwhelmed—with love and joy.
What more could I ask,
than to celebrate within this circle.
I feel totally hugged!
When I'm eighty, you can do it again,
only this time I will expect
to see everybody on their feet,
making dancing fools of themselves.
I love the roses!
I've taken four Polaroid pictures of them.
Wish I could keep them forever.
What a fabulous idea!
May the Lord bless you and keep you, always.

Love,
Mom, Louise

SO, HOW DO I LOVE YOU, ANN?
To My Firstborn
Written in July, 1999

July 21, 1945

You arrived on a summer day about 2:00PM. I wish I had more recollection of the event, but whatever they gave me—I think it was known as "twilight sleep"—put me through with no memory of your birth, just the earlier stages of labor. I was dopey when I finally "came to" back in own bed in the ward. And I challenged the nurse as to why the chandelier in that room had been replaced and admonished them to please rinse out the tuna cans in such not weather. That medication must have made me sound like a babbling brook.

You thrived—you grew. Credit for the fact I was able to breast-feed you goes to the longtime family friend and former neighbor, Martha Jones. Even though she was close to retirement age, she continued to talk up the advantages of nursing your baby. In going to Grandma Mary's to recoup, or "to get a good start with the baby," I felt I had to follow her rules and those of your Great-Grandmother Rhuy—the rule being, according to Dr. Spock, never feed the baby more often than every four hours. This delay caused you to do much crying—and me, too. I did learn later, for Bob, my next baby, to do what was in my heart.

You always had a flair for the dramatic. Even in your preschool days you would prance around in high heeled shoes and carry a purse. Starting school was traumatic for you and I wonder what I should have done to have made it easier for you. Vomiting on the front lawn every morning should have been a clue you needed more help. I don't think there was much counseling done in those days. Just Dad, the coach, talking to Mrs. Hyatt, your first grade teacher. In spite of your anxiety, you ALWAYS did your best in school. Later you would tell me that you felt a real pressure as firstborn to set an example—to toe that mark and scrape those trays.

Music was always an important part of your life, with your music teacher, Connie Workman, in high school and then Cal Rogers in the choir at Ashland College. I recall that I was as excited as you were when, at the last minute, you got to go on the choir tour! To this day you amaze me as you use this talent so well. I'm so proud for what you make happen in your life, creating beauty and order in your home and at church, for the benefit of the congregation and for God. I often wonder how you get all the ideas for the altar and for special events and dinners within the church. It all takes time and money. However, you must feel that it is all part of your ministry. You do it all so well and I'm proud of you.

You (and I) weathered the stage of pincurls galore and what I called your "Bishop Sheen entrances," then learning in the eighth grade that you would not be going to Ashland High School the next year. And the Gary M's of the world lording it over the lowly Mapleton High School Mounties. But you survived and did it with flare! I lost track of how may sets of cheerleading outfits I was involved with over the years—a lot of Golden Flashes before the Mounties. I wonder how you would have done in this later age of girls' sports. When I see granddaughter Laura and her teammates in close contact and so happy to be part of that unit, I wonder if this would have been something you might have enjoyed. However, in your time in school it was cheerleading, Honor Roll, and yearbook. Did you ever feel cheated?

Did you ever feel the pressure of four other siblings in NINE years? Well, I did, but wouldn't take a million for the gift, the experience. I trust you feel the same way.

Recently, you mentioned endearing, pet names. Very probably your dad was the one to have hung nicknames on you. Aunt Betty's "Dear-To-Love" name for you is probably the one most lasting, as she still uses it today when referring to you. And as you might recall, Bill Connery called you—probably in a loud voice—"Onnie James." I don't know where he got this...and he has refuted it—in a loud voice—in more recent times. I think he was about 14 or 15 when his mother died and he sat behind the kitchen door at Grandma Ruthie's and "rocked" and felt pestered by all the kids. Hold to the names you remember, because I've forgotten most of them.

You have had more than your share of illnesses and unwelcome diagnoses. You have had to endure all the uncertainties of the medical field—you have forged your path through the nightmare times, never allowing yourself to be bitter, never allowing yourself to become the victim...and have come out even stronger. You have no idea how many depressed souls you have helped in the past seventeen years. Do you know this—feel it in your heart? It is just one of your many gifts.

You have always been so supportive of me. I'm thinking of the time we sat in the parking lot behind the hospital and I told you of my despair about living with Dad, the toll his dependence had taken on the marriage. I remember that you were supportive and yet made me realize that it was something I could/should do. It was hard to feel love for him as he had worn it so thin with all his actions. I thank you for helping me through those difficult times.

You always tried to arrange NEW experiences when I would come out to California—Robert Pante's salon being the most traumatic! You have always given me the opportunity to think about changes in my life—challenging me to paint, write, communicate with others, to try to step out in life and find new interests. I give you so much credit for working in my life, encouraging me every step of the way, yet allowing me to be the "little dog under the porch" until I was ready to come out on. I just this morning ran across the little brown ceramic dog you gave me in the early days and memories folded over me.

You came home when Jim was in the beginning of the end of his life and that meant so much to me. Those were difficult days with all his anxieties, poor "Tiny Man" [as you called him when you were a little girl and he was a friend of the family.] As you and I bunked on the divided single bed, we developed an understanding of what was ahead. You would always tell me that I could do it.

Remember how I used to say every time I saw you that you had not changed a bit! Well, you are now a few years past the college-coed era, with a few crow's feet to show that you have "been there" and made it. But you are still the same at heart, and that is what counts in this old world. I see the beauty in your mind, heart and spirit.

I love you so much,
Mom

SO, HOW DO I LOVE YOU, MOLLY?
1999

Wonderful things come in small packages. We have heard this for ages, but it is oh, so true about you. Your little preemie body was so well-formed; even though your weight was only 4 lbs. 3 oz., you made a good entrance into this world. Predictions that there was "no life" there before you were actually born, haunts me yet when I think about it. But you fooled all those medical people! You were just a bit in a hurry to be with the family. Guess what I'm saying was that you were a bit fragile, but you came on strong. I loved you from day one!

Most of this you have probably heard before but it bears repeating. One of my clearest memories of you as a toddler is you sitting at my right at our dining table with the wrought-iron legs and benches to match—though you were too little for the benches and sat in your "youth chair." You were never picky about your food, but you did get soooooo tired. I'm sure that meant that you were just past regular nap times. I know you didn't fuss or whine at me. Suddenly your little head with its blonde curls would start to nod and the eyelids drooped down and covered your big, beautiful brown eyes. I always loved your curly hair, so fine and soft. I know you think it has always had a mind of its own, but it is so pretty.

I love it that you have told me about sitting on my lap and listening to my heartbeat—and I didn't even know. We had a wonderful connection, even then. I know you remember some playtimes in the park out front that weren't so much fun. But you did have fun with Mike G. and also when your Cousin Janet would come down. Around the statue and up on the cannon. I hope that the fun times prevail in your memory.

No teacher every complained about Molly—probably you even scraped trays without whining. Your grades were always right up there. I remember your clothes better than the other kids', for even though I made a lot of things for you all, it was your clothes I enjoyed. I especially remember the orange-and-gold plaid—sort of a gingham—that I thought was just too cute for words. And then there were the two corduroy jumpers—one in brown and one gold, maybe? I think Aunt Betty says Cousin Leslie still has them. Oh, and I liked the grey dress with, I think, some black trim.

Through all the high school years you managed to stay focused on not getting into the bad stuff, even with the free spirit L as your best friend. And I was always proud of you for taking the protector role, lifeguard or whatever when your classmates got a bit "high" and out of control. So what made you this way—the desire to please parents, your resolve to do the "right thing." At an age when all the other kids were bending the rules, you hung in there. Wonder if any of those kids remember—or what their memories might be, if they understood or recognized your role in it all.

You are such a good mom. I especially love it that you have had so much conversations, like "Timmy" games and things like that. Both girls are strong in their feelings from being nurtured in decision-making. Homeschooling, even though it was brief, gave them a good start at school. You did that for them. Do you ever think of that as Erin excels at Grove State College in such a difficult course of study and Sara does so well at North Central Technical College? So even though you were and are sensitive at times, you have done your mothering well.

You were with me through all the difficult years as Dad gradually faded away—stopped being with us. You weathered the anxiety and yes, the anger that we both had. It certainly wasn't easy for you to go through this in your high school years, Ohio State and also in nursing school. I just know your presence was such a comfort to me.

When you took over the reins of the Music Boosters Club food service, I was proud. Sort of like-mother-like-daughter—organization, we can do it and do it well. When you have told me over the years that you really liked helping with banquets when I was in charge, it felt good.

You let me know that the strawberry shortcake I brought to the nursing dorm for your birthday was just what you needed. It was fun doing that, and I remember that even Dad in his semi-silent days enjoyed it, too. And then you were "capped" and Glenn came on the scene. What a bonus for our family, and how blessed for you to be so treasured and loved so much over the years. And how good he has been to me!

I just wonder what I would be doing right now, this year, this week, if I didn't have you!! I never hear you complain (or even sigh) over all the miles and time it is taking now—with many more to go. You allow me to think I'm worth it. Your expertise and knowledge are so very helpful in all the medical situations, truly a blessing for me. Your realizing that I was "down" last week and engineering a day which proved to be a nursing home visitation day helped me so much. If it weren't for you—well, I don't know where I would be in all the negatives for me the past year.

You warm my heart, you surround me with your love. And I know you want to help me make my way through these last years when the body parts sort of forget how to work together.

So, why do I love you? Because you were my preemie, my curly-head, my Molly B. who like to be cuddled and read to. For being strong in the face of times of youthful temptations with your friends, for being a great mom and a loving wife—who is also a wonderful daughter.

May God bless you and keep you always.

Love you,
Mom

60TH ANNIVERSARY THOUGHTS FOR MY CHILDREN
Bob & Louise Brownson
Written October 16, 2003

I'm thinking of you all—my five—this morning on this, a special day in my memory bank. Sixty years ago today marks the marriage date for your dad and me. The years fly by so quickly—can it really be that long? Somehow—this 60th year—seems more meaningful than the 50th was, and I don't really know why. Guess it is just on my heart today.

When we married in the house at 827 College Boulevard in Ashland on that snowy day in 1943, never could I have dreamed of the life ahead for me, the changes that were in store for me, for us. Some great joys and much sadness, too.

The joys of all your births and the sadness of the many health problems for your dad kind of roll up together as I try to sort out the highs and the lows of life. I look back and wonder why, and I don't think that does much, if any, good. I'm a firm believer in the fact that what is past is past, best to move on, face the opportunities of another day.

In your "small group" at church, Bob, we are studying *The Purpose Driven Life* and learn that God has our lives planned out. I'm not an accident! So what is my purpose in life?" I needed to take a look at that. I have often thought that I don't have much purpose in life anymore—the five of you are all grown. (However, I do reserve the right to worry about you all from time to time.) Am I just marking time to get to the end of the road? Was it God's plan that I would be a caregiver for three men in the final days of their lives? I'm not complaining for I have learned that through suffering we grow in understanding, compassion, and, most of all, love. I do have a purpose!

I married at 19 (and 1/2)—awfully young by today's standards—but I wouldn't have changed a thing. After all, it was part of the plan. But I had so much to learn—patience, tolerance and understanding, all of which brought meaning and order to my life. And order is big with me. It all brought hope to my life and hope does not disappoint—Romans 5.

Molly and Glenn share this anniversary date. That has always been a blessing to me. I'm wishing both of you a happy day today. I treasure your marriage. I rejoice that you both anchor the home place, allowing us all the happiness of the reunion, our heritage celebration.

I must be very mellow this morning. If it was a bit sunny, I would go out to the woods and watch the leaves flutter down, stand at Dad's memorial site and smell the absolutely wonderful joys of the woods. I'm so glad that this area is at both your back doors, Bob and Frank.

Tomorrow will be the 28th anniversary of Dad's death. May he rest in peace. I have such good memories of the memorial service we had in the woods. I think the date was the 16th anniversary of his death, October 17, 1991. Ann, sending her heartfelt tribute from California, to be read by Frank with little Frankie in his arms. Tina, reading that special letter written by Dad to his folks. The junior-high-age kids in the circle, and Matt being brave enough to tell us all he wished he could have known Grandpa Bob.

Life rolls on—the babies arriving—the grands marry in rapid succession these day—the circle grows. Life is good!

Love you all so much,
Mom

FLUKE REUNION, 2003
Labor Day Weekend

Once again the big weekend is over and I'm feeling a bit sad. All those who trucked in the tables and chairs—those who actually "toted" those straw bales for games and hay-wagon rides—those who roasted the corn, hauling in a special "corn" roaster from the Wooster Fire Department through Josh Brownson—those who washed up the pots— might say "it is well." But for us all, there is a glow as we reflect on the three days. Some came for all three events—some just Saturday—but all had a great time.

Preceding the three-day event this year, Emily, bless her heart, suggested that the "Fluke sisters" gather for a special luncheon—a time for "just us girls." Emeline hosted this wonderful time together. We are indebted to Emily for having this idea!

Each year, those who plan—from the invitations to the actual first-car-into-the-designated-parking-area—wonder, will they come? And they do come. By my unofficial account, 39 attended Friday evening. It is such a fun time to meet and greet everyone as they arrive at the farm. 85 attended on Saturday and maybe 20 on Sunday morning.

The rains came during the day on Friday, but let up and the tent-people came and put up our green-and-white tent—the gathering place for the three days. After our very rainy summer, we were fortunate—not a drop fell during the reunion.

This year Molly had this great idea to involve more kinfolk...and somewhat to lessen her load, which is considerable. To do this, she "assigned privileges!" What a neat idea! Everyone got with the program and came in with "games" and the "stuff" needed to put on these fun things. I did not get to see all the games, as things we're moving so fast. I failed to see the "milking-the-cow" game. How could I have missed that? Guess I was in conversation with someone. I did see the "Horse Races" and the "Kiddy-Wagon-Obstacle-Course" and the "Skillet Toss." The Skillet Toss was a "first" this year and a popular event. A skillet was broken, great brute strength was exhibited by several. Josh won for the men's division with a mighty toss that nearly went out into the road. We thought we might have to flag down traffic for a bit. Tina and Molly McFrederick tried their best to keep the macho guys in line, with no cheating, while measuring the length of the throws. The fairer sex tossed the skillet, too, but my back got tired and I had to head back for the older folks and the lawn chairs. Did anyone actually throw any bales?

Matt and Michelle Brownson were in charge of the Scarecrows—good job, lots of fun for many during this event. The scarecrow "couple" stand there in all their glory by the silos and appear to be viewing the grounds. Many took pictures through all the events—lots of "digital" pictures this year. Megan Martin—one of the newest members of the clan—and isn't she a sweetheart!—was faithful to all the events with her camera. Ofoto—we await your services!

How things have changed since our first reunion in 1981–the year of Grandpa Gene's death and the farm sale. Wouldn't he be surprised by the presence of digital cameras, the cell phones and, ah, yes, the porta-pot, not to mention that a gas well is once again producing on the farm. The farm looks great—wonderful crops this year with the north pasture full of 23 or so mighty good-looking Angus cattle.

The hayrides numbered three this year—a very popular event, as always. Rick Krause drove the first two runs out—the wagon filled to capacity for both trips. Some folks, even very little ones, went out on all three trips, even the one that went out late Saturday night when Glenn drove without lights—in the dark—scary. This trip followed a fantastic fireworks display by Marty and Matt Ritschdorff in the north pasture. Nary Sheriff nor deputy came in to check out what was going on. However, the bull got moved to another pasture when he became a bit uppity about the invasion of his territory!

The traditional bonfire burned in the familiar spot and some corn was roasted in the coals, in addition to the corn in the "roaster" mentioned earlier. Lots of visiting went on, plus some readings from Grandma Mary's book and Aunt Bernice's heart-touching writings about her days as a girl growing up on the farm. Added to the bonfire scene was some "play back" theater under Erin Johnson's leadership. Lots of laughter when she had three folks, picked from the audience, act out "Helen stuck in the barrel"—a memory recorded in Grandma Mary's book.

After a great noon meal of grilled sausages, hot dogs, chicken and all sorts of great food prepared by the local folks, a short business meeting was conducted by President John Fluke. We found ourselves to be solvent—we could pay for the tent and the porta-pot. John has done a good job; it was easy to elect him for another term. Way to go, John! Helen had prepared a History Quiz, with the younger generation reading the answers to her questions regarding their ancestors and events down through the years. Nice touch! Margaret gave an update on the Fluke Family History. How indebted we are to her for her faithful research in the past years. Her ongoing research is invaluable to all of us.

On Sunday, the third day, some of the family assembled to eat a breakfast provided by the Fluke kids: Elinor, Emeline, Helen, Donald and Louise. Then it was time to say goodbye for another year. Goodbyes take quite a while, as we realize our time together is so very precious.

In attendance—not actually Flukes, but so close to the family over the years—were Walter and Edith Brownson and Betty Smith, brother and sisters-in-law of Louise, Aunties and Uncle of the Brownson branch. Walter thanked us for including them, also thanking me for taking him into our "wonderful family many years ago."

The "newest" Fluke arrived early Friday morning, just in time for the official count—Ava Grace Baum, daughter of Ellie and Jason. She even made an appearance on Saturday afternoon, still only hours old.

Another recent addition to our family is the "adopted" daughter of Molly and Glenn—not a legal adoption, but more like a mentoring. Barbara Borkholder, formerly Amish, is now one of ours. Barbara brought her fiancé, Harvey Keim. They will be married in October at the Bethel Baptist Church in Savannah, Ohio.

We have had several marriages and new babies in the past two years, but I'm not going to try list them here—might omit someone. The family grows. Next year we hope the California folks can join us and Sara and Don McIntyre from Estes Park, Colorado, though this is their very busy season on Wind River Ranch.

The family circle remains intact and, the good Lord willing, we will meet again in 2005 at the farm. We, the five children of Gene and Mary Fluke, are doing our best to "age gracefully." Our bones ache and creak a bit, but our hearts embrace with joy our heritage, our roots and our memories of growing up on the Fluke Farm, now 139 years in the Fluke Family.

Louise (Fluke) Beattie

SUGGESTION FOR MEMORIAL SUNDAY
Submitted to Christ Community Evangelical Free Church
May 30, 2004

I borrowed this from Martha Jorden's excellent column "Mental Health Matters," [in the Ashland Times-Gazette] May 13, 2004. Perhaps it could be used somehow in our Memorial Sunday service for it is so true—a valuable commentary on how and why we grieve and how it helps to "remember."

> "May is a time for memorials. The very act of honoring our deceased is part of our affirming. We grieve the loss, and we affirm that they were. They lived and touched our lives. A community that honors its dead reaches back into its own history and promises a continuity of life into tomorrow.

> Today by remembering we serve both the dead and we who grieve.

> We offer an external symbol of our loved one's person. Their names live; their memory is lifted up. We who grieve also are helped by such remembering. We are able to publicly proclaim the life that touched us so profoundly. It is part of our healing."

Louise Beattie

DAY DREAMS AND NIGHT DREAMS
January 31, 2004

I'm not given to many "day dreams," as I think I take life much as it comes—never wishing for the impossible or the improbable. I don't pine to travel, to do more exciting things. I might obsess just a tad over order and general neatness, however. But I don't straighten the fringe on the "throw" rugs after vacuuming, and I don't require that guests take off their shoes at the front door. I feel confident on a bitter cold day that the larder is full—that I could manage to feed hungry neighbors, if required.

So why do I dream night after night that everything is in a real mess with laundry stacked high, meals to prepare, laundry to do for folks who do not live with me, people I don't even know. It is sort of like I'm stuck with living with these people in the dream. I'm NEVER in my own home, but always trying to make some kind of order out of an unorganized, absolute mess. I never know whose home I am in; although, Aunt Betty thinks that in my dreams I am in HER home! Invariably, I lose things—my purse, my car keys or even my car, and thus no transportation to remove myself from the location.

Molly suggested that I try to journal some of my thoughts or memories of these dreams. I believe I dream every night, but not all nights are bad enough to make me remember them past my shower time. When they hang on me in vivid detail past breakfast and I feel worn out—even though I was asleep at least eight hours—I feel distressed. I have a great deal of trouble sleeping and often have to resort to taking a Tylenol PM which I fight doing, and I wonder why I do that too. So, whether I take the Tylenol PM or not, I don't know if I will have the cluttered, messy dreams or not.

Even if I get up to go to the bathroom and think, now I won't get back into that mess, I can and often do go right back into it when I doze off to sleep again. Last night—this morning, whatever—I dreamed that I was apparently trying to rent a very old and crappy house. None of my family was there but I was given a baby to care for. I was away from home during the day, working or running errands, but the baby was at home—seemingly okay! I went to a bank, but it wasn't any bank I was familiar with. I needed to inquire about some investment that I had no papers for but was trying to make some sense of. Of course, the bank ladies couldn't help me. While there fidgeting nervously and wondering why I didn't have this straight in my mind, one of the ladies in the group farted loudly and crudely. She didn't laugh or apologize, nor did anyone even smile or make a joke. Then one of the ladies said to me "My, I remember your dad—now there was a hard-minded man." I was so puzzled that anyone would refer to Gene Fluke in that manner. I had a nasty, cruddy brown rag with me, sort of like an old bath towel!!

Back to the house then—it had open ceilings to the roof, with the log roof-rafters exposed—the bark still on them—junk and crappy stuff everywhere. I was supposed to find the key for somebody, but I searched and searched, went thru many small boxes of junk, but no keys. Two really dimwitted fellows came to look at the house—thinking to buy it—but they didn't. One of them was wearing a tool apron, new. He laid it on the counter, and I can still remember what all was in it. There was even a "tack" cloth along with the usual ruler, etc. Enough for that dream, but I keep wondering—why?

Am I stressed? It is not because it is winter and I can't get out much, because I have this same sort of dream—never exactly the same, though—regardless of the weather or season of year. I DO worry about Bill and his declining health, his problems with breathing, but he is never in my dreams. I have no need to worry about money as we are quite comfortable in all ways. I live in a neat, warm and cozy home. I can't think of anything I need. I do think of "end times" for us both, for Bill especially, but this is never in my dreams.

Years ago—maybe seven—I dreamed some very dark and unhappy dreams about Bob, even though he had been gone for over 20-some years. I had a very difficult time with this until I had a wonderful talk with my pastor's wife, Jeannie. She was able to help me sort this out, and the dreams stopped completely. I think it is strange that my family is never—maybe it would be more correct to say, seldom— in my dreams. I'm surrounded by the most klutzy people as a rule. In my dreams I don't think I'm ever at church, at the grocery store or any place like that—but always in a building that could only be described as a "dwelling" of some sort. Always piles of dirty clothes, and yet in real life I never have a pile of laundry ahead to do and I really *like* to run the Maytag washer and dryer! And then there are stacks of dirty dishes and pots and pans!

Enough for today.

Louise Beattie

REMEMBERING MY SON,
FRANK E. BROWNSON
November 18, 1952-March 15th 2004
Written on March 23, 2004

I have written his name. Now what can I write to tell you about Frank's memorial service? I may be picking the wrong day to start this, because it is the Monday after and life is supposed to go on as we head back to normal—whatever that is—but I'm typing through tears.

It has been said by the multitudes that our children are not supposed to leave this earth before we do. I have heard it hundreds of times in the past seven days. But it has happened, and I know I have to adjust. Having gone through loss before has very probably seasoned me to do my best to make adjustments. I know all the platitudes—he is in a better place, and I do truly believe that. I know he does not have to endure the pain and sufferings of life ever again. Even in my knowing and believing this, I still ache with the loss. Memories abound as I go back in my heart and rethink past losses and try to find some sense in it all.

The memorial service was simply outstanding. I know through Bill Martin the Michigan folks will, no doubt, get a firsthand account of the event. It was so good, too, to have Emeline and Bill there as my family, my sibling representation. It was truly amazing. I always knew that Frank had many friends, but I was dumbfounded by the outpouring, by the cross-section of people from all walks of life who attended. I thought of his dad and the blend of folks who knew and cared about his dad like this.

As I arrived at the church an hour and 15 minutes ahead of the scheduled service, there were already at least 50 cars in the parking lot. Clustered just outside the door was a group of blue-jeaned guys, and I heard one say, "Frank was one hell of a worker." I know it was a high compliment from a former co-worker, probably said within a sort of caucus of Electrical Union guys. I didn't know one half of the folks attending and Frank's wife Sherry reports that she didn't either. There were many from his electrical workers' union, old classmates, his high school football coach from Avon Lake who left a seriously-ill wife to come and pay his respects. Relatives on both sides, MANY cousins, old friends from Nankin that used to play in the park with him—folks telling us that Frank was always so good to them, kept the bullies off them when they were picked on by the bigger, meaner kids. His warm heart came through in all the stories. I wish I could remember more of the conversations, more of the wonderful memories related by so many.

There were two videos made of the service. One from the back wall of the church, the customary one for Sunday services. That one is kind of far away. But Erin Johnson sat right next to me in the front pew and videoed the whole service. It looked to me as though she had gotten everything up close and, hopefully, with good sound.

I want to try to describe the setting, up front on the elevation, three steps above the congregation level. Tina has a friend who is good at putting things together, and together they did just that. It was so very Frank. His deer hide was laid on the communion table and then covered with the "loves" of his life. A little cabin made out of sticks, an arrangement of fall woodsy things, moss, a bird house up on top. All very rustically displayed, backed with a fan-tail from a turkey he shot, a deer skull with the antlers intact.

And centered on the table were his ashes in a wooden box made by Uncle Walter during the days preceding. On an easel frame on one of the tables was a large picture of Frank taken in Florida last year; he's dressed in his usual worn shorts and tattered tee shirt, in his work shoes and holding a fishing pole in one hand and a fish in the other. He was smiling, having a great vacation. There were candles interspersed among the floral arrangements on the steps. His high-school Mounties athletic jacket hung on the front edge of the table and his favorite ball hats cornered the framed picture.

During the hour of visitation, music was played with nature sounds—birds, water, in the background piano, oboe and flute. Just right for Frank. And all during this time pictures of the farm were projected on the front wall over the wooden cross that hangs there. All in all Molly put 150 pictures in the computer projection. Such a nice touch—all the places Frank tramped, his places of solitude, whether in depression or in his joy of the farm and all it meant to him. And because the woods and farm are also Molly's place of peace and contentment, she has all these wonderful pictures. She even had pictures of Frank's footprints in the mud—or snow—and his discarded cigarette butts. She'd ended up following him at different times on her own walking rounds. It was SO touching. The BIG, old stump at the end of the cow lane—the roll of the land—the snow in winter and the crops in the summer. She has it all on film. Not many would know the meaning of this presentation, but family did.

I will try to see if there are any more of the printed orders of service left. However, with somewhere over 375 attending there may not be any. Our sanctuary holds 275. You can imagine the standees and the chairs out in the foyer. The parking lot was filled by 1:00, and our good friends from the church had their hands full. Parking was on both sides of the road to nearly a half-mile away. Some came in to greet Sherry and Frankie and then left, saying they wanted to leave room for family.

I was so proud of my family. They all managed to say all the right things with such love. There is no way I can quote what they said, but let's hope I can circulate the video and that they came through with clarity. Bob sang and played his guitar using a great favorite of his and mine, "Give Me Jesus." Ann read her poem, written especially for Frank, capturing so well the many facets of him, his personality and his life. Tina spoke about her brother in such a loving way and also read what Rick had written because Rick said he could not read it in front of the gathering. Glenn read the obituary and kind of set the order of service— he does this well. Bob gave a wonderful eulogy. His love for his brother came through—so touching with a good blend of humor to help us through our sadness. Molly, who initially felt she couldn't speak, changed her mind and beautifully honored her kindred-soul, farm-tramper brother. And with heartfelt love she read Psalm 23, so fitting for our Frank.

Sherry had asked our family to just go ahead and plan the service as she indicated she didn't have any idea what to do. It was planned here on Tuesday night with the help of our pastor, John Stevens. All plans were run past Sherry on Wednesday, and she was pleased with the planned service. Jim Anderson, one of Frank's oldest friends, was asked to say a few words, and he did a good job. As he left the pulpit, he turned to Frank's picture and the woodsy arrangement and said, "Bye, Bro."

Sherry and Frank's family then spoke with a passed, hand-held mic. Megan, the oldest, couldn't say anything, even though she had planned and hoped to; we all understood. Josh was next and paid a fine tribute to his dad. Frankie was next, and I was proud of him. He told us all how much he loved his dad, how his dad helped him with everything—all the sports and even including homework. He ended his tribute with a very soft, "I love you, Dad." There were no dry eyes. Both Chad and Adam [Sherry's sons] spoke briefly, good thoughts and remembrances of Frank as a "special" dad to them.

Then, as planned, there was an open-mic time. Several folks stood and spoke, but the most touching ones were two 12-year-old boys who stood up in the jam-packed gathering to tell through tears how much Frank had helped them in their lives through summer baseball and Junior High football, as their coach. One boy didn't get up to share—guess he was too scared—but he had called Sherry several times during the week. He has very weak eyes, thick glasses, kind of an uncoordinated kid. Frank had taken him under his wing, actually cleaned his glasses for him every time he came up to bat. On the phone he was crying and asking Sherry, "Who will clean my glasses now?" This would indicate Frank's servant heart. He will be missed by all "his boys," all Frankie's fellow students and friends. The father of one of the boys shared some thoughts, also.

At the end of the service, Rodd played "It Is Well With My Soul"—a sax solo, unaccompanied—beautifully and meaningfully done. He is so talented. The gathering just sat for a few moments when it was over—perhaps a bit stunned by the whole service. Our church people provided refreshments. However, many left directly from the service, not going to the fellowship hall.

This was so touching to me... Sherry went back up front, after all were gone but family, to start to dismantle the "arrangement"—I truly don't know what to call it. Josh went to her van and brought in an ancient, ragged flannel shirt of Frank's and she put it on and wore it, apparently taking comfort from the closeness of that old shirt. She even had me smell it—cigarette smoke and all. A real comfort to her. Last night she brought me one of his old denim shirts—one for me, his mom, my request.

About Sherry and Frankie... My heart breaks for them both. Sherry is strong, she will know what she wants—she will manage. They are shaken, but they will adjust. I was reminded of our dad, Grandpa Gene, who rode on the seat of the horse-drawn wagon taking his dear mother's body up to the farm after she died at the Nankin church; he said he thought the world had come to an end. Sherry is a strong lady. She will survive, but it will take some time. It was hard to move his work boots from the kitchen, where he had taken them off when he came home in pain that Monday morning before he died. And she said she had not been able to even touch the pile of work clothes on the bedroom floor. Oh, the evidences of her loss and suffering.

Many friends and relatives have been very generous with her, and she is so appreciative. She keeps saying to me, "Your family! They have all been so good to us." I know the service was very meaningful to her, though it took great courage and stamina to stand in line and accept all the hugs and words of sympathy from all those many people, many of them strangers to her.

Frankie. He has done well. Devastated and missing his dad so very much, yet surrounding his mom with much affection. I hope he was able to go back to school today and enter back into school life.

About me, his mom... I just couldn't share at the service. Understandable to you all, I know. However, I have been flooded with memories of Frank—thoughts of Frankie and his life ahead. Also of Bob's death and the other losses down through the years, as well. So I'm writing this today—easier for me than talking. I'm feeling my nearly 80 years keenly the last few days and feeling sad, remembering last times and last words. I know full well that Frank is in a better place. My faith tells me that. But neither will he walk this earth, those fields, nor the woods or the back-forty. I just have to keep that memory alive in my mind and heart.

He walked to a different drummer. He walked with a heart of gold. And he will be remembered by so many people. He touched lives and that is good. What will our lives say about US?

Sad, but grateful for his life,

Louise

FOR SHERRY WITH ALL MY LOVE
April 4, 2004

Your beautiful card and loving message came today. I cried some more tears, but that is good. Of ALL the communication I received in the past weeks your words touched me the most. I feel your love—your words hug my heart—they surround me. A strong bond, forever, between us.

As I write this I know I'm writing the words that I might have shared (no, just maybe) with that multitude of friends if I had been able to speak [at Frank's memorial.]This is not to deepen your sorrow, but for you to keep and know how much I care about you—how much I share in your sorrow. My mother's love ranks up there a step or two behind your intense love for Frank.

He was the cutest little boy. When he learned to walk and talk in Portsmouth he used to go to the outside door and call "Here Snowball," a neighborhood white cat. I can't write it the way he said it, kind of like you would call a dog, "Yough"—and it was so cute—the sound of it. He was the most adventuresome of all my five. I lost him once in Nankin and I was frantic. Everybody went out to try to find him. We went to Hank Steiner's filling station—a favorite haunt of his—but he wasn't there. Actually, we found him in the neighbor's garage watching Donnie Steiner, sort of an ornery teenager, change the oil in his old car. Frank was not lost. He just smiled and wondered why mom was so concerned, as he dabbled in the used oil and wiped it on his shirt, not unusual for him with his often-torn pockets and missing buttons.

He wandered the village with his old duffle bag which contained binder twine, old parts to things, and an ear or two of field corn. The day he dropped it in the Shaum septic tank run-off and brought it home to me to try to wash it was a hard day for him. I said it couldn't be cleaned up. I wish I had tried harder—it was such a treasure for him. This was along about the time he discovered the many dead cows hauled out in the woods north of Nankin. I think it was Keener's herd that got sick and died. It was winter and they couldn't bury them. Spring came. What a find! Molly was with him, but not quite so involved. He couldn't resist jumping on them to see what would happen and I guess he broke thru the ribs—what—a—mess! That was Frank.

Then there was "Charlie," the baby woodchuck he brought proudly home, found in a newly-plowed field. He scrounged up a shoe box, but Charlie kept getting out and running around the living room climbing up pant legs. I said it HAD to go. "Take it back where you found it" And he woefully said it no longer had a home, it was all plowed up. He did what I told him, but it was not what he wanted to do. These things all happened on his tramping, wandering trips around Nankin. He was an outdoors boy even then, at maybe ten years old.

You know Sherry I can't remember that he ever talked back to me. I've tried to think of a time, but I can't remember one. He was always loving and respectful all thru his life. In the last few years he took to telling me he loved me every time he called or I called him. I don't know when he arrived at that place in his heart, able to say it. I would guess he always did have the love in his heart but suddenly it became easier— maybe necessary to him—to actually say it. I loved it that he did. In recent years he would always tell me not to worry about him, but of course I still did, for I was always aware of his arthritis-like pain. I worried that it was getting worse as he grew older.

He was a worker! I was always so proud that he kept at all the jobs he ever had—working the long hard hours—and always trying to assist or save the older fellows on the job. I told you this before in the write-up of the memorial service, but I will repeat it, for it spoke volumes to me. Outside the church door the day of the service some guy in the midst of all the blue-jeaned workers said, "Frank was one hell of a worker!" From the mouth of someone who really knew him it was a high compliment. No wonder that the job-people would ask if he might come with them, on to the next job site.

I treasure the conversation we had on the way home from the Cleveland Clinic all those years ago when you told me how much and for how long you had loved Frank. It seemed as though you were but a toddler when you tagged him around and Rick said, "Sherry, Frank doesn't want you hanging around!" He stayed in your heart thru the years and finally you sought him out at Club 42 [where he had been drinking] and walked him out with you. I have LOVED it and as I said, treasured the story, knowing that you surely lifted him out of a continuing downward, unhappy spiral. I remember I told you that I would never worry about the two of you again, not afraid that your marriage might not make the long haul when so many fail. I felt you both were safe with each other!

Fourteen years of marriage. I would have stayed home from my trip to California had I known you two were going to get married the day before my birthday. I'm sorry I wasn't there. It should have been a bigger deal, though I know that Frank didn't think that was important. Fourteen years was not long enough—not nearly long enough—to be sure, but remember YOU made him a happy man. You listened to his perpetual worry and grumbling about financial things, and I know that wasn't easy. You hunted with him, deer, mushrooms, wild turkey all in season and that made him happy. You listened to his "pain" and I know that wasn't easy either, for I have been there and listened to anguish with his dad. You were with him in his dark days and darker evenings—even though "some" didn't think he was ever depressed—but you and I know. Not easy times, but you stuck with him all the way—a good wife—oh, so good. You were his life, you and Frankie.

I know that you can't see any "sunny" days in your future, ever again, but as I have promised you, it WILL get better. I so want you to know that if it becomes too difficult to stay in the woods for whatever reason, down the way, you are not tied to it because the land was once mine. I want what is best for you and Frankie. "Take time to make any decisions" is the frequent advice of many and it is sound advice, too.

Frankie has always been so special to me. I guess his staying with me on Thursdays for that year or part of a year made him extra special as I watched him grow. He cried when he came, but I knew it was because of leaving you, not really about having to stay with grandma. I hope I can continue to watch him participate in his various sports and special times in his life in time to come for as long as I am able.

I want our bond to be tight and that we continue to support each other—we both need each other down thru the years. I will save your note, a real keeper to go in my memory box to treasure always. It truly speaks to my heart. I love you very much, Sherry. You made Frank's life—you were his ANCHOR—his LOVE. I will continue to "hug" the old denim shirt and know Frank is with us both in our hearts.

Louise

A BLUE BIRD CAN FLY
Written in 1993,
Amended May 26, 2004

I started the first grade in the Nankin Grade School in September. It was 1930. I had turned six in May of that year. I have no recollection of that trip to school, how I got there. It may have been via what we called the "kid wagon," a horse-drawn wagon used to transport kids to the Nankin School building. The "kid wagon" had high wheels with the floor as high as a farm wagon and steps up to the back door, as I recall. A small stove was placed in the back of the wagon in really cold weather. Straw on the floor to add some insulation from the cold must have been very hazardous with the burning stove. With windows all around, we kids had a good view of all that was going on at our neighbors' farms all along the dirt road.

Dirt roads through this winding, hilly countryside may have been scenic, but on muddy days in the spring of the year, the horses had to strain to lug this top- heavy, lumbering conveyance through hub-deep mire—slow and messy. In the late spring, after the frost came out of the ground and the mud dried up, the roads turned to dust. It is often said that dirt roads are either mud or dust with a few hours in between when they are fairly decent. The "big girls," high school girls, always griped at us "little kids," because we crawled over their cotton lisle stockings, leaving our muddy imprints and spoiling their day.

The Nankin building was a rather new building and quite a plus for the village. Most of the county school children were still in one-room school buildings. We considered ourselves fortunate. My grandfather, James Fluke, working through Columbus state-house politics, was instrumental in acquiring what was a nice facility for its day. At this point, a three-year high school program was maintained in Nankin with the students finishing their Senior year in town at Ashland High School. The other two rooms in our school housed elementary grades. In my first year I was in the same room with my brother Donald, he in the second grade and I starting the first. Now you have to realize that even then he was an outstanding student, a teacher's dream who excelled in the three R's. And then here comes Louise. Always a B+ student, I did not come up to his caliber of work, hard as I tried. My teacher never let me forget that. Her name was Miss Shook. She was fond of Donald and apparently disliked me. My first grade and also my second are a bit like a bad dream to me. I'm sure there is some scarring yet.

I was promptly put into the "Blue Birds" reading class. I think the better class was known as the "Red Birds"—and everybody knew which bunch were the dummies. I DREADED reading aloud. I just hated it when Miss Shook would announce it was time for my group to go up to the reading circle, a semi-circle of chairs in the front of the room. I invented all sorts of means to get myself up to the dreaded circle. One winter some relatives from Cleveland, people of some means, sent a box of used clothing and one really great dress fit me. It was gray in color and sort of a knit, wooly dress. I thought it was beautiful. It had several buttons at the wrists of its long sleeves, and as I would make my way to the reading circle I would drag those buttons along the rungs on the backs of the chairs as I progressed to my place in the circle. This took place nearly seventy years ago, and yet it as clear as yesterday to me.

In my second grade, my brother had moved on to the third-grade room. Things didn't improve. I was still so distressed over the reading circle. In addition, my teacher was constantly asking me why I couldn't do things like my brother. (Once she even asked me who gave me such a bad haircut. This upset my mother, because she had actually paid to have my hair cut by one of the other teachers, Miss Hoag, in the same building.) This reading problem, reading aloud, became a lifelong cross for me. Finally, in the fourth grade I got a teacher, Miss Kline, who understood me and my problem, as well. I loved her fairness. She was a very tall, thin lady who stood for no nonsense. When the tattlers came in from recess and reported that so-and-so pushed them, she would say, "Well, well, do tell." I'm grateful to her for her insight, for seeing and understanding my problem. It was under her tutelage that I started to read to myself and enjoy it. I still clammed up over reading aloud, however.

Strange as it may seem, I still avoid reading aloud. I never volunteer to read the Bible aloud in Sunday School class. If it becomes my "turn" as the reading progresses around the room, I read, but not with ease, as I still remember the "Blue Bird" time in my life. One time after I was married and we lived with Bob's folks in the country east of Ashland, we were invited to join the Katatawa Community Club. I was promptly asked to be secretary. Great! I love to write minutes...and then it dawned on me that I would have to READ these minutes aloud at the monthly meetings. I nearly panicked. And the truth is I sometimes would feign sickness and stay home because I couldn't face that oral presentation. What a burden for me to carry. In order to overcome this, to a degree at least, I frequently read aloud my own personal devotions from the Bible or other writings. There is no one else here to hear me. I have always thought I read much as I write, and speak, with words and letters flopping around a bit. If I were starting school in today's world, I'm sure I would be labeled with a learning disability of some kind. I've always been glad it didn't dampen my pleasure in writing and for this reason I'm grateful this "Blue Bird" has been able to fly!

Louise Fluke Brownson Conery Beattie

May 26, 2004
I amend this now at the time of my 80th birthday—May 26, 2004. During the interview that Ann and Tina did with me for my party, Ann asked me what I would choose as a "title" for my life! With no time to ponder this question, this writing popped in to my mind. I think it truly tells the story of my early school days in Nankin Grade School and its impact on the rest of my life. I give credit to a wise teacher who helped me to walk through this time when I lacked self-assurance in so many ways. So my title for my life could be "A Blue Bird Can Fly!" I didn't give the credit to God then—but I do now.

Louise Beattie

BLESSINGS FOR MY CHILDREN
On the occasion of my 80th birthday
May 26, 2004

For Ann I would wish you always treasure your great talent for understanding and communicating with people—a talent you have for everyone. And then there is your God- given gift of poetry that has woven us all together in our circle of family—experiencing our joys and our sorrows—how you bound us all together with that Golden Cord. You are a fantastic grandma. You are so wise in your boundaries and input in other's lives. With Larry's retirement may you find peace and contentment wherever you live, whether it be across the Bay closer to Daisy or in some other area. Continue to live life to its fullest!.

For Bob I would wish for you a rewarding final year of teaching, realizing that the fruits of your labors may not be known for some time. You have touched lives. Many of your students don't really know the impact you have had in their beings—at least they don't know that yet. It takes time for teens to develop the sensitivity of acknowledgement in their lives. May you never experience again the multiple stresses of this past year. I'm praying for a most successful colon surgery and recuperation period and better health for the future. Find sanctuary in the woods—a part of your inheritance—blessed with the peace of the wonderful quiet you experience there, remembering your Fluke heritage.

For Tina I wish for you continued zest for life in all the things you do—your beautiful home and landscaping—your gift of holding your gang of guys and Molly together—your ambition and enthusiasm for everything you tackle—making things happen--making homes more beautiful, yours and the homes of others who don't have a clue as to how to put things together. May that gift always be yours. Grandma of so many, you fill the role so well, loving them all equally, keeping their best interests at heart. Retirement? I can't quite picture you retired. But may it be a peaceful, rewarding time whatever you and Rick decide to do.

For Frank You left us too soon. We suffer from the loss of your presence in our lives. And even though I know you are in a better place, I wonder how you are faring. I shouldn't question this, as our God is so capable of anything and everything! Do you know what goes on in our lives? I'm not much into ivory palaces or streets paved with gold. More to the point, are there places for you to hunt there, wildlife on the hoof, mushrooms galore? Is there a fire-pit and chair, a tree stand, or a reasonable facsimile there of? I ask that you be blessed with peace and comfort, ever in God's care. Do you know that you are making a bridge for us all?

For Molly My last born, my preemie, I would ask that the good Lord bless you with on-going good health that might grow ever better as the years go by and that you might feel a real peace in your life. I know that one of your fondest dreams is to become a grandma. May this wish come true and I pray that you will be blessed with several grandchildren. What a wonderful grandma you will be and how totally blessed will be those babies. The Fluke homestead needs some babies to roll around in the front yard whether they come from across the road or across the country. Keep those who feel sad, burdened and hurting in your heart, another of your wonderful gifts.

I pray for good health for all of you. It is hard to see middle- to old-age health problems developing in your lives, but I realize—and am thankful for—the fact that you are all taking better care of yourselves than I did taking care of myself as I aged. May you be surrounded individually by strong family ties and strengthened by your united strong family heritage.

I am so proud of all my children and also the wonderful spouses you chose to share in your lives. (Dad would have been proud, too). You are all so important to me, making me feel very loved. Life after 80? Well, whatever time I'm given, I hope to make good use of it.

Final words on this, my 80th birthday: Love each other always. And this is a quote I love, borrowed from somewhere I can't remember—*Tenderness and kindness are not signs of weakness and despair, but manifestations of strength and resolution.*

May God richly bless you all.

Love,
Mom

MY 80TH BIRTHDAY PARTY
May 26, 2004

It all began with two dozen b-e-a-u-t-i-f-u-l deep-rose-colored roses on the communion table at church on Sunday morning—Molly's touch. Well, actually it all started all those years ago in one of the rainiest spring season in history—much like 2004! I was born the third child to Gene and Mary Flue—not quite so fair in complexion and smaller than my preceding brother and sister. I was born hungry and was sucking my thumb within the hour! The die is cast!

Back to the present. Ann flew home to be with us, even though she had already made the trip home at the time of Frank's death in March. I really had no idea what the girls were planning. I'm sure there were lots of emails and phone calls and quite a bit of secrecy after Ann got here. I had told the "planners" that I did not want another "big" party—just family, my children and their spouses and that is what they did. Perfect!

On the day of the party an "all-girls breakfast" was held at the Lyn-Way with Ann, Tina, Molly and me in attendance, plus Aunt Betty, Laura and Leslie all driving down from Wellington of the occasion. What a fun time! Everybody was in rare form—full of stories and memories. Lyn-Way will never be the same.

At 6PM we gathered at Tina's for a traditional roast beef and pork dinner with mashed potatoes, gravy, green beans with bacon and new red potatoes, tossed fruit salad, rolls and a wonderful chocolate cake. Tina had the table all decorated so well—just handsome—with candles and flowers and using Grandma Swan's crocheted tablecloth overlay. Lovely meal!

Everyone had been given the assignment of writing down ten things they admired or remembered about their mom. Each person read aloud what they had written. We shared both tears and laughter through these readings. I wondered a bit if they were all really writing about me, their mom (or mother-in-law,) as they were most generous in their loving remarks and remembrances. The family gave me a wonderful gift—the prettiest bracelet I've ever seen—a wide silver one with a basket-weave. One the inside was engraved: Happy 80th. Love always, Ann, Bobby, Tina, Frank and Molly. I was truly delighted.

Now to back track. On Monday, Ann and Tina made a video of me, with Ann asking me a list of questions she had prepared. She asked me if I wanted to see the questions ahead of time, but I told her I would forgo that unless she was going to ask me about *War and Peace*. So they set me all up comfy in a chair in Tina's lovely living room and using a borrowed video camera (from Jake), they asked me questions and I answered for 1 1/2 hours. I had sorted of dreaded it, but it went well. The girls told me that I told them stories they had never heard before, like the time I was offered the management of the fabric store in Ashland and I was too unsure of myself to take it on. Missed opportunities! Who knows.

Toward the end of the interview, Ann asked me if I were to have a title for my life, what would it be? After a moment of total "blank," I replied, "Oh, I know! 'A Bluebird Can Fly'." I had suddenly thought of the story of my difficulty in the first grade at Nankin Grade School. Reading was not my forte as a six-year-old. I was put in the "Blue Birds" reading group, and I knew that it was the 1929 version of "Reading for Dummies." The "Red Birds" was the reading circle to be in. Several years ago I wrote an account of this experience, entitled "Blue Birds Can Fly." Enough said at this point. I turned the corner—a term of Dad's—

and in third grade I learned to read books on my own and loved it. Today, I read book after book, but the scars of that first-grade experience caused reading aloud to be a bugaboo for all my life. But I have come a long way. The video was viewed by all after the dinner.

I had a super 75th birthday party. I thought it couldn't be topped, but this one did. It is now two days past, and I am still basking in the glow of family love. My family surrounds me with great love, and I am totally proud of all of you. We missed Frank in our circle as we shared memories of days in Nankin and other places, too, but mostly Nankin, the home you all grew up in. Sherry had been asked to share in the evening, but I understood perfectly her declining, knowing it would make her really sad to be there without Frank.

Losing Frank from the circle has been so hard, a difficult time for us all, but especially for Sherry and Frankie who experience the void in their lives daily. Ann's poem about the Golden Cord tells our heartache, but also that we are sensing, now, the cord's tightening and strengthening our family bond.

I had experienced great love in the celebration of this milestone birthday, and I will treasure the events of the day, ever thankful for my great family as I look forward to whatever God has in store for me. I know He will see me through, for He knows every hair of our heads and each feather on a Blue Bird.

I love you all,
Mom, Louise

TEN THINGS ABOUT OUR MOM
For Mom's 80th birthday we had a special family dinner,
at which each of her children and their spouses shared "ten things."
May 26, 2004

Ann—Ten Things I Will Always Remember About My Mama

1. A Picnic Basket Of Food And A Thermos of Lemonade
   The day of our wedding Larry and I left immediately to make our way to Pennsylvania for Larry's new job. You packed us a picnic basket of food and a thermos of lemonade to take with us into our new life. You let your eldest child go to Pennsylvania and, later, California, without whining or making me feel guilty at all. (Only now that I am a mother and grandmother myself, do I know what a sacrifice that was.) Just as importantly, you came to see us in Pennsylvania and California and moved into our lives just a little while each year, even though I know you don't really like to leave home. And I will always remember with gratitude that you respected my wishes and did *not* come to California as you felt drawn to do during my depression, something I needed to suffer on my own.

2. The Smell Of Spring
   You kept a clean, orderly house with as much loveliness as the pocketbook would allow at each stage of your life. I especially will remember coming home on a spring day each year to find you had done the spring-cleaning of our bedroom leaving it glowing and fresh—newly-polished floors, curtains and bedspread laundered and smelling of sunshine, scatter rugs clean and poofy, windows open and a breeze blowing springtime inside the room. It always gave me a feeling of hope and well-being.

3. A Hollyhock Cake, Bath-Towel Robes, Mahogany-Colored Turkeys
   You made birthdays, Christmas and holidays happen on very little money for a lot of kids, made our special days *special*. The birthday child's favorite cake all dolled up for the party—one year my cake had dolls made from hollyhocks on the top. The birthday boy or girl's favorite meal. Three carefully-chosen gifts for each of us at Christmas—I remember the bathrobes you sewed for your three girls, made from patterned bath towels. A Christmas tree hung with beloved ornaments—a plastic snowman on skis whose backpack once held suckers, an angel tree-topper whose wings you had repaired with tinfoil. Bountiful, festive meals with all the trimmings—oh, those giant turkeys roasted to crispy, red-brown, still miraculously moist and tender. Dyed eggs, jelly beans, marshmallow peeps, a chocolate bunny and a little gift in our Easter basket each year.

4. Your Long, Long Hair
   I always saw your long hair as a sign of a desire to be your own person, not part of the crowd, a symbol of your wanting to express your individuality. And I love that this husband (Bill) has sometimes brushed your long hair for you. I always carry the memory of your body and physical appearance, your neatness and cleanliness, the mole on the base of your neck (later removed) that was just like mine, your hands and clean nails, your embraceable body, your youthful skin, your softness and your strength, your partiality to clothes with detailing—top-stitching, special buttons, darts, unusual pockets or raglan sleeves.

93

5. Terms Of Endearment

As you grow older, you sometimes call me "My Dear" or "Ann Dear." Each time you do, I feel it as an address of a new stage in your mother-love, the cherishing endearment of an elder, my wise-woman mother.

6. Someone Is Home, The Lights Are On, Dinner Is In The Oven, All Is Well

You always provided a sense of security for us as kids. You were always there, always grounded, always sober, always dependable, always a good woman doing her best. Though Dad was sometimes swept away on tides of illness or depression or silence, you were always there as our anchor.

7. AIM, Ark, Watercolors, Daring Older Woman On A Flying Trapeze

You are ripening well, having dealt with difficult times without turning bitter or rotten. You keep expanding your horizons and deepening your wisdom—taking classes, having adventures in California, casting an eye to visiting in Colorado. You allow yourself to be inspired and act on your inspiration—creating AIM (Adventures In Maturity) and the ARK ministry (making bags for Foster kids to use to carry their belongings.) You continue to learn and try new things—taking up watercolor painting, becoming proficient on the computer. You are always seeking positive ways to use your energy—volunteering at Hospice, giving generously to your church and other charities, creating more greeting cards than Hallmark. You welcome the friendship of both young and old, especially loving the vitality young people bring to your life. You are bright, an avid reader. Though you are sometimes hesitant to reach out, you love it when you can connect, love it when you feel comfortable enough to tell a good story and make people laugh.

8. A Woman of Faith, Singing Harmony

I hear your voice in my ear singing old, familiar hymns. You have believed deeply in your faith. What comes through to me most is the sense you gave us that there is a right and good way to live and treat others, and that is the way you wanted us to live our lives. You always describe your faith self-deprecatingly as "simple," but I have always seen you as living your faith as God created and made you, especially you, to live it. "By their fruits you shall know them." And your fruits are and have been bountiful and good. You are a top-flight organizer of anything, and you have employed that for other people's behalf your whole life long.

9. Tea-Dyed Lace, Spaghetti Feeds, 10 Pounds Of Fries

You have always been abundant and creative in your domesticity, believing the 11th Commandment is "Thou Shalt Not Be Chintzy." You are a wonderful cook and you have continued to cook and bake for others even when your diabetes precluded partaking yourself. You baked a literal wagonload of peach pies for Molly's wedding, cooked up 10 pounds of potatoes at a time for French Fries, fixed mounds of shrimp salad for Breezure's (son Bob's) birthdays and fricasseed a parakeet! Oops, forget that...though it is a memorable story in family lore. Your home is always a beautiful nest, always good-smelling and clean. You have designed, sewn, dyed lace for, piled on orange petticoats for, traded dusting and housework for: prom dresses, school dresses, bridal gowns, bridesmaids' dresses and mother-of-the-bride/groom dresses. You are a Goddess of Home Arts.

10. Mama Duck And Her Five Ducklings

Mama Duck walks along, and the ducklings follow. Mama Duck splashes into the water and the ducklings follow. Mama Duck dives and the ducklings follow. You have taught us, by your example, how to live, how to be a good parent. You have loved us through all our trials, respected our individual gifts and talents, loving in each one of us what makes us who we are—even when there were times you didn't understand us. We're still watching and following, Mama Duck, as you teach us to be 80 and older.

Larry—Ten Memories Of Louise

1. Being so welcoming to me and serving up the best roasts I've ever eaten as the family and I sat around the table in the Nankin house when I was dating Ann.
2. Loving her poodles; it planted the seeds for me to accept Topsy into my home several years later.
3. Entertaining and feeding a Nankin houseful of people with seemingly no more trouble than picking up the mail.
4. Being there and doing what was needed during the crisis of Ann's hemorrhage and subsequent stay in the hospital.
5. Giving such warm heartfelt hugs every time she came to visit in California.
6. Being so open to trying new experiences in California—foods, wines, Robert Pante's Dress for Success seminar, Fenton's Creamery, tours of the Bay Area, theater (Petey Fisk), Lake Tahoe.
7. Being such easy company to have visit that I always hated to see her leave.
8. Never wanting to linger over goodbyes at the airport.
9. Liking her sporty cars.
10. Being the best mother-in-law I could ever imagine.

Bob—For Mom —Ten Things

1. Forgiving
2. Vital
3. Vivacious
4. Purpose-driven (softly so)
5. Resilient
6. High integrity
7. Gracious
8. Giving
9. Even-keeled
10. Voted most important in the fox-hole.

Gini—Happy Birthday, Louise/Mom—Ten Things

Asked to write 10 things about you what immediately came to mind were character words or traits: love, compassion, strength, concern, vitality, humor, tenderness, honesty, friendship, morality, spiritual, real, and oh yes, grit.

Louise, you are a person I have always admired in the straight-forward, positive way you have faced life. You see a need—you go after it. (AIM, Ark, cards, financial help, a listening ear.) So many people know you can be counted on—myself, included.

One thing I especially admire about you is your ability to handle adversities or the tough times in life. You do it with such "pluck!" Not that you don't hurt and not that you don't let us know you hurt, but you have the strength to go on, bear up, and look forward with such grace and determination…that "We mustn't cry over spilt milk forever" attitude…so admirable!

Little did I know that day back in '74 when my heart melted over a house painter named Bob that I would also fall in love with his wonderful mom and family. I might call you Louise but know that I think of you as mom…no mother-in-law jokes here.

Tina—Ten Things

Dear Mom,
Here I am at 3:00 o'clock AM. For an hour I have been in my bed unable to sleep because I am mentally making my list and thinking through all that I want to say to you. This is very difficult for me, but I'll try my best…

The top ten things I love about my mom!
1. I admire your commitment to God and the church. What a great foundation for your life and all of your children.
2. You are so soft and loving. Your "hugs" are the best. You have loved us all in a way so unique.
3. You can get the job done no matter how difficult it is. You taught me that I can work right alongside the guys—I'm so thankful that I have your strength and energy.
4. What an awesome cook—food preparation was fun and eating it was even better yet. I still remember coming home from church in Nankin and smelling the roast baking in the oven. That was the best smell and even today when I prepare that meal it brings back a special memory of home.
5. Thanks for all the beautiful dresses that you made for us all. Prom dresses, wedding dresses, and special Easter dresses. I'm amazed today that you tackled such difficult projects. My senior prom dress sticks out in my mind—I had the prettiest dress—and my very own mom made my dress. I still have that dress.
6. Your ability to continue on in life when you have lost someone you loved so very much. You don't give up. Your courage amazes me.
7. Your desire to help those who are less fortunate. Riverside Christian Training School, ARK, baby blankets, teddy bears and the list goes on. You have helped so many—and most of them you have never even met.
8. The beautiful notes that you have written to so many people. You have such a special gift—your words of encouragement have "lifted" so many up!
9. Your wisdom to be able to help us all. I think of the time that Joe was so sick—your wisdom prompted me to seek help! I always thought your intervention saved his life!! Your wisdom and guidance has helped us through difficult times.
10. You have been my absolute role model. I see you as a woman of such great character. Hard working and yet soft and loving. Thank you so much for being such a wonderful mom. I have always looked at myself as a great blend of you and Dad. For this I am forever thankful and I will continue to pattern myself after you. I want my mom to be proud of me! Please know how much I respect you and that I love you with my whole heart.

Happy 80th birthday Mom. You are loved by so many. My prayer for you is that today you will feel completely loved by us all! Peace be with you.

Love forever,
Tina

Rick—Ten Things

Dear Louise,
The ten things that I am about to write represent but a sketch of how much you mean to me. I am so proud to have you as my mother-in-law. You provided me a beautiful little girl and nurtured her to become a great mother, grandmother, and most of all my wife. To you Louise, so much credit is due. The following ten things are but just a few.

1. You always have shown a compassion for other people not as fortunate as yourself.
2. I always enjoyed watching you put on a big meal for everybody back in the day. You always made it happen and got it on the table in such a beautiful way.
3. The cars you drove were so neat, and I loved the way you enjoyed them. The hot little red Comet GT was my favorite.
4. Whenever we came to visit with our kids, you always made up a little "thack" of goodies for them to take home.
5. I love your laughter. Your laughter exudes joy!
6. I admire your deep concern and love for your family. You always seem to know who needs attention.

7. You have always been a hard worker with no complaint. If there is a job to be done, you get it done.
8. I love your beauty. I have always enjoyed the picture of you in your wedding picture, and you have remained just as beautiful at the young age of 80!
9. Your commitment to the Lord, your family, and friends has always set an example to our entire family.
10. Last and most selfishly, I love you because of who you are, but also, you have always loved me.

Love,
Rick McFrederick

Molly—Ten Things I Love About My Mom

1. I can only imagine the sacrifices that you made for me as an infant...you must have been so exhausted with the move to Ashland...and 4 other kids in tow...and Dad probably too busy with a new coaching job to help you much. How did you find time to pump that breast milk?...to give me that extra nutritive boost that, as a preemie, I surely needed? Thanks for being selfless, Mom.

2. I love the fact that you were a stay-at-home mom and were always there when I needed you. You were always there on school days to make lunch for Frank and me. This gave life a degree of security.

3. Thanks for teaching me to sew. You tackled difficult sewing projects, and they turned out well. I cannot imagine sewing my daughter's wedding dresses. You seemed to do that with confidence. You gave me a gift in exposing me to the world of being a seamstress, and I have found much satisfaction in this gift.

4. You are a good cook, and this trait "rubbed off" on your daughters, and in turn, your granddaughters. You were always generous with food. I can still remember the smell of freshly baked bread when I came home from school...a smell that has meant "tangible love" for people through the centuries.

5. I love the way you are able to organize things. You always had your neat little desk...a place where records, bills and letters were carefully kept. Sometimes when I go through my files, I think, "Mom would be doing a much better job of this."...and I try to do a better job of it! Well, maybe I'll get better at this as I get older. I've had a great example set for me!

6. I admire the ability you had to organize BIG events. You were President of the Boosters and that entailed a huge amount of work. I was there watching you do it...tucking away information and confidence which let me know that if my mom could do it, so could I!!! I ended up taking my turn at Boosters, too.

7. I love your "arty" side. It's evident in everything from your water-color painting to your ability to express yourself in the written word. It also comes through in the way you express yourself in your "home surroundings"...beauty, grace, softness of colors and peacefulness. You've been arty for years, as evidenced in your sewing and love of flowers. You have used your hands for many creative purposes and produced many meaningful gifts of beauty and usefulness.

8. I love the fact that you are my FRIEND, as well as my mom! You have always been someone to whom I could bring even my worst problems... you have always tried to help me keep "things" in perspective, reminding me of the *truth*...that things get better with the passage of time...and you are right, they do!

9. You watched over me when I was sick, staying with me even after I told you that you could *"Go HOME."* You were not a stranger to what I was facing, because you'd seen it before in those you loved. Even though you had no personal experience with depression, you had compassion and didn't pass judgement. You gave me hope that I would get well...and I did!

10. I love the fact that you have always been a woman of God. I cannot even imagine what it would be like to never have been exposed to church. I have early memories of sitting beside you at Nankin Federated and listening to your strong alto voice. Over the year, you've grown even stronger in your faith. You have raised 5 kids who know and care about the things of God. We are good, moral people. We are your heritage, and I'm sure that God is pleased.

With love...
from *Your Preemie*

Glenn—Louise, Ten Things I Admire

1. The 1st time that I met Louise–1975–we had burgers on the grill and salad. It was just Bob, Louise, Molly and me. She made me feel at home and welcome. This was my introduction into the family.

2. During the time that Molly and I were dating and I was in the hospital for my kidney stone, Louise came to visit me.

3. Louise borrowed our 1975 Ford Mustang so she could go "profiling." Louise has always liked a "sporty" car, especially one with a spoiler.

4. Louise always loved our children and treated them just as we wanted them to be treated. If they needed to be corrected, she would do it with love and respect.

5. No matter the situation, Louise always displayed wisdom, love, understanding, care and most of all, grace.

6. In 1982, Louise went to North Carolina with us in our camper. We had a wonderful time. We often talk about the time that Erin and I took an unexpected "dip" in the waves.

7. During Molly's recovery from surgery in 2000, Louise came and stayed while I was away from home. She understood the situation and was able to be a caregiver to Molly. This has and continues to mean a lot to Molly and me.

8. From Louise, one of the Fluke children, I appreciate hearing about how she helped Grandpa Gene on the farm. I can identify with milking "a" cow by hand, but she had to milk many cows by hand. Louise has always "identified" with the land and the farm. I believe she still has a screen-saver picture of some of our cattle.

9. I admire Louise and her use of the computer. It is a necessary tool in her life, helping her to stay in touch with others.

10. Louise loves family, being active, getting out and being involved. I hope that when I turn 80, that I will express that same "vim and vigor.

Most of all, I thank you for being the mother of my wife.

Love, Glenn

ABOUT AGING

For Ann on Her Birthday
July 21, 2005

In this process of aging,
I have had time to reflect on my life,
time to question what I have
or have not accomplished,
what I have stood for and the times
I have just plain goofed!

For in my span of eighty-one years,
I have known both sorrow and joy—
the bitter with the sweet,
the happy times and lonely times—
and I realize that all along the way
I had—and still have—*choices!*

I can live in the gloom of life,
allowing it to be my total focus,
or I can choose to rise above it
and become positive,
to look to the future with hope,
knowing that it is God's plan for me
—for I see only a glimpse of life.

In aging I have experienced
the loss of those near and dear to me.
Two husbands, parents, grandparents
and ah, yes, the loss of an adult son.
It would be easy to draw inward
and focus on the negatives of old age
—the aches and pains, ever with us.

I have left some things undone
and I should have enjoyed
the joyful moments more.
I should have taken more chances
—strived for more goals.
However, basically, I'm satisfied,
I have lived and loved life.
God has blessed me. I am content.

Happy Birthday, to my firstborn, Ann

Mom

FLUKE REUNION, 2005
Labor Day Weekend
Points To Ponder by the "Middle One" of the Fluke Kids

Hey, we all made it—all five of us [the Fluke Kids] but not without effort and many miles. We are all grateful for the opportunity to once again be able to be a part of this great event! Elinor Martin, from Michigan, accompanied by Liz (Azoni)—Donald Fluke from North Carolina, coming to Ohio with Mary Fluke—and Helen Fluke from Florida, who braved the Atlanta airport to be with us. We are not as spry as we once were, but our hearts pull us "home" to the farm to be close to all the kinfolk, to enjoy the three-day event held every other Labor Day weekend. Each year is different. Each year we declare this one to be the BEST. And then another one come along and tops them all. What a weekend! The weather was perfect—not a drop of rain—sunshine all the way.

The high-energy weekend started on Friday night with a dedication of the new farm pond to Frank Brownson who died very suddenly on March 14, 2004. This was his "territory"—where he walked, hunted and enjoyed nature. His Uncle Walter Brownson initiated a fund at the time Frank's death to help in the cost of establishing a new pond at the same site as the one Grandpa Gene had built in, I think, 1965. Ann Keiffer so beautifully planned the program and dedication, involving all those attending. Walter launched the event with a fitting tribute to his nephew, Frank—remembering the hunting and Frank's love of nature and how much he had meant to us all. Molly and Glenn had installed a large stone engraved with words of tribute and the dates of Frank's birth and death. At the end of the service, Erin Johnson led the group in singing "For the Beauty of the Earth," accompanied by Bob Brownson on guitar, who also closed the evening with prayer.

Earlier in the service all the kids and many adults lit little votive candles and placed them in tiny white paper boats which were then launched around the edge of the pond, The daylight was fading to dark—the effect was beautiful. The tiny boats, moved by a very gentle breeze, floated toward the east end of the pond. Then each person was given a black, polished stone and told to go to the edge of the pond. At the sound of the hunting horn we were to throw the stones into the water, thinking about Frank and our memories of him. What a heartfelt experience to hear the individual stones going "ker-plunk" in the semi-darkness. Previous to the dedication Molly had provided a "campfire supper"—served off the hayladders. Many of the guests brought in cookies, a wonderful assortment. What a wonderful way to celebrate the life of our Frank—honoring him in this area which was so much a part of his life. The pond has long been a focal point at the farm, in years past and again in this year with the new pond. The "clan" was to feel free to come and play and meditate at this very peaceful spot. By my unofficial count, there were 76 in attendance.

An interesting sidelight... The next morning, someone taking a walk to the pond observed a frog sitting on one of the white paper boats—just sliding along—enjoying the day. Too bad there was NO camera! (The candles were still burning as the last folks left the site Friday night.) Molly and I had made the 65 boats out of folded paper, but we had no idea that they would hold up that well or that they might last into the next day, becoming a method of "froggy transportation." Today—five days later—they were still floating. Sadie, Molly's dog, was retrieving them, bringing them back to her.

On SATURDAY—the BIG day! 87 Flukes gathered to celebrate the day.

The "Assigned Privileges" worked well this year. I will mention some—and forget others, I'm sure. The food first. Salad-making was going on at Erin Johnson's home with Mary Fluke and Erin knee-deep in lettuce. Gini Brownson, Kathy Martin and Dale Fluke were whipping up desserts to die for at the Brownson household. Molly Smith prepared a roaster full of escalloped potatoes. And Louise Beattie and Tina McFrederick marinated well over 100 chicken breasts in the Beattie kitchen on Friday. By mid-morning on Saturday, the prepared food began showing up at the farm. At 11:00 Larry Keiffer fired up the grill and shortly Matt Johnson joined him at a second grill. Add Matt Brownson and you have the crew for cooking the chicken, sausages and hotdogs. By mistake, I had gotten a package of HOT Italian sausages in a purchase mixup. WOW! Surprise to those who thought they had picked out a regular sausage! Forgive me, I'm sorta over the hill. Competency suffers in aging, you know. John Keiffer was very competent with the drinks—preparing gallons and gallons of lemonade. In the late morning, Bob Brownson, with help from others, built a huge pile of wood for the bonfire and corn roast. The actual roasting of the sweet corn was done by Bob with the help of Bill and David Martin. Many "oohs" and "ahs" over the corn—done to perfection, always a highlight of the reunion.

Crafts for the little ones were ably handled by Lynn Ritschdorff and Kathy Martin. Lots of stickers and Play-Dough materialized into some cute things to take home.

Margaret gave an update on the Fluke history. How fortunate we are to have someone as talented and caring as Margaret to keep our "roots" intact and up to date.

Also new this year—a Scavenger Hunt. This was provided by Susan McFrederick. What fun they had with this—an excited gang in teams, each with several kids and an adult supervisor. They worked very hard and fast trying to find, among other things, a four-leaf clover—that, without success. There was even an attempt to hold two clover leaves together. And one guy, in response to the request for a cow patty brought in the whole thing in a plastic bag! I don't know who won.

Hayrides—there were three, I believe. The wagon was loaded to the gills each trip out. Rick Krause had trucked-in his newly-acquired Ford tractor—actually, it was Grandpa Gene's last tractor. In that roundabout way the tractor is now back in the family. On the first trip out, just rounding the curve on the by-road, the rear right tire of the wagon BLEW! Sounded like a gunshot. Joe McFrederick, Steph and little Andrew were just arriving and it "blew" right beside them. It is a wonder that Andrew didn't want to leave the farm right then, but he was a real trooper and had a great time all day and evening. Rick Krause drove the first two loads out, and the Glenn, the final one, after dark. On that one I hear there was lot of "mooing" from the loaded wagon, probably spooking the cows and calves a bit.

Marty brought fireworks from Michigan. WHAT A SHOW! Again, the "law" left us alone. The neighbors didn't report the happenings at the Smith Farm. And the night sky over the sycamores was lit up with color and vibrating with SOUND! Fourth of July celebrations—take a back seat!

Added this year were several new events, and they will be "keepers" for sure. Molly Smith wrote the skits for four PUPPET SHOWS. Three were stories from the Fluke Heritage. Erin Johnson, Susan McFrederick and John Keiffer assumed the roles of various Flukes in the past. What a FANTASTIC job they did. I did so wish that someone would have videotaped it all—the performances, the performers, but the audience as well. The fourth show was about the "Cookie Monster" and a lesson on greediness. A nice way to end it—especially for the kids who made a mad scramble for the cookies recklessly scattered by the Cookie Monster. It was all absolutely priceless. Already ideas are being filtered in to Molly for "next time!" Hoots of laughter, knee-slapping and loud guffaws filled the lawn (the viewing area.) Perfect atmosphere—beautiful sunshine—what a day!

Late in the afternoon—no, really, it was almost dark—we were given a contest to see who might be the "Fluke-iest" of the entire gang. Molly and Ann had devised the game. A cowbell was selected as the "prize"—to be awarded to the Fluke-iest person. First, you had to answer quite a list of questions, such as: Do you hate to be more than four hours away from home? Did you ever eat bread and milk as dessert? Did you ever wear a long-sleeved shirt in the summer time? On the back page of the contest were images of some very obscure, odd, tiny "things" on the farm. The contestants were kind of loosely assigned groups, which soon became "families," which boiled down to the Krause and McFrederick families. Wow! Talk about splitting straws. Neck-in-neck, the whole way, with the Krause family finally becoming the winners. The cowbell is engraved:

The Fluke Family Reunion
Most "Moo-valous"
Award

The cowbell now graces the mantel of Margaret Welch's home on Township Road 754, about a mile-and-a-half to the west of the farm. This is rotating "trophy" to be back at the reunion in 2007 for another contest. Helen and I were teamed together. As older aunties we felt we didn't have a chance amidst the youngest sleuths armed with flashlights and digital cameras used to record and verify the "finds."

Modern day times—things change. Cell phones in use to confer with each other, especially families or parts of families who didn't make it to the event. The Port-a-Pot intrigues the little ones. While perched on the "throne," one little girl—I won't name her, but she is in the McFrederick clan—said, "I just LOVE the smell of this place." We think she was referring to the deodorizer apparently lavishly applied in the sanitization process before it came to the farm. Hmmm...makes me think about the old, authentic ones, our outhouses.

We are all so indebted to Molly and Glenn for all the work they do to get ready for the arrival of the clan—folks coming back to their roots. Also thanks to their auxiliary crew who came in ahead of time and helped no end. Namely, John Keiffer, who mowed the pastures, cut firewood, and who later helped Glenn go to our church and truck tables and chairs, roasters and large thermoses for drinks. It takes lots of legwork to put this all together. "Our" yellow-topped tent—our home away from home—we've had the same one before—came in and was set up by the Lions Club on Friday.

Brunch at the farm was provided by Helen Helvenston and Emeline Fulmer on Sunday morning, with an assist from Ann Keiffer. An unofficial count of 26 members of the clan came to have some wonderful fruit, muffins, and some delicious little rolls made by Pepper and brought by John and Dale Fluke. The goodbyes were not easy, as always. Most folks were on the road before noon. We rejoiced that they all had good weather to head home.

Much thought goes into the preparation for this event. My one regret is that it goes too fast. It is hard to take in all the activity—to hear all that is said—to try to get a minute with everyone to hear about their lives. We see how the little ones of last year have grown and now see a fresh crop on the scene. Six-weeks-old Derrick Baum was the youngest this year. Wrapped in a blanket this year, he will be walking around in 2007—and probably on the hayride.

We were happy the Evans—Marilee, David and Eva—could join us again this year, coming from Texas. They made it for the Friday night pond dedication, as well as Saturday. Gloria Horn came with the Evanses on Saturday—good to see her, too. Pat and Harold Williams from Cleveland came for the Saturday events. First-ever guests were Jim and Gretchen Fluke from Dublin, Ohio. We appreciate all their efforts to join in the festivities and hope they will come again. Pat is the daughter of Mary (Fluke) Dixon. Marilee, Gloria and Jim are members of the John Fluke branch of the family.

An event of the weekend touched our hearts. It was the fact that the courts awarded Sherry Brownson the custody of her dear little three-year-old grandson, Leif. This took place on Friday morning. How timely for the pond-dedication day, as Leif was the absolute darling of Grandpa Frank's eye. We join with Sherry and Frankie in this milestone event in their lives. LUCKY little boy—now with "Bee" and "Mawmaw," for sure.

The youngsters grow—the rest of us just grow older. How glad we were that our dear Elinor could make it here for the reunion, though it took much effort on her part. Thanks to Liz who carefully shepherded her mother down and back in one day. The years take their toll—will we all be together in 2007? The Lord willing, hopefully we will.

I've attempted to recall the things I saw, heard and experienced. However, I know I missed a lot. In 2007 I would like to see a family portrait—all 87 or however many attend—like in the old history albums. I'd also like to see photos of various family units to preserve the day. Now *there* is an OPPORTUNITY! Keep those thoughts and suggestions coming. Just say, "I could do that!"

As I write this I am thinking of all the devastation and loss of life in the Gulf Coast region. I know the scenes of destruction were there in the back of our minds and in our hearts as the weekend progressed. Our prayers go with the people there in these most trying times.

Love to you all,

Louise Beattie

REMEMBERING EMILY JO MARTIN

January 10, 1954–August 19, 2006

Yesterday—quite a day—we said our goodbyes to our Emily—so much to remember and to mull over. Many relatives to hug and many emotions to experience: tears, laughter, and yes, even joy...what a special word.

When I left home at 8:00 AM, Bill said "Have a good time." And then he was embarrassed, saying he should have said, "Have a safe trip." But you know, we all had a really good time. A good time to be interpreted in several ways—even in sadness there can also be joy. Yesterday was much more like a blend of both tears and joy—they can be so closely related, especially in times like yesterday as we listened to the Martin siblings remember their sister Emily with humor, along with grief, and yet happiness and joy, as well. Emily would have hooted at some of their memories; however, she would have known she was blessed and loved by them all.

The Brownson/Smith contingent—and I—arrived at Serenity Road to join the family circle, already present, and eat a fine lunch provided to some extent by close friends. How wonderful to sit around their big table catching up with the family—the younger generation(s) and to meet David Drouillard, Liz's new husband, whom, by the way, is an easy person to know, a really nice guy. Elinor invited us to see Emily's room—intact, with the things that were very much "Emily." Nice to have that picture of her little space in the world in my mind, as I took inventory of her special treasures grouped around her bed.

The memorial service was held at the Pixley Funeral Home in Rochester, Michigan, where Rick, Janet, and Emeline joined us all. Visitation took place in a large room across the hall from an even larger room where the service was held. Lynne and Liz had carefully put together several bulletin boards of photos of Emily and her family down through the years. I was especially touched by the ones that showed her holding the babies—each of her nieces and nephews—as newborns in her arms. What a treasure!

In the gathering of maybe 150, I know there were many old friends of the family in attendance. There were people from the "automobile world" who were longtime friends of Elinor and Bill, though I'm sure that number had dwindled in recent years. There were neighbors from their own street and friends from their church. I did get a minute to talk with Bill's sister Lois, hadn't seen her since the family weddings in the past. Weddings and funerals, they draw families together, often from many miles away. This was one of those drawing-in days, embracing the years of remembrances and shared happenings.

Emily's pastor, Steve Andrews, of the Kensington Community Church, also the pastor for Liz, Lynne and their families, gave the opening words of welcome to all the assembled family and guests. Heartfelt remembrances from Emily's siblings followed.

Lynne spoke first, remembering the "giggle sessions" in their shared bedroom, then memories of Emily riding a bike, her school life and playtime. I never knew she was able to ride a bike. I especially loved Liz's comment about Emily in her adult years, eating out and wondering how she could order from the kiddie-menu and still get a gin-and-tonic!
'

I believe that both Pastor Andrews and Lynne used Psalm 139:13-16 in remembering Emily. It was also printed in her memorial tribute provided by the funeral home.

Liz spoke next, telling more about Emily's life and especially recounting the last few weeks of Emily's life—the hospital stay, the tests, the draining of fluids, how hard it was to try to make her comfortable as she lay confined in bed for too many hours in painful positions, her body distended with fluid build-ups. Liz told of the final day(s) of Emily's life and Emily's coming to terms with end-of-life issues, how bravely Emily faced it all.

Brother Bill spoke last. He and Kathy had driven in from Anchorage, Alaska, 4000 miles away, leaving their RV/caravan trip to head back to be with family. Ten days on the road. They made it home "in time," receiving the blessing of having a day with Emily to treasure some heartfelt thoughts in conversation together. Bill tied it all together so beautifully with scripture and deeply-felt remembrances of this special lady and her life confined in her "mixed-up-bones-body," as she called it. It is always difficult to go to the deep spots in our hearts and express the sorrow and love we feel in the face of emotions that run that deep, but they, her siblings, all three, did it and did it so well. The entire group was touched deeply by their words.

Pastor Steve Andrews officiated for the service. Small wonder Emily, her sisters and their families are involved with such a dynamic church. Pastor Andrews is a genuine leader, a blend of deep reverence for God with spontaneity and humor—a true servant of our Father in Heaven. Two pieces of music were used—sorry, I can't remember the name of the first one, but the second one was a more contemporary arrangement of the old hymn, "It Is Well With My Soul." It was FANTASTIC! About half-way through the recorded hymn there was a technical problem and the music came to a halt. Silence—then chuckles, a nice relief from the gathering tears. And then the music started to play again. Something very unusual happened! During the final two choruses the gathering of family and friends sang along, building in volume with the last "It is well with my soul." It was moving and so fitting. These words make each of us wonder, is it well with *our* soul?

Our special little lady has left us—gone on to be with her Heavenly Father and all those who have gone on before her. I find myself picturing Emily with Grandma Mary and Grandpa Gene and all the others who have left this old world. I can especially see Emily and Frank sharing a quiet and endearing moment together. They were always connected at the reunion, with Frank squatted down by her wheelchair in earnest conversation.

Emily always took in all the events of the reunion that were possible from the limited vantage point of her chair. She viewed it all, the generations, the hay rides, the games, the little ones, the conversations she could hear, the "flavor" of the day. She recorded it all in her memory, everything in order. Our Emily.

Emily's request was that her eyes be donated to someone in need. Hopefully, that someone will "see" because of her bequest. Bless her heart.

We will love you for an eternity, Emily.

Aunt Louise (Beattie)

FOR ELINOR
MY SISTER, MY MENTOR AND MY DEAR FRIEND
March 31, 2007

We always knew there would come this day—a day when one in our circle of five siblings would begin to fold their tent and prepare to leave this life. But I'm struggling—not ready for you to go. If I get to see and talk to you just one more time I will be overjoyed but if not, these are a few of the things I'd like to tell you or maybe tell you again.

Over half my favorite recipes are yours, loving memories accompany each one. It was you who taught me how to cook and entertain, though I never came up to your benchmark. You're the best! Weekends with the Martins were something to really look forward to, whether it was in the days with all our little kids together, our families together, or later with Jim coming, too. I regret that my Bill was never able to travel to 3055 Serenity Rd. You always kept a beautiful home, clean, bright and with just the right amount of lovely "things" to see, taste and enjoy. Water, trickling in the little stream—I thought it had rained softly all night long. I absolutely loved it!

When I was 16 and still biting my nails, I'd look at your lovely manicured, mauve/rose nails and wonder if I could ever have ones like yours. Your clothes in beige, ivory and black set the mark for me. Elegance all the way! Of course, you were always tall and thin and stylish—never could describe myself as such— but you were my example as to how to dress. In our days on the farm we were raised in the era of: an apron for you, as Mom's faithful helper, and me in denim overalls and straw hat, Dad's helper in the fields and in the barn. You know, we both filled our individual roles in a farm family and did it well—without fussing or complaining.

When, Tina, my third baby was born in 1949 I had to came down to Ashland 3 weeks ahead of time— overdue pregnancies are no fun—and then went to our mother's for the required two weeks of "rest and rehab" after her birth. I was SO ready to go to my own home in New London before the scheduled two weeks was up. Dad was sick—his semi-annual ulcer attack—the household was tense. Then you came down from Michigan. Bless your heart! How did you know? I remember you asked me what I would really like to do and I told you I wanted to go home. You asked what would it take to allow this to happen? I told you that my house would need some cleaning, after all I had been gone for nearly five weeks. And off you went to make it shipshape for my return with new baby and two toddlers! And you bought me some kitchen things as a "surprise!" Among these things were two aluminum pie pans. I still have them. They are etched with a thousand marks of pie- cuttings. On the bottom is marked "Brownson"—with "Conery" and "Beattie" added as the years went by. However, every time I've used them I think, "my sister loved me then and she loves me still!" You have always been so special to me!

Your lovely letters and notes down thru the years have always been a joy to receive, a welcome reward after a trip to the mailbox. And I know when you became unable to put your thoughts down on paper, I understood how sad it made you feel. Always written on blue-or pale gray note paper in your perfect printing, a work of art topped only by your lovingly expressed thoughts of concern and love for me and mine, for us all. What a gift that you gave to so many! Handwriting is special—so unique—kind of like the "thought prints" of a person. Yours has always been that for me and our dear mother's likewise.

Even though we have lived many miles/hours apart throughout all our adult years, we have remained "close, "ready to listen to each other's heart, always regretting that we couldn't see each other more often, always wishing we could sit down on the patio face-to-face with a cup of tea more often, but ever grateful for the wonderful, loving bond we have always enjoyed together throughout our lives—together or apart.

We have "circled" each other in times of joy—weddings, births and reunions—and also in times of loss and grief. Today, as I write this, 3-31-07 marks the 26th anniversary of our dad's death.

Just yesterday Molly took me for a ride all around the farm on their "Gator" a *2x4* sort of ATV deal with a bed on the back for hauling things, and I got to see everything—the pastures and fields sprouting green grass, the pond so clean and serene with geese swimming around, the fields with their promise of another year of growth. The wheat is up and looking nice. It was too wet to go into the woods, but the trees are all budded and ready to go. It was an absolutely delightful, nostalgic trip for me! I could never have walked that far. The farm looks so nice, everything is in order—wouldn't our dad be happy to see how it looks and how well cared for it all is? I viewed everything for *"all of us,"* breathed in the fresh, clean air. I was thankful to Molly for making the viewing of the farm possible, also thankful for our Fluke heritage and the place where we grew up. Nice memories, revisited.

We Fluke "five" did alright, didn't we? And you were the best ever "leader"—the rest of the troops followed. You set the mark and I/we all thank you!

Know that I love you my dear, now, today and forever—and forever is a wonderful word, so full of promise for all God's children. Save a seat for me—by you—in the sunshine—in the "garden!"

Always with love,
Louise

MEMORIAL SERVICE FOR ELINOR (FLUKE) MARTIN
April 21, 2007

A very special lady died April 10, 2007. We celebrated her life on Saturday, April 21 as her family and friends gathered around in the same funeral home where we bid our dear Emily goodbye in August of 2006. The day was sunny and warm, the best kind of early spring day—in Michigan or Ohio.

The facilities at Pixley are most accommodating, complete with elevator. A large room on one side of the central hall provided a great place to meet and visit with family and friends. In this room there were various photo-display boards on easels with pictures of Elinor as a child, as a young adult, as a wife, and others of her with children, family and friends all through the years. They were put together by all the girls—portraying our beautiful and lovely lady in all phases of her life. Many floral arrangements adorned this room. Across the hall, where the service took place, lovely flowers from family graced the front of the large room along with other floral arrangements. An 8 x 10 photo of Elinor at age 20-something showed her in all her beauty.

I'm writing this three days after the event and my mind has already allowed much to just slip past, but I will give it a try—trying to relate to those of you who could not be with us all in person, a bit of what the day held for those in attendance. Elinor and Bill's pastor, Rev. Dr. David E. Wheeler from their Congregational Church, officiated for the service, welcoming everyone and tying the service together with scripture and prayer. Early in the service he had us all recite the 23rd Psalm, not something we do very often—but very nice.

Young Bill, Liz and Lynne each very lovingly told us about their wonderful mother's life—what she meant to them. I'm told that their very thoughtful, loving words are recorded, and, therefore, you will all be able to hear their remarks in their entirety at some later date. I look forward to being able to hear their words again myself. After Bill told of his memories of his mom, he then incorporated the written thoughts of Elinor's siblings, brother Donald and sisters Emeline, Helen and me, Louise. We were given the opportunity of sending in our thoughts ahead of time.

Liz and Lynne followed with equally moving memories. As I've already written, you will be able to read/hear all the above mentioned remarks in their entirety. But tell me—did our sister never raise her voice? Hmm...couldn't be said about me! How about the rest of you?

To my siblings: Our sister and husband Bill raised four wonderfully, talented and loving children. Elinor would have been (ever so humbly) very proud of them all.

Lynne spoke of the faithful care her dad provided for their mom, especially in the last few months as Elinor gradually failed. We all know his life will be very lonely as he adjusts to being alone after all his care and devotion to Elinor. The entire family was so faithful to their dear wife and mother in the final weeks.

During the service and at young Bill's request, my son, Bob (Brownson) played guitar and sang "Give Me Jesus." When he sings this song at our church, I usually tear up at the last verse when he sings the words "and when I come to die—give me Jesus." However, as I thought of my dear sister it just seemed so right—

no tears fell as I pictured God welcoming Elinor into His world for all Eternity and knowing, too, that Elinor is now reunited with Emily for whom she has "searched" daily since Emily's death in August.

The pastor remarked about all the talk of the farm and Nankin, Ohio, their importance in Elinor's life and also within the circle of kinfolk. He told of traveling from Oberlin, Ohio to wherever—maybe to Route 71—and driving through Nankin, and he said, "You know it doesn't amount to very much—it is a very tiny town—one you could miss in the blink of an eye." He said now that he knows that the roots of this dear lady and her family are firmly planted in that village it has become important him. A recording of "It is Well With My Soul" was played at one point during the service—a very fitting hymn.

As family and friends left the service to go upstairs to a beautiful, catered luncheon, John Azoni played his guitar and sang. It may have been an original number—hopefully we will know later. I didn't find out for sure on Saturday.

Those attending from Ohio were Emeline Fulmer and her family (Rick and Marti Krause, Margaret Welch and Janet Whitlatch), Louise Beattie and family (Bob and Gini Brownson and Molly and Glenn Smith.) From Wisconsin, came our cousin Jeanne (Swan) and husband Gordon Garnett—so good of them to make the long drive to attend. Those who had time to linger around after the meal enjoyed a fantastic time in reminiscing together before we hugged goodbye and headed home. Memorials and such events are sad, but so strengthening and uniting for a family.

Our circle of five has been broken. We lost our leader, our mentor and our dear sister. I'm picturing her at peace—all the anxiety and confusion gone. In her last days the family told us that she was asking to be taken down to the farm. When asked what that would mean to her, she haltingly told them that she would "be safe there." Doesn't that bring tears to your eyes? Safety in the rolling hills of north Ashland County—two miles north of Nankin! So many things she had forgotten entirely, but this she still carried indelibly imprinted on her heart and in her very confused mind—carried them into her very last days—the fleeting memories of her parents, Mary and Gene and the farm. Both her roots and her safety!

The "Serenity Prayer" was printed in her memorial leaflet. I know this had great meaning for her. I'm glad it graced her in memorial.

> God, grant me the serenity
> to accept the things
> I cannot change,
> the courage to change
> the things I can
> and the wisdom to
> know the difference.

Elinor truly had the God-given gifts of Acceptance and Courage. God also gave her the valuable gift of Wisdom and she used it so well. Another dear soul enters eternity. God love her.

Louise Beattie, middle one of the five Fluke kids.

FLUKE REUNION, 2007
Labor Day Weekend

Another reunion has come and gone. This one topped them all. I know—we keep saying that each time—but it was totally true. The sunny skies—not a drop of rain—with 70 degree temperatures, not 90—and with enough rain in the preceding weeks, we were blessed with green grass and blue skies—a perfect weekend. This was the largest reunion ever. For those who care to read no further (in case you are already bored) there were 36 at the Friday night gathering, 107 during the day and at the Saturday noon meal, and 38 for Sunday morning brunch. What a delightful three days.

Molly kept us all informed as to plans—and the "assigned privileges" took shape. Her emails and updates were invaluable as the weeks, then days, rolled by as we anticipated the reunion. What did we do before email and the host of exchanged email addresses?

The reunion started early this year with a fence-building project. Someone had suggested that it might be a nice way to start the reunion, with a project. So on Thursday the "guys" started. I'm going to list names for this project—forgive me if I've omitted anyone. Bill Martin and David Drouillard came down from Michigan by motor-home and camped at the pond. John Fluke, from North Carolina, came in early to assist in the project, joined by Rick Krause, now back living in the area. John Keiffer came in early from California and David Evans from Texas. It was reported that Glenn was a "slave driver" and that Bill Martin got a blister on his heel from his "work" shoes. It seems they hadn't had much use recently! Fun time! Yea, fence crew! David Drouillard mowed the pasture, and Bill Martin, the back-40, to give the homeplace the final touch-up. The porta-pot arrived all ready to go and also the tent—green-and-white this year.

When John and Dale Fluke arrived on Thursday, Dale brought along the most beautiful flowers from her garden—I mean, tubs of flowers. They graced the welcome-to-all back porch area and the tables under the tent.

Friday evening as the clan gathered at the farm, they began with a supper for all—hot dogs and coneys, chips and cookies. What a great time for the kids to get reacquainted, for the older folks to touch base with their siblings and cousins with cousins. A new "crop" of babies (five were added since the last reunion,) some new spouses and boyfriends and girlfriends were added to the mix.

Saturday morning the Martin family held a very heartfelt, intimate memorial service at the pond for both Emily and Elinor Martin. Emily died on August, 19, 2006 and Elinor on April 19, 2007. A stone bench centered between two red maple trees is engraved with their names and dates of birth and death, as well as words of love and endearment. Elinor's final spoken wish was to "go to the farm" where, she indicated, she would feel "safe." May they both rest in peace in this very tranquil and special place.

Saturday noon Donald Fluke gave a blessing for the food and the day, using a prayer that was so apropos for the gathering. I now have a copy of those moving words. It was so timely.

But hang on while we fix the food. I'm getting ahead of myself!

Food Prep Committees—functioning as "privileges"—consisted of:
Salads—Erin Johnson, Chair, with Mary Fluke Liz Drouillard and Ann Keiffer.

A roaster full of tasty potatoes—Molly Smith.

Chicken/Brats/Hot Dogs—Louise Beattie, Chair, with Tina McFrederick and Helen Helvenston, who all worked Friday afternoon to marinate the chicken and get it ready for the grill.

Grilling—Matt Johnson, Chair, with David Martin (and maybe others)—great job Matt and crew!

Drinks—John Keiffer and Darcy Keiffer made gallons of lemonade!

Desserts—Gini Brownson, Chair with Janet Whitlatch and Margaret Welch who made a great assortment of goodies, delicious.

Corn Roast—Bob Brownson, Chair, assisted by Rodd McFrederick, Matt and Dan Brownson, a huge bonfire built by Bob where they roasted 12 dozen ears of corn, fantastic! The bonfire was in the pasture this year—out through the garden gate. This all took place around 6:30P.M. The cows had a field day with the cobs.

Business Meeting—John Fluke was re-elected President and Treasurer; Bob Brownson, Vice President; and Liz Drouillard, Secretary. A new venture for 2009: It was suggested that a committee be named—like in, volunteer—to offer suggestions and assistance in putting together the reunion for 2009. Those who volunteered were Ann Keiffer, David Drouillard, Janet Whitlatch, Erin Johnson, Susan McFrederick, and Marty Krause, with Glenn and Molly Smith as consultants. This is a HUGE task—much planning is necessary. A committee could help immensely to ease the burden of the volume of things that need to be done to make the reunion "happen."

Family History—Immediately after the business meeting Margaret Welch gave us an update of the Gene and Mary Fluke family history. We are all indebted to her for her diligence in keeping the records. During her most interesting presentation of information she gave an update on the Victorian farmhouse built by John Fluke in 1877–at the other end of the township road from the farm. Given permission by George Hammer, the present owner, Margaret has been able to take pictures of both floors of the house, still in solid condition and being considered for the National Register of Historic Place in this area by the Ohio Historical Society. She displayed the pictures for all to see. Margaret also brought a wonderful contest of "Farm Knowledge"—all sorts of native growth, plants, weeds, etc. The contest was won by Dale Fluke. Many of the little kids took a part in this and to their delight, for participating, they were given bandana handkerchiefs which they wore all day as headbands, head wraps or around their necks. Great contest, Margaret!

Crafts—Lynn Ritschdorff assisted by Meredith and Elise helped the kids make several neat crafts. I think it might have been a bit difficult to hold the kids' attention for long stretches of time because there was so much going on.

Family Pictures—New "privilege" for 2007 was accepted by Joe McFrederick who so willingly took the pictures of family groups and family groups within families, as well. These photos will be offered online where all can purchase the ones they might want. Good job, Joe! Something we have needed to do for some time.

Storytelling in the Barn—Another new "privilege" this year, presented by Ann Keiffer. A little straw bale arena was set up on the barn floor for the kids, little and big. A winner for both the little ones and the adults. It was fun watching the faces of the adults at story time as well as the kids'.

Corn Hole Tournament—Another new game, set up by Dan and Laura Brownson. I never heard the outcome of this, but I know it was going on until almost dark with much laughter and keen competition.

Hayrides—Four for the day. All trips out were FULLY loaded, with Rick Krause driving the tractor for the first three rides. The first one "tipped" a bit—maybe quite a bit—back beyond the pond and some panicked—just a tad. On the second trip out, Sadie, Molly's Lab, leaped on the loaded wagon, after exiting the pond and shook water on them all. More shrieks! Glenn took the last load out after dark.

Puppet Show—Written and directed by Molly Smith, this was, again, a huge success. I believe there were five skits in all, 1) Philip and Mary Fluke Homesteading in Orange Township, 2) The Courtship of Gene and Mary Fluke, 3) Horse Quakes, 4) The Formula for Making a Fluke, 5) Madame Johneese—with fantastic makeup hints. It was a totally hilarious skit done by John Keiffer and Susan McFrederick with much ad-libbing by John. You had to be there to experience the fun and laughter.

Scavenger Hunt—Molly again put together another group of digital camera pictures of small and obscure things around the farm. The diligence by many groups of people was amazing. First, you teamed up with others—small groups or families—and off you went. They all worked so hard—even the young kids. Leif McFrederick, 10 years old, was totally "into" this context, and I believe his groups was one of the group winners. This popular contest went on all afternoon and ended after the corn roast and supper. Perhaps four groups got all the answers right—amazing! Janet Whitlatch's name was drawn from the hat as the winner this year. The rotating prize is a brass cowbell engraved with the words: The Fluke Family Reunion Most Moo-valous Award. Molly was surprised that some do manage to find these quite obscure objects depicted in the little pictures issued to the participants. Great contest! I marvel at the effort they all went to, to find these objects.

Family Memorial—After the corn roast, mentioned earlier, came cleanup time. Daylight faded away and we all headed to the pond for a family memorial time. I have no idea how many went—some on the last hayride and many by car. Ann directed us each to take a little paper boat—made earlier by Darcy, John and Ann—place a votive in the boat, carefully light the candle and gently place the boat in the water, remembering all those who have gone on before us, our loved ones and ancestors. The boats drifted toward the south side of the pond. What a sight! The kids were decked out in neon bracelets and necklaces that added to the "color." I believe I heard that John Keiffer got a picture of the lighted candles and kids' neon adornments all in the same picture. We all sang "Amazing Grace," accompanied by John Azoni on his guitar. David Duke, from Texas, sang a beautiful gospel song. What a meaningful service! Tina reported that San and David Duke (Tina and Rick's guests from Texas) were moved by the whole day, but especially by the service at the pond. They had never experienced anything like that day or evening. In their area, Waxahachie, Texas, their city has an enforced curfew that does not allow them to be on the streets after dark. It was an awesome time for both of them.

The John W. Fluke family was represented by Molly Evans, son David Evans and his wife Eva from Dallas, Texas. Jim Fluke, his wife Gretchen, Cicely and Jeremiah came from their home in Columbus.

Other guests included the Dukes mentioned above, Uncle Walter and Aunt Edith Brownson, Aunt Betty Brownson Smith, and Richard Blank, long-time Fluke family friend.

Bill Martin, Senior, Elinor's husband, made it down from Michigan—and withstood all three days. We all appreciated greatly his effort. The four remaining children of Gene and Mary Fluke—Donald, Louise, Emeline and Helen—enjoyed this very special weekend together. Our physical stamina lessens, but the whole weekend had much meaning for us all. God willing, we will be there again.

Much has been imprinted on my mind. However, many details slip by. Have you ever noticed how difficult it is to try to explain this event to others outside the family circle? The title of Aunt Bernice's book, *You Had To Be There,* still holds true for all these very special times in our lives. You had to be there under the tent, eating sweet corn, looking for the artifacts of the Fluke family, listening to the history, catching up on each others' lives to get the full picture. Watching the lighted boats head out across the pond as we sang together—remembering those already departed from our family circle, those who have already crossed to the other shore—was an especially meaningful time for all gathered together under the stars.

Until we gather again, blessings and love,
Louise Beattie

CITYWIDE CLEAN-UP
Place Your Refuse at the Curb
April, 2008

For a person who feels keenly the "distress of mess" I look forward to this day in spring when I can tote my no-longer-wanted items to the curb for this specific, week-long event. The first few years I lived here on Avalon Drive I noticed that very few residents put anything out at the curb—not even a coat hanger. But after being here for nearly eighteen years I'm finding quite a bit that I no longer need. Time to trim the sails and get rid of the unwanted, unneeded cargo, my accumulation of those things I once I thought I had to have—dearly needed—desperately wanted, but what I realize now were either poor buys or things I really didn't need. So soon they seem like excess baggage! (Today I actually saw an old television set at the curb of my neighbors across the street! Maybe they felt the pull to buy a new set—"direct TV." We can no longer say the tubes are shot. And so we hoard or attempt to hide our poor, short-lived choices of an earlier day until this special week. Citywide clean-up week—southwest section!

So my concrete angel—now dissolved at the knees during last summer—had to go. I had guarded her so carefully, even bringing her inside for the winter months. She was, no doubt, made of inferior material. I had bought them for all the girls, and I did notice that all the others had this same weakness in the knee area and departed their assigned garden spots early. Perhaps they had all knelt too many times when we weren't looking! The city fathers had specified "no cement" in spring pick up, but surely they didn't mean angels!

And then there are those artificial flowers in cute baskets or pots assembled by little Chinese grandmothers. The arrangements turned out to be inferior with that strange- bright-hue-of-green stems that soon loosened their grip on the leaves. Now I'm left with a mostly leafless assortment of green stems with a few drooping blooms.

Or what about the el cheapo—"small amount of assembly required"—arrangement of plastic tubes that should have become a framework to support a black bag to hold yard trimmings or fall leaves, but didn't have enough support to stand on its own, let alone take on the spent mum blooms or the tough wintered-over Bradford Pear leaves. And oh yes, they even send you two of these handy things for the price of one. Now both reside at the curb.

Or that cute little wooden reindeer. I had wanted one ever since Ann acquired one in San Mateo many years ago. It stood so perky in her TV room. Well, mine was a challenge from day one. Again—some assembly required. Insert #1 leg in #1 leg-hole. None of the four legs fit into their assigned holes and it continued to fall down with the slightest nudge or even a gentle breeze. I even tried wedging masking tape in the holes, to no avail! A crown of red berries adorned its head. Cute, well, maybe, but even a few drops of rain caused the red berries to leak "red" down its wooden-bark chest and over the wobbly front legs. It would have made kindling for a stove, but I was ashamed to cart it off to Matt and Erin's. Now Ann's no doubt came from some really neat store or catalog on the west coast and mine came from Collection's Inc. There in might just lay the difference. So "Rudy" too resides at the curb awaiting the city truck.

And then there is the wicker basket/hamper with matching lid that is a carry-over from the Conery household. I'd painted it ivory in hopes it might brighten up a bit. A worn- down broom. Some old, beat-up flower pots. A filter from the furnace. Avid collectors from anywhere are allowed to go thru all the trash and retrieve anything they might need or want. Let me tell you I haven't seen one person going through my discards—at least not yet. Heaven help the poor soul who decides to work on "Rudy!"

One discard was a cardboard box clearly labeled "Free Garage Sale." Yes, I actually did that one year and it was a <u>huge</u> success. People were totally amazed at the *free* stuff—everything! Some even insisted that they donate—money! When the day was over—at slightly after 1:00PM—only an old pair of shoes, a belt and a wire coat hanger remained in a cardboard box in front of the garage. No trip to Goodwill or Salvation Army was required. I just secreted them in with the garbage and trash the following Monday morning.

As I get older, I realize—now—that I need less and covet less as the years go by. And oh yes, "curbing" means less to dust. So I kind of move around what I have and keep my dear cleaning lady guessing. The clutter of our lives bogs us down, especially me, in our smaller 1200 square feet of condo living area. Periodically, I purge my closets of collected materials from by-gone days. Things seem less important today than they did 10-20 years ago. Papers containing Christian "personality" tests of years ago don't mean much in today's world. I think I'm still an "S," as in being serving-minded, and I think I was classed as a "golden retriever" in the animal world. I forget what that meant. But does it matter anyway with my eighty-third year nearly spent? My folder on "Back Problems" won't be of much use to anyone. However, I might save that folder for Molly—my medically-minded one—who feels she is destined to follow in my medical/physical footsteps. Though hopefully not in the "back" area. Down through the years and three back surgeries later, I'm just so glad to be walking and "doing" on my own with minimal pain.

I've thrown away some "journals" in the process of purging as the years have gone by. Some things best travel to the landfill than to be around for others to read. Therapeutically, I was helped by the writing of my thoughts at the time. A few remain that I hope might be of some value to family as they remember Mom. I have saved special "boxes"—one for each of my girls, with especially the "written words" they have sent me, the milestone events of birthdays, anniversaries and reunions and some through their growing-up years. Each "child" has his or her own photo album, and I think each grandchild as well. In this day of prolific digital pictures all the little ones are well represented on the various family computers.

So I am sorting out the best material things to keep, the written word, for one. Memories can't be sorted. Mine will be there only for as long as I can keep them straight in my mind. With the telling of your own individual memories as they occur or by writing them down, they will be remembered far longer in the family circle. I challenge you all—my children, grandchildren and great grandchildren—to write down your thoughts and experiences. Keep the memories alive and someday in the dim future someone will say "my Great-Great-Grandmother or Grandfather did or said something very much worth remembering." Remember the Philip Fluke family and how much it all means to us now!

Louise Molly Beattie

GOLDEN RETRIEVER

In Louise's "White Binder" she still had a copy of the personality test she took at church. Of the four personality types on the test her responses gave her the classification of "Golden Retriever."
She wrote in the margin, "That's me!"

Golden Retriever
Loyal
Even keel
Enjoys routine
Good listener
Sympathetic
Nurturing
Tolerant
Non-demanding
Avoids conflict
Dislikes change
Adaptable
Thoughtful
Patient
Deep relationships
"Let's keep things the way they are."

Wants to go deep into relationships. Expresses tremendous loyalty to those they love. Listens attentively to the problems of others. Is sensitive to the needs of others. Will carry the emotional burdens of others. Desires peace at all costs and is people-oriented at the expense of speaking the truth.

GROWING UP
My Home, School and Farm Life
in North Ashland County, Ohio
Written in 2008

Lately, for some reason, I've felt this need to write. I hope it is not just because it has been a rather long, slow winter—void of much social time! In this line of thinking, I'm reminded that I have often wished my Great-Great-Grandmother Mary Summers Fluke would have recorded her thoughts in 1816, when she and her husband Philip Fluke left their home and family in Lancaster, Pennsylvania area to head for the unknown in Ohio. The promise of land to homestead beckoned the Philip Fluke family. All we have is what is written in the *History of Ashland County* by George Hill, MD, dated 1880. It must have been a terrible ordeal for them all, but especially a difficult time for the women. It is written that the men labored clearing land and to keep the wolves from the door, not to mention contending with the Indians [as they would have been called back then] who were not to be trusted. But what about the women? What about the illness of the small children, the bitter cold weather in winter, the homesickness for family in Pennsylvania, and the lack of social connections? It must have been heartbreaking at times. So I'm writing my own thoughts of growing up in rural Ashland County, beginning in 1924. Maybe some grandchild will be interested in my ramblings.

Earlier, I had written of my birth on the Ruby place—the third child of Gene and Mary Fluke, eventually the "middle child" in a family of five children. It has been said that the middle is not the best place in the birth order, but I don't give great importance to that. I was not the oldest, where much is expected of you, but neither was I one of "the little girls."

I was shy, with little confidence and a B+ student. I have written about this elsewhere and will not belabor it here. It was hard for me to talk to anyone outside the family and I never had a really close friend. Not through either grade school or high school. Guess that would class me as a loner. There was Grace, with whom I would walk downtown at noon in my high-school days, but she was not a confidant.

Testing in school always caused me panic. Following a super-bright brother didn't help my confidence level, though it was never through him that I felt inadequacy. Helen tells me that she experienced the same thing in chemistry class with Mr. G—when he admonished her, saying "You are the sister of Donald Fluke?" For me, it was Mrs. O. G. (teacher of some history course) who asked why I didn't get grades like my brother. Wonder why those teachers felt the need to compare—in front of the whole class? Great intellect was not my gift, but I'm hopeful I have collected a bit of wisdom in my walk through the years.

I always took much satisfaction in finishing a job or any assignment and that has gotten me through many times in life. I liked "order" in things, even as a child—things lined up properly. I like my living space in order, clean and fresh-selling

Sense of smell—this reminds me. My sense of smell has been my delight, but has also caused me much consternation as well. It can be both real and imagined. Grandma Swan also "suffered" from this affliction of an acute sense of smell...and my own mother, as well, in later years. Different odors bring back past, vivid childhood memories even today. The smell of horses and often cows brings a comforting feeling to me. As a kid at home, I could smell the cows grazing the south pasture some distance from the house. The smell of new-mown hay—dry and filled with sunshine, ready to bail—takes me back to a time in my childhood. The smell of a pig eating corn off the cob was good, but *not* the mud in the pig pen! Odors could be a factor in my bouts of homesickness when I was not on the farm. One of my least favorite odors would be the smell of potato bugs, also my least favorite job. We always had quite a sizable patch of potatoes, and when the plants became covered with bugs, it was one of the jobs of we kids to take a stick, go up and down the many rows and rap on the plants to get the bugs to drop in a basket that we held under the foliage. The basket was dumped at the end of each row, and later the bugs were burned by Dad. However, the most detestable smell came off the bugs and became imbedded in my negative-odor memory.

I was a poor speller, but by the eighth grade I knew that I liked to write even at the cost of fighting my bad spelling. I got past my "elly to bed and elly to rise, makes a man helly, welly and wise"—a sample of my spelling in early grade school. For eighth grade graduation I was given the assignment of writing the class prophecy. I was delighted—it felt good to put words together. Somewhere in grade school days I got a spanking from my dad—the only one I ever got from him. I was balking on something in my homework, and he told me to "get it done." I stomped my foot—ever a no-no with Dad, and he turned me over his knee for a few whacks in the right spot. I don't recall that it hurt; however, I never forgot it. Get it done—finish the job.

I never learned to roller skate or ice skate, but I do remember having wonderful times during noon hour, sledding on Ford's hill across the street from the Nankin School. What fun! I still believe there was one particular part of the hill that was straight up and down! The school had its own little hill, and even though it wasn't much of a challenge, we spent a lot of winter noons and recesses there, too. I will never forget all the wet mittens piled on the one large register in the hall, hopefully to be dry before going home. I tried to learn to ski in m high school years with the Brownson family, but fell on my behind on a little stump and that quickly took the fun out of that.

Fishing in the north pasture was fun—fishing for little "sun fishes" or was it crappies?—with a homemade pole (stick) and a bent pin. There were too boney to eat, but we did fry them and did try to eat them. We played a lot in the barn, though Dad didn't go too much for swings like the Koppler kids had in their barn just up the road. We played in the straw shed and on the straw stack if we could get away with it.

There were always cats and kittens galore in the barn, and we named them and lugged them around. One cat—I think she was Donald's favorite—was named "Delcie Capi Zerbino Pretty Heart." I don't know where he got these fancy names. Another we had was named Tommy, but we felt obligated to change the name when Tommy had kittens. One dog that we had for years was named General Nuisance—Dad picked out that name, I'm sure—but we kids called him General. When I was 16 or 17 Dad allowed me to buy a dog of my own. I had long wanted a dog. So I bought Sarge, a German Shepherd. He didn't last long—he was hit and killed on the road by a boy from up the road. Dad told me that Sarge would have probably gotten mean, as that breed of dogs usually got that way.

I learned to work. At ten I learned to milk, was assigned my two cows to milk, morning and evening. Summer time wasn't too bad, but in the cold, dark and ice of winter it was a challenge to get my cows milked and hope I was lucky enough to get the one lantern shared by four of us to carry the bucket of milk to the milk house over the ice and snow in the dark. I was in a real hurry to get this done and get back to the house for a breakfast of buckwheat cakes or fried cornmeal mush, and then make it to the bus on time. I was always proud to work with my dad, but I know it was not easy for Donald, who often found it difficult to work for my dad who usually gave directions just *once*.

When Donald was in the service in WWII, I left my job at Faultless Rubber Company—cementing life belts for the Navy—and helped Dad for a whole year on the farm. I was his right-hand man, and I recall, with pride, helping him cut and "shock" a sizable field of oats. It was my first experience shocking grain. I still find myself thinking about just how it was done—like, how many sheaves does it take to make a shock? Not vital information in 2008. Now, only the Amish bind and shock grain.

I was in 4H for several summers, though I wasn't too interested in making an apron or a pot-holder. (I had my own special teacher at home, Grandma Swan.) The girls of that day didn't get to be involved with animal 4H projects. That, I would have loved! We never "showed" animals at the county fair, though I thought that would be great to be part of the fun the kids had during fair week. One year I was obsessed—in my own mind only—with wanting to be in the milkmaid contest. I know I never mentioned it to Dad—just knew it was not something I could expect to do.

Which reminds me of when I was a junior in high school and dating Bob, who was on the starting-five of the '41 Ashland High School squad. Bob's team had a very successful year and the team went to the district tournament. I got invited by Bob's parents to go with them to Sandusky to the game. I was very excited. The folks gave permission. I went and the team won. The next week they were to go to the next notch up on the tourney ladder and again I could ride with the Brownsons. When I asked Dad for permission, he said, "You went one evening; that is enough." You have to understand my dad was never involved in athletics, didn't know the thrill of sports competition and tournaments. I, of course, didn't go. Some folks down through the years have asked, "Didn't you argue with your Dad about it?" No, I never did. However, I was allowed to go to the finals at the Ohio State fairgrounds, where they lost the first of three possible games to get to be state champions. The season was over. I cite this only because Dad's word was final, and I understood his viewpoint—maybe a short while *after* the disappointment of missing that second game.

Dad and Mom were very fair-minded people, moral and just. They were very hard-working people who did their best to raise five children. They weren't especially demonstrative—Mom more so than Dad. Dad teased all those he was fond of and that may have been his form of love. He rubbed whiskers with his grandchildren—another form of love. I'm sure he was raised in a family that didn't do much hugging. Dad and his six siblings lost their mother when Dad was 12 and the youngest was only 3. They were raised by a stepmother who must have been overwhelmed with the task and wasn't a very loving person. That unhappy time of life left its mark on Dad. But in her writings—*You Had To Be There*—Aunt Bernice notes some happy and interesting times in that family's growing-up years on the farm.

In the years since my dad died in 1981, we have held family reunions at the farm every other year. And in them I have experienced great happiness. I know it has become increasingly more work for Molly and Glenn, the current owners of the family farm and the reunion hosts—to organize these fantastic events scheduled to spark the interest in the younger generations and to keep interest keen so the younger folks will build this three-day event into their busy lives. However, for my generation, it means so much to us as we all remember the wonderful Fluke reunion of 1937 at the same farm. It was nearly a week-long affair. One of Dad's sisters lived in California, Aunt Betty Quackenbos. She and her family came "home" for this event. All the family was there. What a fun time! The food was special to me, a 13-year-old farm girl. I was impressed with "cold cuts"—we'd never had anything but plain old bologna. Potato chips in five-gallon tin can and olives galore.

Dad had borrowed a pony for the week from the Marshalls next door. What a thrill as we took turns riding day after day, up and down the by-road. It must have been one very patient pony. The boys of the combined families slept in the attic, the girls on the second floor. I don't know where the adults slept. I have no idea how Mom got all the week-day meals together. I know it was no small task. Five-year-old Billy Quackenbos from California was in his glory with his own "cow stick," learning about rounding up cows and all sorts of farm happenings. Sadly, we never saw Bill again. They could never manage another trip back to Ohio. I recall how he had so wanted to take his "cow stick" back to California, but it didn't happen. We Fluke kids later hid his stick in a hollow tree and from time to time checked to see if it was still there.

The reunion of 1937 was a growing-up time for me. That summer I would learn about family love and concern. My grandfather, Jim Fluke, was in failing health and very probably that was the reason for the get-together. It was on one of those summer days at the reunion that I realized that small groups of the adults—in twos and threes—were gathering in the pump house and when they came out you could see they were fighting tears. Their dad was heading into end-times, and they realized it might very well be the last time they would all be together. It was the last time. That reunion brought a gamut of emotions for me. Happiness, yes, but it also caused me to examine the deep love and concern within a strong family circle as the generations age. And it caused me to know that the family circle will ever be changing, losing loved ones through death and gaining through birth.

Now days, in 2008, the babies just keep arriving—steadily—and the preceding generation has passed on. They have left the circle, but their influence and memory stays with us. The little ones are just starting their lives. Some are finding their wings, some just finding their reason(s) for life and their way in this world with both its hopes and its faults.

May God's blessing be on our forefathers and foremothers and also on the many who are following in their wake, joining the family now.

Louise

HIGHER EDUCATION
Just a Bit Beyond High School
Written in 2008

To go to college was not a dream of mine. My brother Donald carefully plotted his course of study, partially attained through his time in the service and progressing on to a Doctorate at Yale. In high school I gave some thought to studying to become a nurse, but the thoughts of taking Chemistry led me to bypass that route. I have done some nursing in my time, but it has been through the avenue of family-needs only. The medical field continues to fascinate me, though—diagnosis and treatment and new ventures in the medical field. It is perhaps where I have my best memory retention for my age.

We four sisters knew that would be little or no money from family for college, so we chose our different ways. Elinor, the oldest, took a business course and became a secretary. Emeline managed a year at Baldwin Wallace College—I think with some financial help from Grandma Swan. She should have had the opportunity to go further. She also became a secretary. Helen did take Chemistry and made a good try at nursing school, but eventually learned that it was really not for her. She ended up working in the field of radio.

In the summer of 1942, right out of high school, I went to work for a local doctor, assisting with office surgery and giving injections, as well as all other day-to-day things required of me. I was only 17 years old with a paycheck of $9.00 a week. I roomed at the Business and Professional Women's Club for $2.25 a week, spent $5.00 for groceries and had $1.75 to blow on ice cream cones, breakfasts at the doughnut shop and, oh yes, various necessities!

After that first summer I took a job at The Faultless Rubber Company, cementing life belts for the Navy—my WWII effort—for $.43 an hour, while still living at this club for older, single, working women. Not much into social connections at that venue. My sister, Elinor, roomed there, too, for a while, and I loved that. It was great fun. In the spring I left the life-belt job and went home to help my dad on the farm. (Donald was in the service.) After the summer field work was finished, I went to F.E. Myers Pump where Bob also worked—Bob, in the testing department and I in the nozzle-and-spray department. We were making plans to get married.

On October 16, 1943 I married Bob Brownson and shortly thereafter I found myself busy raising a family while Bob went to college, his longtime dream. He finished in 3 1/2 years, attending winters, summers and nights, all while teaching History half days at Jeromesville High School. After graduating with honors from Ashland College in August of 1948, he took a high school teaching/coaching position in New London, Ohio. There, he started his successful football coaching career. In the fall of 1952 we moved on to Portsmouth, Ohio where he found great success. Then finally, he went back to his Alma Mater, Ashland College. There, he taught Education courses and went on to have another undefeated football team. He won the Ohio Coach of the Year award three times in his coaching career, each one for a different level, Class AA High School, Class A High School and then College. As a family we spent four unique summers at the University of Wisconsin as Bob acquired his Masters Degree in School Administration. He *loved* to go to school.

Elsewhere in my writings I have told of Bob's major surgeries and the poor health that ensued. Sixteen difficult years followed the surgeries and a devastating depression that took over his life. In the fall of 1971, the "powers that be" at Ashland College suggested that it might do Bob good to go back to school and make a start on his Doctorate at the University of Akon. He was in favor, but said he couldn't do it unless I would go with him. And I said, "And do what?" To which he answered, "Anything in which you have an interest."

So I had this bright idea that I might take some course work in the Food Service Management program and combine it with my numerous years of volunteering for the Mapleton Boosters Club money-making projects, all dealing with food. I thought I might be able to teach at the Career Center. So off we went to Akron. I learned that my volunteer service would not transfer into anything. However, by then I was caught up in the course work. After a couple of times of being called out of classes to take Bob on rush trips back to Samaritan Hospital in Ashland, he gave up on it, just felt he wasn't well enough to take on all that was entailed. However, I kept going.

I soon learned that the actual food classes were fairly easy. I did get reprimanded once for changing the location of the racks in the oven—apparently, a no-no. I turned in reports that were okay, but I didn't know anything about bibliographies and/or footnotes on my papers. Luckily, I had a great woman professor who helped me with this. I didn't like Accounting, as it took me way too many hours of homework to make it all come out right, only to get to school and find that the 19-20 year-olds in my class were working theirs out all the while sitting on floor outside the classroom door just before class started—and got it done! Food-buying, sanitation and all that were a breeze, but I realized what I really liked was "Human Relations." That opened up more avenues of thought and writing more papers. Words, thoughts and ideas—I loved it.

In those days I was driving a "hot" car—a Comet GT with many "cubes" and lots of zip! It was RED, and in those days, back when I had more confidence and daring, I pushed it a bit. I was flattered when the "kids"—the guys in my class—found out what I was driving and followed me to the parking garage to ask all sorts of questions about the "cubes," etc., none of which I could answer. Just imagine me at age 47, already a grandmother, trying to discuss youthful automotive interests with the students. It was the year that one of the very popular records of the day was "Bye, Bye, American Pie," all about "driving your Chevy to the levee." Today when I hear some of that music, I have a flashback to my stint at UofA.

Another funny thing that happened at that time: I was very probably a curiosity because of my age in the Food Service Management program. When the "kids"—boys, again—learned that I was from Ashland and that my husband was Athletic Director at Ashland College, they asked many questions about Ashland's most recent (maybe current,) very controversial basketball coach, Bill Musselman. Not only was he a very successful, winning coach, defense was his specialty. However, he was also into "entertainment," ball-twirling and fancy stuff before the game, during half-time and even in the 48 minutes of the game. Great, crowd-pleasing stunts, of sorts, during the game when his team often held their opponents to 30 points. He made a name for himself, at least state-wide. So the guys, these UofA college kids, were asking mainly one question, "Why would your husband hire this fellow?" Remember, I said Musselman was very controversial in the news media. Guess the answer I gave them was that he WON games! Musselman went on to coach the Timber Wolves in the NBA in later years. He died at a rather early age.

So I drove into campus for the school year, through rain and snow—all kinds of weather—and often home after dark. I especially remember the white-outs, the blinding snow storms, following semi's and being so glad to hit the West Salem exit, out of heavy traffic. That was the negative part of that year, as I never really like to drive that much after dark.

At this point I didn't quite have enough credits to have Sophomore status, and I knew I was going to have to give up school, because I truly needed to get a paying job. Bob was, by then, working very little. It was then that I went to work for a second doctor, Dr. Darrin Huggins, in family practice. This was a good job for me. I guess I would have been classed as the office manager. I manned the phone, made appointments, accounted for the daily money intake and pulled the charts for the day. The doctor was an unusual man, quite before his time, as he was into computers and looked up all sorts of medical things on the internet. Other local doctors tended not to like him and some patients felt that by his looking up information he didn't really know his stuff. Who knows!

Dr. Huggins was very good to me. I worked for him for seven or eight years until he went half-time with his practice, following the death of his 16-year-old son. Dr. Huggins was also Coroner for Ashland County and was called out to an accident scene, only to recognize his own pick-up truck involved in the crash and his own son, the driver, dead. This experience took so much out of him. He later gave up his practice and moved away.

I had surgery in the fall of 1975, during the time I worked for Dr. Huggins. I was off work for 5 weeks. Every week he brought me a paycheck when there was no agreement for him to do so. One summer Molly was down in Hazard, Kentucky, involved in missionary work at Riverside Christian Training School. Bob was not doing well, and the Dr. asked me if I needed her at home. When I indicated that I did need her, he volunteered to fly his own plane down to Kentucky to bring her home. He did just that. I think he was probably an R&R pilot (River & Railroads.) He flew his plane down around those Kentucky mountains, located the airport and flew her back. I met them at the Ashland Airport, so very thankful to have her home. It was Dr. Huggins who took Bob as a patient in the last few weeks of Bob's life, when another doctor had given up on him. Dr. Huggins rode with Bob in the ambulance to the Cleveland Clinic, where Bob died 12 days later. Needless to say, Dr. Huggins was very good to me. And employment in his practice was most helpful to me.

I learned a valuable lesson while working in that office. I was the "mother" figure on the staff, and one morning while I was pulling charts and getting ready for patients, I was irritated with the two office girls who were eating their breakfasts in the lab and combing their hair. So "mother" went back to the lab and asked, "Do you girls realize that you are wasting the doctor's time?" The one girl immediately answered me with, "You made your point." There was no argument, no more words, we all went back to work and it never happened again. But that little episode made a lasting impression on me. I applaud that girl. I've used her words in helping to diffuse other situations in later years. A quick way to end a trivial argument: You made your point.

A couple years after Bob died, after the doctor's practice went to half-days [and consequently more limited income for me,] I desperately needed a different job. Through a couple of old Ashland College friends I was able to get a job in the Registrar's Office. I felt like was back in the old college-friends circle. It was within this group that we had had social friends. In the summer Bob would invite some 40 people to the house for sweet corn, hamburgers with homemade buns, a variety of salads, with carrot cake and pecan pies for dessert. I always fixed all the food. It was a fun time with personnel from the coaching staff, business office, admissions office and registrar's office. It was through registrar's office friends that I was offered this job. Those were the good old days.

While in the employment of AC I was entitled to take course work—for free. While there I took an Art class I really enjoyed and several others of interest to me. I acquired enough credits to add to my U of A work and made it out of Freshman class status. I now had the equivalent of one year of college. It might be difficult to tell what the experience did for me. It was interesting; most of all, I received quite satisfactory grades, which gave me more confidence and helped me to get past thinking that I could not make good grades.

I was fortunate to get through my working years with interesting jobs—not big pay, but interesting. In 1982, I tried for higher wages than AC paid—a bit of greed. I interviewed for yet another job in a doctor's office and got it. I was so pleased, but soon learned this doctor had a serious drinking problem. It was a new practice in town, an OB-GYN office. There I was, office manager, sometimes assisting the doctor, bookkeeper and cleaning lady. I stayed for 13 months, should have left after the first month. I called my former boss in the Registrar's Office at AC to ask if I could possibly return to my old job as transcript clerk...and it turned out I could. The gal who had taken my job was transferring to another job on campus.

If I had it to do over, in these modern-day times, I would train in some medical specialty field, the field that still holds much interest to me.

Am I sorry I didn't go to college at age 17? No way! It was fine with me the way it turned out.

Louise

WHAT MAKES A SPIRITUAL PERSON?
In a Letter to Ann
August 17, 2008

Dear Ann,

I had a good weekend—no wedding or childcare assistance to be involved in. So maybe I'm sort of ready to tackle the spiritual/religious question.

You asked two questions:
First: What do you think makes a spiritual person?
I think it is one who believes in God and lives accordingly—a moral person who lives according to God's principles, believes in salvation and the forgiveness of sins and recognizes the pain and suffering in others and who is willing to assist in reaching out to those in need. I do not think it is one who reads the Bible daily or memorizes massive amounts of scripture and pops up with them for every occasion.

Second: How would I recognize someone who is or isn't a spiritual person? This question is harder for me, but I believe it would be by watching how he (or she) lives their lives. Is this individual <u>consistent</u> with the principals of goodness and mercy as they associate with others, willing to forgive, operate with fairness and honesty in the caring for and working with others? Do their lives have meaning? Do they show the fruits of their labor? I know "fruits" is perhaps an overworked word, but I can't think of a better one to use. It "says" it for me.

Very simplistic but that is me, what I believe. I'm making a copy of this, but I will probably want to amend it or make changes. That is "me" too. Flip-flopping has its place.

Always with love,
Mom

LETTER TO MY SISTER-IN-LAW BETTY
January 18, 2008

Dear Betty,

Today your wonderful story "My First Love Affair" arrived. Betty, you write so well. I know you have told me about this writing several times, but I never thought I would actually get to see and read it! Good job! It is easier for me to *write* my response—thus, this letter.

Along with your story arrived a DVD of Ken Burn's WW II—the 3rd disc. I've been crying over the first two discs, feeling so moved by the events of that war that I lived through, but never really understood. And now I know that we were not allowed to REALLY know what was going on. It also seems pretty clear that the guys [going to war] often didn't really know either what was taking place.

Oh, yes, we viewed the news reels on Saturday night at the "Ohio" theater on East Main Street and had a hamburger and Pepsi at the Sanitary Dairy restaurant afterwards, but I didn't really "feel" the horror of what my classmates were going through in Saipan and Normandy and all those other terrible places. I have been thinking lately about all those who gave their lives or sacrificed their health in all those various godforsaken places. The fact that your brother Bob didn't "go" and all his friends did I'm sure play some part in his emotional (that might not be the right word) instability on down through the years. He was "rejected' twice in Cleveland with a chronic shoulder dislocation. He didn't talk about it, but it must have taken its toll. As I've listened to music of those days—the 40's—in the background of the DVD's, I'm finding myself in tears. We were dancing up above Pelates (sp?) while the guys were being killed in the South Pacific. The music of the war was simple; it was sort of "cutesy." But NOW it really touches me so much in my mind association, 65-66 years later, me, an old lady of 83.

But I digress. Because of the WAR, because of Eslie's injury, he came to Crile Military Hospital and the two of you met. We so often hear said "God works in strange ways." Did He make this happen or did He allow it to happen, to progress to the point of pulling you two together at the same place at the same time? I didn't recall that your courtship was that short, but I surely do remember your wedding—at the farm—with the family gathered round—Ann, only five months old. We were all so impressed with this new guy in the family. He had it all—a handsome blonde fellow from the "south"—quiet spoken—good sense of humor—and so kind to us all. We loved the way his southern words came out, like when he would say "Guff" station for Gulf. I wonder what he thought of all our mid-western idiosyncrasies, but he seemingly weathered all the Brownson humor and the sometimes not-so-humorous Rook [card] games—hay making—lack of water and all the stuff we all went through at the farm. Bob and I spent four years there and I still count it as some of my "best time" years. Grandma Ruthie—God bless her soul—and Grandpa, too—how did they put up with us ALL? Popcorn in the new kitchen, the wood range that Bob bought at a farm sale—which I always said kept me alive through the nausea and the cold winter of 1948 during my pregnancy for Tina.

I sort of lived your life along with you in those days, but your writing it all down made it a lot clearer and it means a great deal to me. The cot-sized bed at your first apartment—our visit there to see you and Eslie—how you washed little Annie's white shoe strings and polished her white shoes. And later the converted-school-bus trips to and from Mississippi always seemed like such an adventure to me—me, who could never quite allow myself to leave home. (But, you see, when we lived at the "good old place" it was "home" to me and I was content). I don't think I ever really got to take a good look inside the bus. Wish I had done that. Your kids must have many wonderful memories of the happenings in all those miles. I do recall that there was a lot of mechanical trouble along the way. I guess when the schools sell the buses they are pretty much "over the hill." However, Eslie was a "fixer" and you made it. I just don't know how you all stood the heat of the summer on the road and in Mississippi. And I thought our summer vacation together in Upper Peninsula Michigan was hot!! You were pregnant with Laura, I think. I remember the heartfelt conversations you and I had in the wash house, shower house or whatever it was. We were washing out diapers—where did we dry them?—on the bushes? Ha. No, I guess we strung up lines somehow. Those were fun times. I think that was before the "bus" days as I think we both drove station wagons and the boys all slept in them at night. Ward and Virginia Pfeiffer had the "quiet" cabin down over the hill!

I will be waiting for your second "love story." It is SO important that you write it. Is it started? If you write it, I will type it for you.

You introduced me to your brother! I felt loved by the Brownson family. Sadness and loss have taken a toll on our lives. We have both lost husbands and adult children. Tears and sorrow could have broken us, but instead I think we were made stronger by having gone through these tragedies. At this ripe old age of 83 I do wonder some days how much longer we have in this old world. And I also wonder also what kind of a world our generation—and the next—is leaving for all the little ones that keep arriving so frequently around me.

Thru it all you remain like a true sister to me. You are a better communicator than I—so much better at frequent phone contact—always clear in your thoughts and questions and in your concerns for the big Brownson family circle—ever vigilant in keeping "family" events in order. Hang in there my dear. You are so loved and much needed.

Always with love,
Louise

NEVER HAVE WORDS WITH YOUR PASTOR
(Unless His Theology Is Way Off the Mark)
January 20, 2008

Over 30 years ago, while attending an Assemblies of God Church, only a few weeks after the death of my husband of 32 years, I became angry with the pastor during a scrmon in which he was extolling the wonders of "loving your wife." The words he said that inflamed my thinking, more probably my emotions, were: "Wouldn't you just like to take your little woman and put her under your arm and...."

In truth I don't remember how the pastor finished that sentence, but because of my being emotionally drained from my loss, my husband's death, the pastor's flowery little homily left me just plain inflamed, up in arms over what I felt was an offense to me and to others, men and women, who have experienced loss. I totally lost the point of his sermon. I could see that my daughter-in-law was upset, but I could hear in her disapproval, her question, "Where is the scripture in all this?"

And so as I exited the building, I told the Pastor that I hoped he would never preach a sermon like that again. Very presumptuous of me to assume I was the only one who was receiving the message. There were probably thoughts in it that were very loving and kind. Well, needless to say the pastor informed me that he would not allow "you or your family" to dictate the sermons he should preach. My daughter-law must have made her thoughts known as well. So, after that I avoided him—at the bank or wherever and got in another line, I left the church and went back to my former church. Safety among old friends?

However, for me, I learned a lesson. The exploding anger I felt, and then expressed, gave me <u>no</u> satisfaction. What right did I have to express my emotional thinking to this man? I was embarrassed by *my* actions and unpleasant words. I made a vow with myself to *never* again allow myself to be in the position of judging a pastor on his sermon. He has a right to use his own phraseology in putting his sermon together.

In the 30-plus years since, I have observed up close some really difficult church brouhahas where longtime church members have spoken terrible words of hatred, unjust words, undeserved words of condemnation, but I have tried to remain loyal to the various pastor(s) who are usually good men, being persecuted. Often, it is personalities against personalities. I have seen the health of pastors (and their wives) virtually destroyed by these vicious conflicts.

I will remember my pledge to be faithful, to stay calm and use positive influence only. I learned from my poor judgment of 30 years ago. Words, once spoken, can never be taken back. Unless the teachings are against God's ordinances, I will do my best to continue to be a quiet, positive influence, for I have witnessed the toll taken on lives on both sides of one of these unpleasant controversies. "Let everything you say be good and helpful, so that your words will be an encouragement to those who hear them." *Ephesians 4: 29-32*

Louise M. Beattie

The Fluke Family
(Clockwise from left: Gene, Louise, Donald, Elinor, Mary, Helen, Emeline)

The Fluke Family Farm

The Farmhouse in Later Years But Before Remodel
Owners, Glenn and Molly Smith

1945

Bob Brownson

Frank & Ruth Brownson
Bob's Parents

Wedding, Louise and Bob Brownson

Louise's Favorite Picture of "Her Five"

The Brownson Family
with Rick McFrederick & Larry Keiffer

Louise and Jim Conery

Louise and Bill Beattie

The Soirée for Louise's 88th Birthday

REGRETS—LOOKING BACK ON MY LIFE
February 6, 2008

I'm eighty-three—will be eighty-four in May—and the time left for me might be short, but who knows? It is a bit difficult to look ahead and think of things I wish I might yet do in my life, but I do sometimes look back and wonder what I might have done better. Regrets—I don't really have too many. Those that I do have I try not to look at very often. However—just for the record—I will list a few of these regrets and my thoughts regarding them.

Recently I read a great article in the AARP magazine, entitled "Woulda, Coulda, Shoulda" which made me wonder a bit about my life—all the accumulated years—the good times and the difficult times. What more could I have done, what things should I have done differently with my life? Oh, yes I wish I had "spanked" less than I did, but more than that I wish I had talked more to my children—asked them what more they needed—what made them sad—what made them happy and what worried them the most. I do wish I had listened better and harder. I wish I had read to my children more—comforted and searched deeper into their hearts and souls. I was busy—sure—but I wish I had tried harder to better their lives. They all live good lives—a good bunch—a strong family circle. But what could Mom have done that would have made their lives better?

Was Ann old enough that I could have asked her deeper questions as to why she had such a traumatic time in her starting the first grade in New London? Her teacher told her dad that her behavior was caused by her difficulty in cutting the apron strings with her mom—me. It never seemed to me that that was the reason, but I really didn't know. Her sickness and gagging and throwing her lunch box in the front yard as she left for school with her dad certainly showed both her frustration and her anger along with sadness. Did I put too much pressure on her—my firstborn? I should have dug deeper. As an adult she greatly stressed herself with an extremely high-powered job and a session of depression followed, causing her much emotional pain. At that time I felt I should go California to be with her, but my minimum-wage job was all I had. She has urged me to stop my worry about that, but I still wonder if I made the right decision.

I didn't seek out Bobby enough in his growing-up years to find out just how he felt after Little League baseball losses. Or in high school, the pitfalls he experienced as the quarterback for the first football team of a new school system—a new sport for all the kids. This was an experience that didn't always go well. He experienced injuries—like a "pointer bruise"—with the coach very slow to remove an injured player (Bobby, in this case) because there was no depth at any position, especially at quarterback. Things like this can be major negative events in kids' lives. I have mentioned this to him in his adult years and he tells me that I was the *one* who *did* talk to him. Did I just forget? I hope I did better than I remember.

Tina's hair fell out as a sophomore high school. Alopecia by diagnosis, and the dermatologist asked me if all my kids were high-strung. (He had already seen Ann for an undetermined rash.) Tina was mistreated by the older cheerleaders. She was voted in on the senior squad, the youngest on the team, the only one who could turn cartwheels, which didn't help her to fit in. Jealousy? No doubt. Did I talk to her enough about this distressing time in her life? After high school she became a student in Columbus working for a degree as an X-ray technician. However, she missed Rick—the love of her life—and asked to transfer back to Mansfield. We paid the extra money to allow her to make the switch. We were okay with her changing schools, but did I talk to her enough about this time in her life?

A bundle of nerves might describe Frank as a youngster, as I look back—frequent visits to the bathroom—everywhere—between innings and time-outs in sports—on the way to anywhere. He was never really a "fusser"—out loud—and in many ways was a loner, tramping around Nankin with his old duffle bag filled with his gatherings from the village—an ear of corn, hay-baling twine, stones and other treasures. However, it was his frequent nightmares that I think about the most. Something caused him great anxiety and manifested itself in these reoccurring, frightening dreams. Many years later, as an adult, he could tell me a bit more about the dreams and they were dark and very scary, as it seemed like he was always trying to escape from some dark place where he would find himself trapped. Was it his dad's many years of poor health that helped to cause this fear and distress? Frank was only 7 when his dad spent eight weeks in University Hospital in Columbus undergoing three surgeries back-to-back. His dad's life, the subsequent surgeries, the ups and downs of his dad's troubles were a very distressing time for us all. But I think that perhaps Frank was affected the most as a youngster. I should have tried harder in the earlier years to draw him out, to help him verbalize his mental anguish and the bad dreams.

This, too, was a very difficult time in Molly's life. In the declining years of her dad's life she and I lived through difficult times together. The uncertainties of life, the fear and, yes, anger, too, we all experienced took its toll. Molly's bout with thyroid cancer in 2000 and the depression that followed were probably the hardest times of her life. I tried to be there for her and with her, but I often wonder if I did enough. In some of her darkest days I stayed with her—she didn't ask me to and, on occasion, she would tell me I should go home, that she didn't need me to stay. But I didn't go home. And later she could tell me she was glad I stayed. But did I talk to her enough—did I encourage her enough? However, in all honesty, she and I have a very strong relationship, and I'm sure we both grew in understanding of and concern for all those who wade through the minefield of depression.

Did I do enough? Did I understand enough the depths of Bob's life and suffering. Sixteen years of poor health. And as I have said, they were hard years for us all. How tragic it must have been for him to live in that dark state. He gradually gave up almost completely on the things he did best in life—teaching and coaching his high school kids and college students. It has been said that after great success, he may not have known how to go beyond those powerful times. He had the misfortune to have hepatitis in 1948, which the doctors in Columbus said might have caused—those many years later—a block in the splenic vein. Apparently, over a ten-year period, a block formed, requiring a nine-hour surgery in the spring of 1959. If he had regained his health, he might have had some more productive years. In all honesty, I believe I played the role of an enabler through many of those difficult years. I was trying to protect his image! Could I have handled things differently? I did the best I could at the time. I will try not to go back and "live" there.

In the article I read in AARP were listed the five most common "life regrets" for women.
1. Education
2. Career
3. Romance
4. Family
5. The self

Education: Did I want more education? I first thought I would like to be a nurse, but the challenge of even looking at Chemistry deterred me from that. Later I would spend many years in the medical field in physicians' offices, family practice, working in the office-management area. I liked it, and I always felt I was good at the work. In today's world—if I were coming out of high school—I would go for training in the medical field. My last employment was in the Registrar's Office of Ashland College, now Ashland University, hired in as transcript clerk. I was among old friends, a good fit for me. My native clerical skills and liking for order stood me well there, too.

The only course work beyond high school for me was a year at The University of Akron when I was 51 years old. The Ashland College administration suggested that Bob's self-esteem might be improved if he were to go to Akron and take some course work toward a doctorate. And since he always did like to study and take classes this seemed like a good idea. He urged that I go with him and take something that I might have interest in. What would I like to do—what could I do with my limited experience? I decided that I would give "Food Service Management" a try. After many years in food-service volunteer work at Mapleton High School, I thought that just maybe I could take some course work in that field and combine it with the volunteer experience, hoping that I might be qualified to teach at, perhaps, the career center. I soon learned that would never work—really impossible to use volunteer work to help in obtaining a degree. About three weeks into the quarter and after a couple of rush trips back to Ashland and the Samaritan Hospital Emergency Room with Bob, he dropped out. I continued on for the whole year. At that point I knew I could not go on in school as I really needed to find employment and I went to work for Dr. Darrin Huggins—my first paying job since cementing lifebelts for the Navy in 1943-44 at Faultless Rubber Company for 43 cents per hour. Dr. Huggins' office was a good fit for me and I stayed with him for nine years until the doctor decided to limit his practice to half- days.

Career: I never had one and that is quite okay by me. I do sometimes wonder what might have happened if I had taken the fabric-shop management job when it was offered to me by Nate Strauss, somewhere in the late sixties. In truth, I was afraid of the challenge. So I will never know if that might have worked. I felt sure I was meant to be a wife and mother, and I devoted my time to that. The year Ann was married, in 1966, I started to work in the gift court at Gilbert Furniture. I can't recall how I got that job. That lasted only until I was really needed at home. Bob was not well, but could gather himself together to makes speeches and I would drive him to various parts of the state. Life became a struggle, hard to keep positive in my thinking.

Romance: I don't think I can count the crush I had on Paul Hughes as a freshman at Ashland High School. He never knew I existed. I started to date Bob as a sophomore at Ashland High School; Bob was a junior. Our first date consisted of my meeting Bob after his basketball game and going to the Sanitary Dairy restaurant for a hamburger and Pepsi, and then he took me home. He was a good student, strong personality, had many friends, and participated in football, basketball and tennis. His coaching days were heady times—his "hey days." We had a very good life until poor health took over for Bob. I have always wished that we could have had better times for more years. And then there was Jim Conery, my engineer, self-made man, absorbed in his work. It was a good marriage that lasted almost 10 years, until his death at age 86 in 1996. Now my life revolves around my Bill Beattie, my cattle-hauling guy, honest, always fair and kind. He suffers from poor health. He had open-heart surgery in November of 2001. COPD and CHF determine his limited ability to do the things he always liked to do. Three good men. I've been fortunate.

Family: I have been blessed. I am the middle-child of five children, and then I've had the privilege of having five children. I learned "family values" and the worth of "finishing a job" from my wonderfully moral, loving parents. The loss of son Frank nearly four years ago still brings an ache to my hear. He left us all too soon, at age 52. The family grows by leaps and bounds—fifteen grandchildren and in another month there will be 31 great-grandchildren. People ask "How do you keep track of them all?" I tell them that I have them all listed on the computer and in my weekly planner.

Travel: I've not done a great deal of that, but have been privileged to make many trips to California to see Ann and her family. Even though I enjoyed these trips greatly, I do not pine for travel to other areas of the world. I'm not comfortable to be away from home. I like my own home when the sun goes down and my own bed at night.

The self: Hmm…. Let's see, for starters: I wish I could have had more self-assurance, perhaps realizing that I was capable of achieving more in my life. I feel I have some talents, but often I get the feeling that they are on the "small" side—no big talents. I can sew—did lots of it all through the years, like making all the dresses for my three daughters' weddings. But I consider it only a "so-so" ability (no pun intended.) I would like to have been a better typist. Always a secretary, I could have used more skill there. It would have come in handy. I enjoy watercolor painting, but do not consider myself an artist by any means. Writing is something I really enjoy along with making personalized greeting cards for family and friends.

However, one area I think I do have some ability in is to be able to maintain self-control in dealing with the most sensitive things in life. I handle emergencies pretty well, but do weep over any broken relationship and at sad movies. I have had much experience in dealing with all the issues that come along with a big family—serious illnesses, being a caregiver and the dealing with the finality of death several times. I believe that in experiencing the traumas of life you become stronger if you choose to allow yourself to grow in that period of grief and sorrow and not let it defeat you to the point that you just continue to wallow in the woes. In developing this control I wonder if there is a downside, because I think I tend to damper down on some of the happiness of life, too. I'm too much on guard for what just might come along next. Between Bill and me we have well over 100 people to be concerned about—several new babies and a toddler with serious health problems to work through in the past year, the diminishing health of the eighty-plus-year-olds in our family, including the two of us. I am hoping that I can hang onto as long as possible this strength which I feel is God-given.

Also in the AARP article was a section addressed as the "regrets of life" and the need for letting them go. And this is the part that spoke to me. It was suggested that we write down these regrets, the things we didn't get to do, the things we feel we missed. The suggestion was made that we work on "letting it go" in four ways.

1. Write it down—forget it.
2. Consider it final
3. Give up looking at the dark side.
4. Do something about it.

So, I'm writing it down—expressing my thoughts—considering the benefits of this process of examining my thinking in things from the past and in my day-to- day thinking at my present age—a good strategy for learning to leave regrets behind. Regret—and our acute desire to avoid it—is a major part of healthy living. Regret is not something that is just a curse or a nuisance to our daily living. It is an indicator of our minds' trying to guide us through complicated day-to-day living.

We struggle with what we did wrong or what we didn't do. But can we fix it? Surely not in those things that happened decades before! I tend to think the sooner I accept the finality of a decision, the more satisfied I will be with the results, good or bad. The fact that I haven't given up on them entirely, though, shows that I still struggle to some degree with the "what ifs" to some degree. So I'm going to give more consideration to the past as being over, done, final.

The AARP article suggests that rather than dwelling on how your life might be better if you had done this or that, think of the ways in which it might have gotten worse. I feel a bit uncomfortable with this concept. It seems to me it is still in the negative scope of thinking, tending to dwell on it, rather than letting it go. Age makes a difference in how and why we experience regret. The young are more likely to regret the things they *did* rather than the things they didn't do. As we age, this tends to reverse itself. However, I tend not to stay in the "things I didn't do" for long. I'm thinking of travel, which I never did much of. But then, after all, I never wanted to leave home even as a kid. I got very homesick on childhood trips to both Cleveland and Wisconsin to visit relatives. These were intended to be broadening experiences for this little farm girl! I would lie awake at night and wish that Uncle John would come along in his cattle truck and take me home.

"Do something about it!" the AARP article says. "Go back to school"—not anything I would ever remotely want to do at 83! Nor take up modern dance—also too late for me. However, even though my energy and endurance levels have lessened, I will keep searching for things that interest me and for ways I can be an encourager to others, even if it is only in my own age group. I will read to find out new concepts in understanding and findings in modern-day medicine, healthcare, rights for seniors, how to be a friend, a better mom, grandmother and great-grandmother. To keep active in my little corner of the world is my goal.

Treasuring the days ahead, may I be worthy of the gift of the days given to me.

Louise M. Beattie

RHUY HANNAH WILSON SWAN
My Grandmother
November 13, 1865–August. 27, 1952
Written February 12, 2008

When I think of a life hereafter, and my belief is that there is one, I visualize those who have gone on before. High up on the list of those I truly look forward to seeing and to knowing again is my Grandma Swan. Her life and her personality have always intrigued me greatly. I admired and loved her very much. I left home and married before Grandma came to live on the farm. However, my memories of her in some of her earlier years, there in her little house in Nankin, are quite vivid.

One of my earliest memories is of the funeral of my Grandfather Swan, her husband Charles, who died June 8th, 1928. At the time of his death and funeral, I was four years old. I no doubt remember the day mostly because the younger four of us children, Donald, Emeline, Helen and I were baptized that same day. Uncle Alfred, my mother's brother, from Madison, WI., a Congregational minister, baptized us using a beautiful silver bowl, a family treasure having been used for many baptisms over the years. Elinor had been baptized earlier, probably as a baby. The baptism took place in Grandma's Nankin home after the funeral service. I can see that living room very clearly even today. Grandma was a neat housekeeper. I don't recall that she was fanatical about it, just orderly in her fashion. In the era before davenports or sofas there was a day bed in the living room, sort of like a cot, a flat couch, not too comfy to sit on, but great for naps.

Grandma had a radio, a battery-powered one at first, then later an electric one. Nankin had electricity long before FDR programs brought it to the farm in the early 1940's. She also had a refrigerator and ice cube trays in which she made a sort of "junket" ice cream. We loved it! How great to stop at Grandma's on the way home from town, Ashland, on a hot summer day and have a treat of vanilla ice cream or even ice water.

Her bedroom was always very neat with comb and brush laid out on an angle on her dresser. Various little glass dishes arranged on the dresser top, as well, nothing fancy, but they just meant Grandma to me. A very small room next to her bedroom was referred to as the "bathroom;" however, there were no fixtures, Instead, like everyone else in the village, she had an out-house at the rear of her little lot. For some time she managed a small garden. I think she hired someone to spade it in the spring. She kept the garden for several years, mainly because Grandpa Swan had always kept a big garden, something he enjoyed doing.

She had a basement, and I remember mostly that it had a dank smell like old overshoes, "rubbers" as we called them back then. Her rubbers sat on the basement steps and I probably thought they caused the odor. It was probably just typical old-basement smell—such a very different odor from our farm basement. But then, in ours we separated the milk from the cream and took care of the cleaning of the eggs. Grandma had a coal furnace and we heated with wood. All created different odors.

Grandma Rhuy minded greatly the heat and the humidity of summer. I've never been very fond of a hot summer either. Perhaps I inherited this intolerance from her along with an intensified "sense of smell". She fanned herself in church, the Nankin Federated Church, which always had fans in the hymnal pockets, compliments of Gilbert Funeral Home. I have always been "against" fanning in church. In my belief about this, I always discouraged my kids from fanning as well. I think I thought fanning was giving in to the heat and all the motion seemed anything but peaceful. Better to grin and bear it—my motto. To this day I try to think "cool," and it helps. Of course, now days I'm in an air-conditioned church! In China in her earlier years Grandma suffered so from the climate there. Heat and extreme humidity were very hard for her to bear. I believe she writes about it in her book, about writing letters home from China with a towel under her arm to catch the perspiration.

Also in her living room in Nankin, she had one of those bookcases with doors that raise up and then slide back in over the tops of the books. If I wasn't really careful, I would get them jammed. This always scared me a bit, though I don't recall that Grandma ever scolded me about getting into difficulty with the doors. She also had a "Morris" chair, the forerunner of the recliner of today. I think both the Morris chair and the bookcase ended up at the farm in our home but don't know of their demise or later history. I was impressed with them then.

It was great to go to Grandma's house from school, for lunch, from time to time. I think we were allowed to do this when Mom ran out of lunch supplies. What a joy to look forward to—having lunch at Grandma's! She usually fixed canned vegetable soup—we never had that at home. There must have been a sandwich or maybe just store-bought bread—and I loved that, a real treat from homemade bread for us. And she would have dessert—often Jell-O with tapioca in it. I have a warm spot in my heart just remembering being with her on those days.

Grandma sewed for us all and was a very good at it, though sometimes I used to long for something bought from the store. She even made coats, not very tailored and a bit "bunchie," but made with loving hands and a desire to keep us warm. She often bought the fabric herself. When I was in high school, I wanted so much to have a light blue corduroy two-piece suit. She bought the fabric at Penney's—bless her heart—and made it. When I tried it on, it fit well and looked nice, except that she had misjudged the lay of the "wale" in the corduroy and two panels of the skirt appeared darker that the rest. This was my first lesson in working with wale and one I never forgot over the years as I sewed for my girls. I complained about it to Grandma, but she told me "no one would notice." She remained firm about it, and I wore it with confidence lacking, but a lesson learned.

She made me a "spring" coat one year, tan with a large dark brown plaid design. I loved it and wanted to wear it as soon as it was finished, but since it was still very early spring, and the weather cold, my mom said I couldn't wear it until the temperature reached 40 degrees. True spring seemed a long time coming that year. She made prom dresses, and in my senior she made me a white organdy dress for my senior prom. I think it was the last dress she made for me. Probably I was now experienced enough to make my own.

When I was about 10 years old I started to sew, learning to make many things. And it was through her teachings that I learned the basics of sewing on the little old Wilcox and Gibbs chain-stitch machine. This sewing machine had quite an interesting history. It was turned by hand and therefore lent itself well for taking along on their trip to China, prior to 1900, so Grandma could sew for her family while there. My Molly still has the little old machine as a keepsake on a shelf in her sewing room.

Grandma gave careful instructions in sewing. I never felt pressured, unlike when I went to Cleveland to visit my dad's oldest sister and was under her instruction as she felt she must teach me how to sew, making doll clothes. Aunt Edna quite often made me rip out everything I did and "do it right." As I think back, doll clothes are very small and extremely hard to do, especially for a 10-year-old. I don't recall that Grandma Swan made me tear out work. If she did, I don't recall it. At least I never was discouraged by her methods of teaching. I have a vivid picture of sewing with Grandma at the dining room table at the farm, me sitting on the east side of the table—the same spot always—and cranking away on the machine with the light coming in the window from the east over my shoulder. She taught me well and inspired me to always try more difficult things as I progressed. If not for her, I don't know how I would have managed all the clothing for my three girls—prom dresses, homecoming outfits and all the dresses for all three of their weddings, including all the bridesmaids' dresses. I've always been so thankful for the heritage Grandma gave me.

In this same period of time, when I was 10 years old, I also was old enough to join the barn-chores crew and to start to milk my assigned two cows morning and evening. It is a wonder that sewing "took" with me, because I was always a bit of a tom-boy and spent much of my time outdoors on the hay wagon, involved with the harvest work and helping to bring in the cows from the "forty"—the cow pasture— every evening.

Grandma must have had very little money, existing on a minister's-widow pension. However, she never seemed "poor." though she must have been. She owned her little house, ate and cooked well, gave to the church, bought us all watches for high school graduations, remembered all our birthdays and Christmases with small but nice gifts. I never heard her complain about the lack of money.

I've always admired her liking for the finer things of life—at least I would consider them to be the finer things of life, at least for that period of time. She read a lot and subscribed to the Cleveland Plain Dealer— it came in the mail. She kept up on current affairs. In later years when she lived at the farm with Mom and Dad I'm sure she was the only one reading that paper. As I think back, did she not share it? Would either Dad or Mom have cared to read it? Maybe they had no time for more than a quick scan of the Ashland Times-Gazette. And maybe they didn't even subscribe to that with our limited, uncertain income.

One day, somewhere in this period of time, Grandma called Bob back to her bedroom at the farm and asked him what I felt was a very interesting question for a woman of advanced years with no apparent athletic interest! "Bob, now I want to know what you think the chances are for this controversial new football coach at Ohio State University." That was Woody Hayes, the legend of OSU football! I was amazed, Bob, too. How did she have any interest in the field of college football? She sensed the controversy and was curious enough to ask for Bob's opinion.

When I went down to Nankin to visit her in the summertime—we took turns in staying at Grandma's house for a week at a time—she taught me to play solitaire. I recall when I promptly "won" a game, Grandma said I probably did something wrong. I probably did. My, she would have loved to play solitaire on the computer—none of the laying out of the cards.

She listened to classical music on her radio, and I remember I was impressed as I thought this was probably something "grand," even though it made me extremely sad, even to the point of tears. As I look back I realize the music was intensifying my homesickness when I stayed with her. To this day I do not really care for classical music. It still makes me sad. I was not good at being away from home, not even to go to my dear grandma's for a day or two or a week. While I was there on a visit she would sew up some play clothes for me and referred to them as "sun suits."

She was quite tuned into her neighborhood in Nankin, keeping track of Gerti S. and several others, whose names I can't recall. Somehow I felt she didn't really approve of them, but maybe I got this from my mother's comments regarding Nankin neighbors. In later years when Grandma moved to the farm with my folks I understood that my mother felt Grandma "talked too much" in the village.

Looking back, I have the feeling my grandma would have been able to take care of herself longer. I felt she should have been allowed to remain in her little house but then I didn't know of all the circumstances, the furnace to fire and all the concerns involved. There was a lot of tension at the farm, competition between Mom and Grandma over the ironing, dish washing, etc. I'm sure Grandma wanted to be helpful, but Mom wanted to be in charge—two strong-minded women trying to share household responsibilities. I'm sure that Grandma resisted to some degree when approached about leaving her house, and I don't know just how strongly. I'm sure it wasn't easy for any of them. Grandma was known to have wondered— out loud—why Gene (my dad) was hauling manure (today) when the wind was wrong and the odor great? Conversation between Dad and Grandma was very limited—meal times were pretty silent. My dad had a great sense of humor, but I think he did not use it with anyone he didn't really like very well and this would have included Grandma. Grandma cried at Mom and Dad's wedding—not too unusual, really—however, it seemed to be of great importance to Dad who felt it signified that she was not happy with Mom's choice of mate. I would believe that Grandma was very sad at giving up her little girl, one she had catered to and I'm sure sacrificed for. She had lost her first daughter to whooping cough in China

Mom has told me that Grandma quite frequently ripped apart wool dresses and suits of her own to remake them into clothing for Mom. This always made me sad, though I'm sure Grandma just wanted her daughter have the best she could provide for her on a meager minister's salary and she became quite adept in the making and remaking of clothing. She wanted the best for Mom but never insisted that Mom eat vegetables or any food she didn't really like. According to Mom, Grandma never required much of her in helping with household duties, either—living proof that you can be a great housekeeper even if you were never required to clean your room. By example, we can all be taught orderliness—maybe —or is it just what suits our own fancy down through the years?

I always picture Grandma in many shades of blue, mostly navy, some prints, usually in the darker shades. Sometimes she wore black, but mostly blue. She liked interesting necklines with brooches and various pins, often with ruching or lace trim at the neckline. I can't remember that she ever wore necklaces. She had rather prominent ears that she liked to have covered by her hair. Her hair was long. I don't think I ever saw it down, but always "done up," softened by being puffed up a bit on the top with bangs in earlier years. Her hair was probably dark brown. not unlike Mom's (or mine.) But mostly I remember her as being gray, graying in the same way as Mom and I—a halo of gray around the hairline all around the face.

She very much liked "nylon" dresses when they first came on the market, as they were so easily washed, with no ironing required. Again, it seemed like they were mostly navy, often in small prints. I can't remember seeing her in a skirt in the 1940 and 1950's, only dresses. However, in her earlier years she would have worn skirts and shirtwaists, like the blouses of today. She wore sensible shoes known as Enna Jetticks (sp?), though I vividly recall she detested these same shoes and referred to them "as old lady shoes." In the front of her book is a picture of her in her rocking chair in very sensible shoes. I wonder if she liked them or did she just give in and dress in old lady shoes in order to not buck the expected dress of senior ladies of the day.

I loved her "smell" and the smell of her room at the farm. I can only describe it as a sort of lavender smell. I'm sure she never wore perfume in her life, but she always gave off a scent of lavender, maybe soap, clean and fresh.

Though I'm sure I shouldn't ever say (or write) this, but I think I had a special place in her heart. Maybe it was because we both tackled what was laid before us and I admired this in her. The illness and early deaths of spouses, we shared. Grandpa Swan had to give up preaching when he was still fairly young. He was "asked" to leave his last church charge. I'm sure this was a real blow! They moved back to Nankin to be close to Mom and our family. He died after a long decline with dementia, which I'm sure is what we now refer to as Alzheimer's disease. In order to attempt to sooth him in his dementia anxiety, she would rock him in her arms and sing the old hymns of the church. Watching the non-elderly decline in dementia and/or in depression is a difficult thing to experience. I also recall that Grandma herself stated that she would like to be cremated, but decided that it would be very disturbing to the Nankin church folks of that day, the 1950's.

She liked to see things resolved, as do I, and was sometimes impatient with the unresolved things of life—me, too. She had strong opinions and she spoke her convictions. There were things she wished she could do or could change, but she was bound by the tradition of her generation.

In her memoirs she made a small mention of working in the women's suffrage movement, and I believe she referred to it as "fun." I do wish she could have enlarged on that—how she felt—what it meant to her—what she hoped the goal for women might be.

Did she have fun? Little mention of fun times, of humor or joking is in evidence in her book. It was all serious and the careful recording of the events in her life. Perhaps happiness was overshadowed by the joyless times she had in her life—growing up virtually unwanted. Her mother died at the time of her birth and Rhuy Wilson was baptized over her mother's casket. Her dad was a traveling woolens salesman. Not easy for him to take her, so she was shifted to various aunties and uncles as the early years went by. After her father remarried, she was summoned to come live with them to help with additional children, where she became the virtual "hired girl," with no pay, of course. Her early life was a most unhappy life which always brings me to tears when I read and reread her book.

She dearly loved her children and grieved deeply over the loss of Elizabeth in China, as I mentioned before, and Frank, her oldest son—five years old—who died on the way home from China. Frank contracted diphtheria from a playmate on the ship while they were crossing the Pacific coming home. In her book she writes, "I wrapped my firstborn in a blanket, kissed him goodbye and gave him to his father. It was the last time I saw my firstborn." They had gotten off the train in Minnesota. but could not get their baggage off and were staying in a hotel. Grandpa Swan was in search of a hospital who would take Frank in his contagious state. He stayed with Frank and attended to him. Frank died in the contagious ward of a Minnesota Hospital. Grandma and her remaining son, Alfred, three-years-old, traveled on to Ohio by train. She was far along in her pregnancy with my mother who was born soon after they arrived in Ohio at an auntie's house in Cincinnati.

To have sacrificed two of her children to an alien society after spending what seemed, to me, like fruitless years in missionary work, seems so dreadfully sad. What pain—what deep sorrow! Her only solace could have been thru a loving husband and his missionary-family circle there with them in China. What support the good Lord must have provided for them all. However, I have wondered, did she ever blame God? Did she ever blame Charles for taking her to that "heathen" part of the world? Did she censure herself for joining the movement to bring Christianity to the people who hated and feared the "devil eyes?" ("Devil Eyes" was the name the native Chinese gave to the Americans.) When they left for their seven-year commitment to bringing Christ to the Chinese people, Grandma felt she would be of much use as a physician. Little did she know what would be required of her. In her work she had to be content with only the "doctoring" of the Swan family while they lived in China.

I wish I could remember more—wish I had talked to her more—asked her how she really felt about life, its joys and disappointments—how she felt about her children and how she really felt about the missionary movement and her commitment to it all.

My last communication with her was so poignant. She had had a stroke. It was August, 1952. She couldn't speak; however, her mind was still keen. She became extremely agitated and seemed very concerned for me as she struggled to communicate with me. I asked Mom if she might know what it was Grandma wanted to say or ask. We were moving to Portsmouth, Ohio, good move for Bob as football coach, but we couldn't find a house to rent. The A-plant (atom bomb) was being built in that city on the river and rental housing was out of sight, almost non-existent. Grandma remembered this with concern, with me pregnant for Frankie, my fourth child, due in November. I leaned over her bed and whispered that we had found a place—a little white lie—as we had only the vague promise from a sporting goods business man that we could rent his summer cabin 10 miles west of Portsmouth on the Ohio River. Grandma settled down, apparently assured that we had a place to live. In truth, we did move into that summer camp on the river, a place available because everyone else had moved back into the city after Labor Day. The kids and I spent six weeks there, all by ourselves, with an outhouse and a back- porch shower—really outdoor shower—while Bob worked feverishly in extreme heat to get his new football team ready for an early September season opener. I knew I had done the right thing—a white lie—that was okay. Two weeks later my sister, Helen, and Jack Kirsh so kindly drove down to get the kids and me to attend her funeral.

Grandma Swan was a moral lady—she believed in fairness—organized her life and family well. She provided a solid, positive role model for me. Her frankness got her into trouble on occasion in the church and in the village. One could never call her wish-washy. Had she been born 75 years later, she might have lead a different life. She lived her life with conviction and purpose. I have always been proud to say my maternal grandmother was a doctor, graduating from medical school in the late 1890's! She was trained in a day when there were very few women doctors, an unusual profession in her day.

She was a powerful and meaningful factor in my life, a role model no doubt. I will always admire her strength and determination as she walked thru her life with its many obstacles, disappointments and great losses. I honor her memory still.

Granddaughter: Louise Fluke Brownson Conery Beattie

STANDING BY MY MAN
Gathering Strength for the End Times
February 2, 2008

I have just finished reading *Strong at the Broken Places* by Richard M. Cohne. He writes of enduring MS and tells the stories of five ordinary people—and aren't we all just that, ordinary people, all of us, with "terminal" illnesses, living out our lives to the best of our abilities? Some will leave this world sooner—some later. At the end of the book the author suggests a website for further information and suggests that we write our own stories. This is my story of struggles through the difficult times—when lives decline and in the brokenness.

I lost my first husband, Bob, in 1975. He was 52 and I was 51. Sixteen years before his death he had a very complicated surgery to try to correct bleeding from the esophagus caused by blockage in the splenic vein—all this from, perhaps, an unknown cause. It was 1959—three surgeries in all, the first being 9-1/2 hours long—8 weeks in Ohio State University Hospital, complicated greatly with a staph infection. This all took a terrible toll on his life expectancy. He survived the ordeal and was allowed to come home by ambulance with a gapping 10-inch open surgical site surrounded by many irrigation tubes! He survived this complicated ordeal and had 16 more years of life; however, they were not good years. Several more surgeries followed—several related to the original renal shunt with splenectomy surgery, others not. In addition, serious problems developed from the overuse of pain medication and alcohol adding to the dilemma. And then depression took over.

My daughter—the youngest of our five children—was still at home. The four other children were adults living away from home. She and I together tried to weather life with this well-educated man, a popular professor of education and a highly-successful football coach who was gradually losing his grip on life. This extremely gregarious man gave up on life by inches until he became virtually immersed in silence. In October of 1975, a day after our 32nd wedding anniversary, after yet another bout of esophageal bleeding, he died in the Cleveland Clinic after 12 days in a coma. This time the surgeons were not able to make the corrections or to pull him through.

In the sixteen years he was given after the first surgery, I pondered how best to try to help him with his life—what I could do—what should I do—what should I have done differently? Gradually he had to give up on teaching. Students had waited for several semesters to get into his popular classes in the Education Department at our local Ashland College—now Ashland University—a small private school in Ashland, Ohio, 60 miles south of Cleveland. A popular, talented teacher and very winning football coach was giving up on life.

I know now that I was an enabler. I've always hated that label but know that that was what I was. Being so anxious to protect his persona I tried to excuse and work around his frequent failures to make it to teach his classes—his failures to keep commitments—and his changing personality. He loved public speaking and spoke all over the state. I would drive him to the various athletic banquets where he would give a totally inspiring speech entitled *"The Price of Excellence,"* only to have him end up asking those in charge—after the evening's events—to take him to the local emergency room. He would plead a terrible headache. I was both extremely scared and emotionally exhausted. In addition, I was embarrassed—not a noble trait, but nevertheless, true.

One very foggy winter night I remember driving him home from a speaking engagement and to hear on the car radio the announcement of the assassination of Martin Luther King Jr. My passenger was sleeping in the car as he usually did after every speech. I was shocked by Dr. King's brutal death. We rode in silence. During the next few days I listened frequently to that inspiring part of Dr. King's very moving speech—*I Have a Dream*—discussed over and over on radio—and I wondered where "our dream" was headed.

My husband's sleepless nights still haunt me. His playing of Joan Baez's records over and over and hearing him tap out his pipe in the glass ash tray at 2:00AM night after night—knowing of his extreme unrest—his depression and the relentless insomnia would obsess my mind. I tried to talk to him, often with no answer. The daylight hours—while I worked my $5.00-an-hour job in a doctor's office—found him prowling a three-county area hunting for shabby country doctors who would willingly write out a prescription for pain or for cough syrup containing narcotics. Both frustration and embarrassment dogged my days and I wondered what was in his heart and soul. This talented man with many great words in his head could not, would not, verbalize his torment, pain and fear—to me—to anyone. Psychiatrists would ask me how I thought he was doing. Oh, I know, it was just a ploy to hear what the wife would relate. Medications —hospital stays—electric shock treatment—to no avail. Modern medications might have helped, and I lament they were not available in the late 1960's-early 70's. It was a nightmare—especially for my youngest daughter and for me—a nightmare I would re-examine and relive in dark dreams many times in the 30-plus years to follow.

The last couple of years were the worst. My fear was that he would take his own life. I would rush home to see if his truck was in the garage and, if it was, to then look for him around the house. I checked the mileage on the truck and on the sly I even called a couple of doctors to see if he had been there (and he had.) I was tormented because I could not make a difference. He died from yet another bout with blocked blood flow—a haunted man, his true feelings locked in his soul.

I am a firm believer that we can grow in understanding and concern for others through our own battle with pain, sorrow and all adversity—if we will allow ourselves to seek God's guidance. I was raised in the church—joined the church when I was twelve—but spent many years of my life being a "busy" Christian—in charge of the church kitchen, doing mundane things like that, but not really experiencing a deep commitment with Our Lord. However, in 1972 after several of my children accepted Christ into their lives and I saw the difference it made, I wanted the same for my life. At a Bible study at my daughter's home, I sought out Christ and made a new recommitment with my life. My one fear was that I would fall back into my indifferent ways. That never happened, and I feel I have gained strength to survive not only the low spots of my life but to show more concern to others in the low ebbs of their lives.

Eleven years after Bob's death in 1986, I married again. Jim was a widower, an old family friend, an engineer, a talented man in his field of pumps, an expert engineer in moving both water and sewage. We had some very good years before congestive heart failure finally took its toll. He died in 1996 at the age of 86. I watched his downhill go with much apprehension—knowing full well that being a caregiver was not an easy role. He spent his last 5 months in a nursing home—not where he wanted to be—and under the care of Hospice. His son told me, on the night his father died, that I had given his dad 10 more years of life. But I wondered anew if I could have made those end times better for him, just as I have wondered about Bob's life.

In 2001, I married yet again. I knew that Bill had had a heart attack some ten years earlier, but he seemed to be in fair health. We were both 77 years of age with similar life experiences and with many mutual friends. In a few short months he developed major heart problems and went through open-heart surgery. It was a serious surgery for one who had had a previous heart attack; however, his recovery progressed fairly well, though it did end his days of employment in the cattle-hauling business and take him out of his outdoor environment. He is a good man who has made me feel cherished—a very special word. I can't imagine life without him, but I constantly find myself wondering how much longer this kindly man with both CHF and COPD can hang onto life. And I pray that I will do my best for him.

In the spring of 2004, my younger son, Frank, died at age 52 of a violent form of sepsis pneumonia. He went to work in the morning—home at 3:00PM, not feeling well—in the emergency room at 6:00PM and gone by 8:00PM. Our children are not supposed to leave this world before us! His death was the exact opposite of watching death by a slow decline of health. And such a shock! Another sorrow to get through—another tightening of the family circle. Another time of experiencing God's supportive love.

To those who stand at the bedside and do the "watching and waiting" (and the washing and feeding), I have much empathy. I know long nights when you listen to the difficult breathing and wonder if the sun will rise in the morning and will our loved one still be with us. I know long nights of "listening" to the insomnia and depression in earlier years of my life.

In this the winter of 2008, I pray every night for more patience, more understanding, but always thanking God for these good men in my life. My faith—it is my anchor. God is good and ever-present. He *can* make us "Strong in the Broken Places." May God bless all the caregivers everywhere who struggle to get through each day—and every night.

"I stand by my man" and know that a multitude of others are doing the same, [standing by their loved ones]—an enormous circle of humanity all over the world who do their best and give their all.

Louise M. Beattie

THE BIBLE—ON AGING
And My Thoughts
2008

Ecclesiastes, Chapter 12

1 Remember your Creator in the days of your youth,
before the days of trouble come and the years approach
when you will say, "I find no pleasure in them"—

2 before the sun and the light and the moon and the
stars grow dark, and the clouds return after the rain;

3 when the keepers of the house tremble, and the strong
men stoop, when the grinders cease because they are few,
and those looking through the windows grow dim;

4 when the doors to the street are closed and the sound
of grinding fades; when people rise up at the sound of
birds, but all their songs grow faint;

5 when people are afraid of heights and of dangers in
the streets; when the almond tree blossoms and the
grasshopper drags itself along and desire no longer is
stirred. Then people go to their eternal home and
mourners go about the streets.

6 Remember him—before the silver cord is severed,
and the golden bowl is broken; before the pitcher is
shattered at the spring, and the wheel broken at the well,

7 and the dust returns to the ground it came from, and
the spirit returns to God who gave it.

8 "Meaningless! Meaningless!" says the Teacher.
"Everything is meaningless!"

The Conclusion of the Matter
9 Not only was the Teacher wise, but he also imparted
knowledge to the people. He pondered and searched
out and set in order many proverbs.

10 The Teacher searched to find just the right words,
and what he wrote was upright and true.

11 The words of the wise are like goads, their collected
sayings like firmly embedded nails—given by one shepherd.

12 Be warned, my son, of anything in addition to them.
Of making many books there is no end, and much study
wearies the body.

13 Now all has been heard; here is the conclusion of the
matter: Fear God and keep his commandments, for this
is the duty of all mankind.

14 For God will bring every deed into judgment, including
every hidden thing, whether it is good or evil.

This scripture was given to me today by my dear friend, Bonnie Graves, on 8/21/08 at our Thursday Bible Study.

My thoughts:
Our demise is gradual—our bodies lose strength, agility—our sight and hearing lessen as we head steadily toward our death—our lives become fragile, easily broken. However, our Heavenly Father tells us this is "meaningless." Such is life—but only on earth! In our eternal life with God, there will be no struggle—no pain—no tears. Eternity with God—that will be truly meaningful.

What I fear most in aging is giving up the feeling of "being of worth by doing." For some reason this has always been so important to me. Too frequently I measure my worth by what I can still accomplish in my life, what I can contribute: a casserole, a pie, a hug. What am I worth to others? I fear becoming a burden, not carrying my part of the load, especially when I am no longer able to take care of myself.

So what can I learn from this? I need to gracefully coast toward the exit, wrapped in Ann's "petal white" blanket, surrounded by the love of family and friends.

Louise

THE ELECTION OF 2008
October 14, 2008

I voted today—absentee. It is done. What a year in this hotly-contested race for the presidency! Why anyone would truly want to be president is beyond me. The heated campaign has generated much furor, great excitement, and some division in family and church circles, causing me to have this need to write down some of my thoughts in regard to this super-charged election year. I truly feel that Barack Obama is the best man for the job. I do like his calm, pragmatic approach in the debates and in his eloquent speeches throughout the campaign. His calm composure throughout these months is commendable.

I am writing this because I have felt so strongly that I'm on the opposite side of the Obama vs. McCain debate from the majority of my family and my church family—so much so that I feel compelled to attempt to put down some thoughts that I have worked through in the long months of 2008.

Raised a Democrat, I was only 9 years old when Franklin Delano Roosevelt in 1933 came to the rescue of the farm folks, as well as providing assistance for the unemployed men wandering the country, with the 3C program. It provided jobs building roads, digging ditches, improving the infrastructure, and in addition, making life better, especially for farm families. I have recently read that FDR, in his first 100 days in office, instigated these new programs directed to give assistance to the poor and the lower-middle class. In our family, we gratefully accepted a new government-built outhouse with a concrete vault. I think we may have referred to it as the WPA! Gone was the drafty shanty with its smelly environment. But most of all, it was the coming of electricity, the rural- electrification program, that changed our lives for the better. No more noisy gasoline, pump-up lamps by which to do our homework. A flip of the switch provided *light*! And we could now pump water with an electrical motor, pumping it to the barn and the chicken house, not to mention to a "bathroom" with toilet and shower. Actually, the bathroom came after I left home in 1942, but things were definitely improving! So all my life I've been grateful for F.D.R's involvement in improving life during the forties, in wartime. Milking machines were such a time-saving, labor-saving device for the farm family, running water a godsend in our lives. However, I never truly understood how all this happened within that critical time-span in America.

I have never voted the "straight ticket" and tried all my voting life to try to decide who would be the best person for the job and to vote accordingly. Over the years I have lost my vote many times. When Walter Brownson campaigned for a county commissioner position in 1988, I switched over to being a registered Republican to lend support to him in the primary. He didn't make it; however, I didn't bother to change back to being a registered Democrat until the primary of 2008. It was sort of like going back to the barn— that is farm-speak for finding security and comfort again, close to our roots. Initially, in the fall of 2007, I felt I should/could support McCain and I sent a contribution to his campaign, which I have regretted all of 2008 as I was bombarded with requests by phone calls and in nearly-daily letters asking me for more donations, which I declined.

So I'm feeling like an outcast in church (though my stand is probably not well known) and partly in family, as it would seem that nearly all are hanging their hats on the pro-life issue. In my heart, I don't think that either candidate is truly pro-life. I really don't think that McCain, if elected president, will attempt to overturn Roe vs, Wade. He is pro-life, because that is the Republican stand in the "base" of the party, and he desperately needs the evangelical-church vote. So what do I really think? I *am* pro-life. I can hear the boo's [as I write this,] but I'm not at all sure that it is an out-and-out, black-and-white issue. Being a mother of five children whom I have loved dearly, I would never, ever have given a thought to considering an abortion. However, with seven pregnancies and never an extra dime I can only imagine to some slight degree the anguish that goes through the minds of women who are feeling a bit desperate. And I believe that some women should not become mothers; there are those who are totally unfit for the role of motherhood. Of course, in a perfect world, all pregnant women would carry their babies to term and their babies would in turn be available for adoption. But in this no-so-perfect world where the adoption process does not work well and is very costly and burdened with a great amount of red tape, it is extremely difficult to adopt an American child even in the best of circumstances.

However I need to say that I *do* support, regularly, our local pro-life center and have for years! I have been pointedly asked why [I support the center,] if I'm willing to vote for a pro-*choice* candidate. So here are my thoughts on this. In an ideal world, we would all be pro-life, but this is far from an ideal world. I believe that a fetus is a "life" from the moment of conception. I also believe an abortion might be called for if the mother's life is threatened, but I'm confused—isn't that [exchanging] a life for a life? I'm not quite willing to say never. What about incest and rape situations? I find this hard to view as a clear-cut issue. Thankfully, pro-life centers are available to all who care to walk through the door, where they will receive words of encouragement in carrying this baby to term. In time, if this pregnant woman can actually "see" her baby by ultra-sound, she is much more apt to view this pregnancy as her child, her baby. A real plus!

As I have previously said, I do not believe this is entirely a black-and-white issue which would not seem the consistent view of the "church." I'm not totally comfortable with this evangelical view. To those who may ultimately wish to abolish Roe vs Wade, I would ask if they would be willing and comfortable allowing the back-street butchers to flourish with infection and hemorrhaging to become common-place again? This issue of abortion has been with us for all of time—and we will continue to ponder it again and again.

In regard to war, I truly think that the Bush decision, backed by McCain, dragged us into this current war without just cause for doing so. With over 3000 lives lost and mega- dollars spent, it is still so disheartening and does not justify the poor reasoning for going there in the first place. I see us headed on to Iran and/or other places with McCain, whose training and expertise is in the military. He is a survivor, valiant in his years of captivity, to be sure, but he is also a "fighter" —the very thing I feel sure he knows how to do, which he could well do in the future, if elected. Of course, no one can truly say what any one candidate will actually do when in office. We have to go on past their records, stances taken when in situations of power and leadership in prior times. I don't feel comfortable with McCain's history nor with his age, and therefore, I am not pleased with his choice of running mate. Surely he could have done better. Sara Palin's brash, folksy manner does not seem at all presidential to me. How would she fit into the possible situation she might find herself facing one day? Her lack of experience in foreign policy is distressing. Her demeanor is not calming or reassuring.

America and the entire world desperately need sound, moral leadership, a leader who can inspire unity, someone who can inspire the sacrifice of individual will for the good of the country and the entire world, someone who can pull the splintered parties together, purge the greed and corruption in all the high places and bring us back to a good life once again.

While in Colorado in late September, I visited Sara's church-also Evangelical Free--and liked what the pastor had to say in regard to the political scene. He said 'Pray about it, weigh it all carefully and make a heartfelt decision". (I'm sure he meant "vote for McCain,") However, I have voted for Obama/Biden. My prayer is that together they can do what the Lord requires of them, to make this country a better place, strong again and re-inspire the world.

I have the following little quote posted on my refrigerator. These words have been a guide and inspiration in my thinking for many months.

What America Needs

What America needs now is someone with ability not just to manage the world, but to re-inspire its inhabitants again. Only by such re-branding can we get out the hole we are in.

Author unknown

Louise Conery

A CHANGE IN CHRISTMAS GIVING
December, 2008

At age 84, I found myself downsizing my condo last year, beginning to shut down my life, putting away the way-too-many pictures of family members that came along with my husband's and my "combined" family that totals over 100 people. In addition, I was cutting way back on the household "pretties," many them gifts of loving family members over the years. After filling a big carton, I made a decision. Something just had to be done about this accumulation. A heart attack in September furthered my resolve to continue the downsizing project.

Our combined grandchildren number 27, the great-grandchildren 44. We no longer attempted to "gift" these generations; however, we both felt the heart-tug to give to our own children, the combined number of 8. So a decision was made to give $100 to each of our children to be "gifted" on to others. I named it "Gift It Forward" and ventured on writing letters of explanation to each of them.

We were amazed at the thoughtful way in which these gifts turned into benevolent giving. Some went as far away as Africa, to the Kiva program in loaning money to enterprising women striving to build a small business to help their families and their small communities to have a better life. One gift went to a lady who wanted to borrow money to buy calves as she built a small herd. Another to a woman who wanted to borrow funds to buy fabric for her small-business endeavor, again in a very small village. Some went for "gas" cards for local people. Some went to assist those who have recently lost their jobs. Others gifts were used to assist in much-needed home repair and the painting of walls for a woman living alone on a very small disability income.

Needless to say we were delighted with the outcome and the testimony from our children indicating that they enjoyed the opportunity to pass the gifts on to others was all very gratifying to us both. I believe this will be a repeat for the Christmas season of 2009.

I refer to this as a "GOD THING," for He is the greatest giver of all!

Louise Beattie

FLUKE REUNION, 2009
Labor Day Weekend

We all watched the weather forecast. It called for sunny, clear days with day temperatures in the mid-seventies—all three days! Fantastic—just what we needed for this every-other-year event.

Folks gathered in on Friday evening at Rick and Marti Krause's lovely country home—a new and special change for this year—where everyone enjoyed a wonderful meal provided by Rick and Marti and served out in their backyard. Bill Martin surprised us all by arriving with his fiancée Sheila. They are to be married later this fall. Sheila made the rounds of the family in great style. Wonderful connections were made by all as we circled our lawn chairs for a time of fellowship around a bonfire. During the evening many checked out Rick's tractor collection—impressive! There must have been about 50 attending, though I never tried to make a count. What a great way to start the festivities.

Liz and David Drouillard arrived a couple days ahead of time and were of tremendous help to the Smiths in getting things ready to go, like painting the new doors of the machinery shed, clearing out the barn floor, and mowing with the zero-turn mower, among many other things. The tent and other "facilities" arrived on Friday. Glenn and Matt Johnson trucked the tables and chairs from our church on Saturday morning. We were ready to go! The parking area was already filling up.

Molly instigated a new event for this year, called "speed greeting." It was a really neat idea, but not many held still long enough or took time to get to know each other in this way. We do need to try this again.

Another new activity this year was a "bucket auction," John Fluke's idea to add some much-needed funds to our coffers. Larry Keiffer was in charge of this and did a super job along with many helpers. Nearly everyone brought something for the auction—some were Fluke family keepsake items and others were personal art and craft things. It was a HUGE success, lots of fun, adding $500 to our depleted treasury.

Let me back up a bit. Time out for a wonderful noon meal with all the side dishes, catered by Barb Bates. This was a new idea and so well done, very well accepted by all—with the family bringing in desserts. And what a selection! Hamburgers, brat sausages and hotdogs were grilled by Glenn and Matt Johnson. A fee was charged for this meal, $4.00 for adults and $3.00 for kids. Let's keep this idea, as it freed up the kitchen from all the food preparation, leaving more time for visiting and games.

In addition, Molly hired two great kids from our Youth Group at church, Rachel and Nate Kline, who not only toted and carried many things, but kept the kitchen cleaned up ALL day and helped with watching toddlers—especially Jake, Raif and Lena. Another good idea.

Margaret Welch provided a wonderful scavenger hunt for the kids. She was dressed as Miss Sunflower and made a real hit. The hunt was confined to the general farm- buildings area to keep the kids in a safe place. No traipsing off to the pond. I don't know who actually won this event, but Leif and Maya McFrederick seemed to be very observant and quick to identify various clues.

Ann Keiffer again provided "story-telling in the barn," assisted by Erin Johnson doing improv, acting out the story without any prior knowledge of the story. Meanwhile, the "Gator run" was shaping up in the pasture with Meredith and Elise Ritschdorff in charge. They had volunteered to take on this first-time event, and, with clipboard in hand, signed up blindfolded drivers paired with "sighted" passengers who gave the directions about how to drive the Gator course. It was one of the older folks suggestions—hmmm, me—and if the girls hadn't stepped up to the plate, the Gator run would have been axed from the agenda. Nice work, girls! A really fun time with only a couple of slightly mashed straw bales after a few wide or wrong turns.

While the Gator run was in progress, Pepper gave a demonstration—to the more sedate lawn-chair group in the yard—of how she twirls her Indian Clubs. She was a national champion in her youthful days! We had always wanted to see her do this and she performed well even with an ailing shoulder. Good job, Pepper!

Somewhere in this part of the afternoon Rick K. loaded up the hay wagon and took a big group off on a hayride for a tour of the pond area and the woods, too, I think—always an event enjoyed by all ages.

Gini Brownson gathered up a gang for the Corn Hole Tourney that was progressing in lively fashion until Matt B. was summoned to assist with the corn roast in the north pasture, just outside the gate. Bob B. and his family hosted this event. Wow—talk about tasty corn—just a tad burned, the way that makes it perfect. We will remember this always. Lots of butter on the lips and chins—a bucket of soapy water and towel to the rescue!

Okay...the puppet show is shaping up on the new front porch. Hurry now, as it is starting to get dark! Erin J. and Sara Mc. did great job with the puppets as they performed from skits written by Molly S. Some were "standards" and some new.

Then it is off to the pond for the annual memorial time, headed by Lynne Ritschdorff, who volunteered and planned the service. Again, the hay wagon was loaded up and those who rode to the pond got to experience the lovely, cool evening with the full moon beaming down on them all. With torches placed around the north and west side of the pond, one for each of the beloved family members, now deceased, going back to the 70's. Lynne read the names aloud as a torch was lit for each person. She then invited each person to light a candle, already placed in the little white paper boats, each in memory of someone dear to them. The candlelit boats were quietly launched at the water's edge. Silently they drifted out from the bank, a beautiful sight along with the light from the torches. Erin sang a lovely song, "A Way Down the River" from the Alison Krauss album, "One Hundred Miles Or More," as Bob accompanied Erin on guitar—just right for the occasion. This is always a heartfelt, binding time as the generations remember those who have gone on before. Before I went to sleep on Saturday night, I counted (by family) 74 attendees for the Saturday event.

Sunday morning, back at the farm, all gathered for a wonderful brunch prepared by David and Liz. We also enjoyed Pepper's Butter Horn rolls. For some, brunch is one of the most meaningful times of the reunion. Time to reminisce—time to share remembering the events of the weekend—and finally a few tears and last hugs and goodbyes before folks started on their long drives home to North Carolina and Michigan. Others, from California, Colorado and Florida, were on flights home on Wednesday.

Ahead of time, in the planning stage of this gathering, we wondered if the health and age of the remaining Fluke "kids" might make this their last reunion. However, after it was all said and done, we are thinking that just maybe we might be able to make it for 2011—the Good Lord willing. The number of canes increases, and we are all a bit tottery, but the enjoyment is still there, more in the viewing than in actual participation. It is so heartwarming to see the younger generation(s) having a good time and everyone enjoying their heritage and memories of the Fluke farm!

My personal treasure from the reunion was a black-and-white snapshot of Grandpa Jim Fluke and me taken at the time of the reunion of 1937. I never saw the photo before. It was provided by Margaret and used in her scavenger hunt for the kids. It was one of the clues, and I think the kids had been told to find the "girl" in the picture. Leif gave it a long look and pointed at me, saying, "It's you, Grandma." I snagged onto the picture as I have no photo of me with my Grandpa Fluke. Aren't memories sweet?

I know I truly speak for all the. family when I express my deep appreciation to Glenn and Molly for sharing with all the Flukes their lovely remodeled home and all the farm's wonderful memory spots—the pond, the woods, the barn and the front porch swing. Everything was so special and unique for each one of us.

Until we meet again!

Louise Beattie

MY 85TH BIRTHDAY
Written in June, 2009

The actual date, May 26th, is now past by more than six weeks. So, what took me so long to record this event? Well, I don't really know why, except that at this time in my life things tend to pile up in my "to-do" box just a bit. In truth, I just kept putting it off. Not that is wasn't a nice family party—as it was great! However, it did end abruptly with a "BANG!" More about that later.

I didn't want a big party—like, at the church with a big "SURPRISE!!" Or being asked to reminisce from a rocking chair about the good old days. This is not my way. When Molly asked what I would really like I told her just my family and spouses plus Walter and Edith and Betty together for a meal. Tina and Rick hosted the event at their house with this nice group around their lovely table and Tina, Molly and Gini fixed a wonderful meal much enjoyed by all. Rick borrowed Luke's movie camera (or is that referred to as a video camera today?) to record the conversation around the table after dinner. Many old family stories were told and Betty, at our urging, did her famous telling of "Mrs. Pitts and her Baby Snakes Hissing in the Pit"—flawlessly, I might add. It is now recorded for all time.

Molly had made me a very special gift—from the whole family—one of her wall-art creations, a framed picture, incorporating a 5x7 space for each of my five children. Each space featured a black-and-white photograph depicting the talents, gifts and interests of each one of the five—Ann, Bob, Tina, Frank and Molly, with just a bit of color worked in, an unusual technique! It now hangs above my computer where I can see it every day and marvel over and over how well it portrays their individual life interests—what they give and share with others in their lives including me, their Mom.

As we were laughing and sharing a fun family time around the table, a storm was raging on outside—a strong bolt of lightning and very heavy rain. Suddenly the phone rang. Tina answered. It was Karina in tears telling Tina that Luke had been cleaning out his gutters and was down off the ladder when a bolt of lightning struck him as he was standing there in the yard watching the storm. It came down a tree and entered one foot then exited through his hand. Fortunately, it must have been a glancing strike only. Everybody jumped up from the table and the guys hurried to get the cars out of the driveway so that Rick and Tina could get a car out and go to the aid of Luke, Karina and their family. After a trip to the ER, which took ages, he turned out to be okay, but it was a very tense time for all. It is a miracle that he is alive and suffered no serious injury. He said he had never heard such a loud "bang" and he experienced a "burned taste" in his mouth. The bolt traveled through his lawn and into his shop doing some damage inside that building. So that is why I wrote that my party ended with a "bang!"

In all honesty, 85 isn't really much different than being 80. However, I do notice that I tend to lose some vigor as the months go by and it is harder to keep appointments and pills in order, but I can't complain. Will I make it to 90? Only the good Lord knows. In the meantime, I will attempt to keep the two of us, Bill and me, in "working order," ready for each day.

Louise Beattie

SCUTTLEBUTT AT THE CHIROPRACTOR'S OFFICE
(And Other Places)
April 27, 2009

For several decades, the place to get your latest information regarding community, acquaintances, friends and even family was the beauty parlor. You found out the physical, medical condition of man (or beast,) who was dating whom, and—heaven forbid—who was stepping out on whom. But men don't go to beauty shops—or didn't in the old days, but there are barber shops with a wealth of information being passed from barber to client from chair to chair. And so the world goes around. I've been cutting my Bill's hair lately. Wonder what all he has missed?

However, I've learned, since I married a Beattie, of another gathering place where much news is passed. Ah, yes, the chiropractor's office! Your back is aching, so naturally the Beatties, each in turn, head out to the chiropractor of their choice for an "adjustment." I doubt that the chiropractors ask questions about family members, but the people in the waiting room—old friends of the Beattie family do exchange info—especially regarding "Grandpa's fall" and "how he is doing."

It goes like this. Grandson, Dusty, goes to see Dr. C., probably for an adjustment. Old family friends, Dick and Barbara C. are in the waiting room. They ask about Dusty's "Grandpa" and get a report. Some days, or maybe weeks later, Dick and Barbara return to the chiropractor and meet granddaughter, Devon, who is in for an adjustment and get another report on the progress of the healing of Grandpa's back. Yesterday Dick and Barbara turned up at our front door and reported that they had been keeping a check on Bill—at Dr. C.'s office! I thought this was so funny and then just this morning son Jim calls to tell his dad that he had been to see Dr. C. that morning and he had discussed his dad's back with the doctor. Like, was there anything the doctor thought he might be able to do for his dad ? Now, Bill has a possible compression fraction in his lower back from his January 8th fall here at home while he was attempting to put on his house slippers. X-rays in the ER indicated a very much out of whack, back-out-of-line, old compression fracture from way back. All to the extent that they couldn't make an exact diagnosis. But possible compression fracture, that sounds probable.

Now Bill knows that I'm not really sold on this sort of back therapy. Having had three back surgeries and a fusion of three vertebrae, I cringe at even thinking of getting up on that table for any pulling or twisting. However, Bill just might consider it. It is a strong pull when you have faith in the re-alignment process and your whole family does, too. Jim did tell him that it would be "pricey." I think Jim meant the x-ray very probably was not covered by Medicare, but maybe it was the whole thing—x-ray and appointment—that would be pricey. That might be enough to make it not something Bill would want to try. Anyway, I rest my case, for now.

Another place to get a wealth of information is on a stool at the lunch counter of our local eatery, the Lynway restaurant. In a few minutes you can find out not only the price of milk (it's down), but also all meat and everything related to cows (dairy, fats, steers, feeders, even "canner and cutters".) And of course, information about pork, too—not the kind we have heard so much about in present-day political circles, as in "pork spending," but the edible kind! Then too, you can find out how that local hay auction went today, how it all sold and who brought in "thin" hay for sale. You can further find out if Simonson Builders got any jobs to do or even a bid, who is working and who is not, and that Pentair (the old Myers

Pump Co.) is laying off 30 more people today. All this goes on over a plate of the "cube-steak special"—a mound of mashed potatoes, a serving of well-cooked beef, two slices of toast cut diagonally, and ALL covered entirely with very dark brown gravy. Just to view it makes my recovering, post-heart-attack heart skip a beat as I eat my side salad or bowl of soup!

Lyn-way is a hang-out for not only for work men, but also for the elderly. One day I counted three "walkers" and five canes and two wheelchairs (one manually operated and one electrically powered) making their entrance in one noontime span. And not all these came in on the senior-citizens bus from Wellington. You won't find a Cobb salad or a spinach salad with grilled chicken. No siree, but you can get a great bowl of chili or potato soup in addition to the new local news of the day.

Take the news where you can get it, especially if you are weary of CNN and the stimulus-package deal and who is now being ousted from that special cabinet position because they forgot of pay their taxes. Don't you wonder about all the short memories of so many of our elected officials and appointees? We women can get our news in the toothpaste aisle at Walmart or the waiting line at Aldi's and maybe even at Bible Study. Christian author, Max Lucado, just has a way of drawing out our innermost thinking when he discusses "barbaric behavior" in our study of *Facing Your Giants*.

And don't forget the old party-line telephone. I'm sure you could learn a lot from listening in if you didn't do too much heavy breathing and give away your presence. But hey, if your house was on fire you could summon help in a jiffy.

I'm not too interested that the Cleveland Browns traded Kellen Winslow today. Are you? However, I am interested that a gallon of 2% milk at Aldi's is now only $1.99.

I hear that newspapers are in trouble. Small wonder when there are so many other ways to get the news!

Louise Beattie

MOLLY TAKES ON THE GREATEST GENERATION
AND WAL-MART ALL IN ONE DAY
Written by Molly Smith -- October 20, 2009

The huge bargain bottle of shampoo sat on my shelf for three weeks. DARN! I'd gotten the wrong kind...the kind with conditioner in the shampoo. I knew it wouldn't work. My curly hair needs a conditioner that doesn't have to fight with shampoo. What is it with putting shampoo and conditioner together, anyway? Does that make sense? I can just see the two converse entities working to defeat each other on my scalp. I needed to take this $5 bottle of ooze back to Wal-Mart and get a refund... buy the right stuff that gives my hair a smooth sheen...calms the raging snarls.

I grabbed the fat envelope that holds the receipts. I noted that the envelope was too fat, a bad sign that I have not gone through the receipts and itemized their content. My husband, Glenn, has always had this dream of making a budget, and we are giving it a go one more time. It's my job to wrestle with the Wal-Mart receipts, categorizing the long lists of items, trying to decipher the cryptic code used by the store to describe the items I bought. Here's an example of the coded angst I faced: CHXMX HNYNUT. Some of you will decode this immediately. I know what it is, because I ate it. The rest of you will have to guess.

Anyway, I sorted through the receipts till I found one that said Shmpo—$5. I put the shampoo into a rumpled Wal-Mart bag and headed off to the store to complete my mission.

I know the rules of Wal-Mart. If you have a return, you need to go to the "Greeter," just inside the doors. Greeters are usually nice older folks. At least they used to be nice older folks who said "Hi" to you when you entered the store. When you had a return, this nice person would apply a *Smiley Face* sticker to your bag. You then went on your merry way to the Service Counter where they straightened out your problem.

Policy has changed at Wal-Mart. Now the *Greeters* watch with eagle-eyes to see if you are bringing a package into the store. It's their job and they take it very seriously. They don't say, "Hello," anymore. I, being the nice person that I am, made small, cheerful talk with the greeter...a kindly gentleman with a bar-code gun. My greeter now scanned my item and put a bar-code sticker on it. Then, my barcode, shampoo and I headed to the Customer Service Department to wait in line.

The line was five-deep with one service agent in attendance. She was involved in a lengthy telephone conversation, her back turned to the foot-shifting lineup. I knew this was going to take a while, so I made the fateful decision to do my shopping first and take care of the DARN shampoo later.

I was in an efficient mood as I moved through the store getting, CHXMX HNYNUT and EQ FHS. By the time 20 minutes had elapsed I was through the check-out and headed out the door. Just as I went through the first set of automatic doors I saw it! There was that DARN rumpled bag with the shampoo in it! I made a u-turn and headed to the CUST SERV. There was no line this time! I was feeling lucky. I handed over the shampoo and receipt. The sticker had fallen off and was stuck to the bag ... a nuisance to retrieve. My agent threw the bag into a vat of bags and pressed down the heap. She was pleasant enough and I was appreciative as she checked out my receipt and handed over the $5. Done...or at least I thought so.

I turned around to leave, noting that now there was a line behind me. My timing had been excellent. As I started to maneuver my cart out of the congestion, I noted an older man (not my original greeter) dressed in uniform (A Wal-Mart uniform, that is). It took me a moment to realize that he was standing in my way, *on purpose.* I wondered if he'd seen me drop my keys or something and was trying to be helpful. Wait...no...his face was not pleasant like the face of someone who wanted to help me. This face was that of a World War II veteran looking for a battle. He was facing off with me and his face was literally 12 inches away and angry-looking. The crowd in the line-up gathered in close as they sensed the confrontation. I suddenly realized that this man saw me make the u-turn at the door and had been following me...waiting for me to complete the shampoo transaction.

Now here is where things heated up. I literally felt my face get hot as this Wal-Mart soldier accused me of...something. I was so mad that my ears kind of shut off. I knew it had to do with that DARN shampoo. I explained that I *HAD* the bar-code sticker...had realized as I was going out the door that I had forgotten the return. He was not believing me and not backing off. My Customer Service agent was rummaging through the heap but could not find my sticker!!!!

I pulled out the "big guns" and asked for the store manager by name. "Would you please call FRED," I told the flustered CUST SERV agent. I know Fred because he attends our church. My Greeter seemed jarred a bit. "Well, go ahead if you feel the need," he said gruffly. "I do feel the need," I volleyed back. This was a full-fledged attack...some weird sort of scene with the on-lookers waiting for blood. The soldier turned on his heels and headed out to rendezvous with Fred before Fred made it to me.

By now there were quite a few people in place for the standoff. Fred was very businesslike as I told him his Greeter had been rude and inappropriate in word and in deed. "What did he say to you?" he asked. Not having instant, auditory imprinting I stood there and just looked dumb. I could not remember. I just knew it was an accusation done in front of a bunch of people. I was embarrassed.

Fred had his manager's hat on. I don't know what I was thinking asking for Fred by name. Now I thought he might say something personal to me like, "Sorry this happened." Instead he just stared at me, no hint of recognition. Fred was seeing a side of me he had never seen before. Maybe he didn't even recognize this irritated person across the counter from him. Maybe I should have gone off to the Wal-Mart slammer instead of making an issue of it.

I turned to leave and Fred followed me out. He quietly told me that I was not the first one to have problems with this particular Greeter. He said that greeters are not supposed to confront people in public like that. They are supposed to do it more privately. There was no apology from the manager. Maybe he just didn't feel the need. Maybe that's the way it works best at Wal-Mart. I was not sure if I had won the battle or not. It didn't feel like a victory.

Now I have a sort of post-traumatic-stress-syndrome. I find myself having flash-backs...doing clandestine returns to Wal-Marts in neighboring cities. My heart races when I look at Greeters with their guns. I don't trust their smiles...not even the sweet-looking ladies. I've been carrying around a vinyl sink mat in the back of my car for weeks trying to do some "return therapy." So far...no good.

I have not seen The Greeter again. I wonder if he got canned or just had to go on a furlough until the store policies are more firmly planted in his mind. I am fairly certain that he thinks ill of me. I guess the feeling is mutual. He probably thinks he was just doing his job. I did not want to be made out to be a thief. I made my point.

This event was a blip in the grand scheme of things...a tiny battle. I look back at my anger. I didn't yell or punch anybody, but I certainly was assertive. I wonder if I could have done it in a nicer way. I hope I never have the chance to try. You never know what life holds for you right around the corner. Who would have guessed that the shampoo with the conditioner already in it would have caused such a snarl.

Molly Smith

LOUISE'S STORY FOLLOWING UP
ON MOLLY'S WAL-MART STORY
October, 2009

This time it's a "Greatest-Generation" 85-year-old female shopping at the local Wal-Mart mercantile. Where else are you going to get your "lite" soup, the heavy-duty denture cleaner for your husband and your panty liners all in one-stop shopping?

Ah yes, I was also looking for something to put on Miriam's grave in memory of the anniversary of her death 10 years ago. Mums...you can't grow wrong with mums. So I parked in the first available parking space just outside the Garden Center. I went in and viewed the many pots, ALL looking a bit past prime, decided against a purchase and made my way on into the store. I finally selected an artificial red geranium. It looked pretty good and would last through, until time to do Christmas at the grave site. I ended up in buying a second one for my outside patio for next summer. I'm trying to cut down on watering, but they will probably just look cheap in both places! So on with my shopping. Tylenol for the aches and pain, Equate Stomach Acid Reducer for Bill and Lebanon bologna for me who ever needs "spicy" for my sandwich. I rounded out my cart with a good supply of low-fat, lite yogurt and checked out at register #25 closest to the front door. You know—handy for "out the door" and into the car, I thought.

And then I remembered I parked at the Garden Center entrance, so off I trucked with a cart that "thumped" with every wheel turn and headed for the right exit. When I got to the doors a "Greeter" from the "Greatest Generation" was sitting on an overturned bucket—you guessed it, "dead heading"—a term I learned from Tina who diligently "dead heads" her flowers daily all summer long—the bedraggled, fore-spoken mums. He with some effort got up off his bucket and limped over to my cart. And then it dawned on me that he was suspecting me of shoplifting the assortment of stuff in my car, even though I quickly "got it" and hauled out the receipt for the items. He pondered it for some time, poking through the various bags until I told him that I had parked at this exit but had checked out at the front. No greeting—no bye, for sure! But no voices were raised—no blows were struck—Fred wasn't summoned, and I made a clean break for it out the door and escaped to my 10-year-old Buick and hurried across the road to buy some "damn green beans" at Aldi's. But that is another story! Some days you just can't win.

Louise Beattie

179

LETTER TO LIZ
Thoughts after John & Laura's wedding
April 12, 2010

My Dear Liz,

What a delightful day! How great to be there with you to see your John marry Laura and to sit around the same table with my close relatives from Michigan. It was a true honor to be included in the day. Memories of my dear sister Elinor waved over me all day long. Oh my, how she would have enjoyed the day with us all. To see her beloved John so happily married, to see John, for whom she had great concern in his earlier years, find such a great soul mate with similar interests to his. I do thank you for sharing that most precious story of the letters—was it daily letters?—Elinor mailed to John in his difficult grade school time of life and his joy in checking out the mail box upon arriving home from school. It is so like her—her love and support of him and her way of conveying that love and concern to him. Many of us received letters from time to time with similar wishes for better times for us. She hated to share her problems, but was always there with her loving support and not just in letters...

When Tina was born and I was at Grandma Mary's for the "required" two-week recovery time, I wanted to go home to New London so much. I recall she asked what it would take to make that happen. I remember saying, "Oh, my house needs a good cleaning." (I had to be at the Brownson's—Bob's folk—for three weeks prior to Tina's birth.) So she went to New London and cleaned my house—even bought me two pie pans and cupcake tins. I still use those pie pans and remember that heartfelt assist she gave in April of 1949 every time I use them!

But I got side-tracked there. Sorry. Thanks for sending the pictures yesterday. I have poured over them a couple of times already. I don't really have many of the names of those involved, but can put some people and families together.

Such a pretty wedding, Liz. I loved all the dresses. Both Laura and Lauren are such beautiful girls. The flowers added such a spring-like look and contrast to the handsome black dresses. The groomsmen sort of "spelled out" John's and Laura's combined lives, somehow. Nolon—I'd like to know more about him—and the impaired young man—what a testimony as to how John and Laura both related to that young man. I believe I heard that Laura had been involved in his care at some time. (We have a young man in our church congregation much like this young man, quite given to making sounds—no words—especially when excited or distressed.) And the delightful young (flower?) girl. We met her in the restroom before heading home, and she was so dear—offered Molly hand soap from the dispenser bottle. The two of them had a nice little conversation about the little girl's lovely dress and hair. I'm sure this was a very special day for her. Again, John and Laura, reaching out to those on their life path, so refreshing in this selfish old world to see their heartfelt concern for others in various walks and places of life.

I was intrigued by the history of the church—Baptist and then Genesis. It is usually difficult for older traditional church members to adjust to drums, the amplification of sound and the raising of hands during exuberant worship—though I'm very fond of the beat and find joy in singing this type of music. You mentioned the Nankin Church—I remember mostly that there were differences after federation of the Methodists and Presbyterians, as to whether to take communion at the altar rail—I think that was the

Methodist preference—or in the pews, as Presbyterians preferred, I believe. The Presbyterians won out! I was only eight years old, so I certainly wasn't tuned in to the details of worship. It would seem like it is all working for Genesis—but no doubt some tension. Pastor Beau, his remarks to the bride and groom, so right on, I love it. Not read—he was thoroughly invested in his heartfelt thoughts, you could tell. I loved the music—singing "Great Is Thy Faithfulness" is always special. Sitting in the lounge area and listening to them practice set the stage for the ceremony for me. While there I noticed the "knocked off your axis" brochures in the little lounge. I can imagine Beau did a great job with that. Would have liked to have heard him. Maybe you can tell me more about it sometime, not now.

I am so glad that it all worked out for me to make the trip. Molly and Glenn are a blessing to me. It was good to hug you all, but especially you, my dear, with whom I have this blessed bond with my sister, my mentor, whom I have admired and loved all my life. In hugging you, I feel her presence, her person, and the memories flowed over us both. We will remember the day, always. And she "knows" and smiles in the glow of the day!

Hopefully you have been able to make good connection with an orthopedic doctor today and get the attention you need—soon! Do keep me/us posted as to scheduling and plans. May you heal up well!

I was honored to be included in your day.

I, too, love you forever—isn't that a special thought?

Aunt Louise

A LESSON BEFORE DYING

December 10, 2010

It is something we all have to do—there is no escaping. To some, death comes suddenly, for others we march on into our eighties and wonder every so often what will be our demise. My mother lived well into her 96th year—not quality years, with dementia gradually taking over her failing body. And I felt she had probably lost any attempt to factor in the fact that she was dying. She seemed to live only for the faces of her children. She smiled with recognition, though I'm not quite sure that she could put the right name with the face. And because of the way her life ended, my "goal" in life was not to live that long. However, knowing that I might not have any input into my end times, I've often had thoughts about my death in the ever-nearing future because of the rather negative factors within my total health picture. A diagnosis of diabetes in 1998, a heart attack in 2008, then struggles with pesky, elevated cholesterol and triglycerides lead me to think that I would probably die with the stroke and my main hope was that it would be a "big" one. But such seems irrelevant now. It is not the path I'm finding myself on this December of 2010.

A variety of things have happened and I find myself with the diagnosis of Non-Hodgkin's Lymphoma—an inoperable growth in the abdomen. I'm now in the process of further testing to determine if the cancer has traveled elsewhere. Many scenarios are lined up in my mind causing me to examine my thinking to see where I am in all this and to try to work out a plan for the rest of my life. I know full well that God has the BIG plan for my life, but I think He also might want me to take some responsibility in working through the complicated course of possible treatments as presented to me thus far. I'm aware that the final decision of treatment will be mine. I could hasten my death or prolong my life—by my decision.

Foremost in my mind is that I do not want to live my last six months of life (or whatever)—if that is the oncologist's plan—in serious, full-go chemo if I'm to suffer a poor quality of life for the remainder of my days—filled with nausea, diminishing strength, no appetite and much pain. I do not think it is worth an overly aggressive battle for a remission if healing is not to be. And yet I truly feel I need to try in some fashion to "kill the beast in my belly"—if possible—and not to reject the whole chemo therapy. I will know more about this next week when we—Molly, Tina and I—will have our "chemo teach" session with the oncology staff. I am impressed with the staff—all very well trained and all very kind and caring. This will all be summed up on December 20 when we meet with the oncologist, Dr. Khan, who is in charge of my case. That will be the day of decision. I need to remember that I'm in charge—the earthly decision is mine. I pray that I make the best decision(s) possible!

I never thought much about getting old until I reached this stage of the game. There were always those "older yet" folks. Perhaps it was always this way. And just now as I write this, I'm watching five small boys slide down the slope behind the condos having a great time on all sorts of plastic sleds and saucers. I'm watching all kinds of "fun" happening, sportsmanship being learned, great competition, trying to stay on their icy track and I'm thinking this is a lot like "life." They are there in their place in life—growing up, with all the things kids love to do, learning as the go. I'm still learning but it is not quite so much fun on this "icy slope." However, I will make it. It is all a part of the big plan!

I had a long talk with Ann this morning after some rather disjointed text messages last evening. A good old-fashioned phone call can really fill the bill—better than the last line of a long text maybe!

I know, absolutely, totally, that my family surrounds me with love. I am blessed.

Louise Beattie

MY TESTIMONY
God Is Patient and Faithful
March 19, 1010

Throughout my adult years in my "home" church I was a very "busy" Christian, teaching Sunday School little ones, forming a church nursery and overseeing the church kitchen for all dinners. However, I did not truly "Experience God" in my heart.

In 1972 I watched, with delight, as three of my children accepted God. I saw God becoming an integral part of their lives. What a joy! I wanted—yes, even yearned for— this very experience in my life as well. One night after a Bible study in my daughter Tina's home, the leader of the study, a man whom I did not know, George Reese from Mansfield, led me to the Lord. I made a new commitment to my God. The only apprehension I had was that I would slide back into being just a "busy" Christian again— although it never happened. I've stayed committed.

In spite of this new commitment, I'm ashamed to say it took me 21 years to finally leave behind my life-long, mainline church, my long-time friends and some close family relatives and withdraw from this church where there was too much stress and unrest within the congregation to allow for heartfelt, peaceful worship. I didn't know where to go, so I followed Rick Fischel to Christ Community Church in 1993. Rick was a former assistant pastor at my home church while he was a student at the seminary, and he was and still is a good friend. It was difficult to leave this church where I had spent my whole life thus far, especially when my paternal Great-Great-Grandfather had helped to form the church back in the early 1800's and a century later my maternal Grandfather preached there in the 1915-1925 era. The roots grew deep. Family history and ties were strong. It wasn't easy to walk away.

In those, my "busy" years, I lost my first husband, the father of my children, and knew what it was to be lonely, alone and to be on a very limited income. However, it was in this period of time that I was moved by a sermon about honoring our God with our "gifts" that I began a tithe. I was making $3.85 an hour and my one extravagance was a Wendy's hamburger from the drive-thru on Fridays.

At this time it seemed so right—to give tithing a try. And it truly was an awesome experience to see that it was not only possible, but so fulfilling. I have never wavered in my conviction regarding the value of tithing—this honoring of my God—this adherence to the words of scripture regarding the giving of 10% of our income to the Kingdom!

Now, at nearly 86 years old I often feel that my days of serving are nearly over. Now I am limited in what I can do physically. I am no longer able to help with the cleaning or painting. I can't tote a filled roaster or even carry a small child.

Ah yes, I sometimes feel that the true elderly, like me, are very often nearly "invisible" in this modern-day world. And then I have to take myself in hand and remember that I can always pray for individuals and for situations within the church body and in the community. I can also offer encouragement at times to those who just need to be both remembered and reinforced in their lives whenever possible, regardless of age or status in the church or station in life. Every individual has needs. It is our responsibility to be aware and to offer that "cup of cold water."

I love the song we sometimes sing in "Worship and Celebration" time, the one with that great line that says—*"I want to sign Your name at the end of my day."* It is my goal to do just that and I rejoice in those words. It *is* my prayer at the end of my day.

Louise

CHRISTMAS IN THE 1930'S

Bill and I grew up in a more humble time—both farm-raised and the children of hardworking parents. Ah, yes, during the depression! No fancy Christmas presents, no "themed" Christmas trees. No large-money gift items, for sure. But the excitement and joy was there.

One Christmas, I think I was ten years old, my siblings and I "made" our Christmas tree! We never had a real tree. An elderly aunt who lived on the next farm allowed us to cut some boughs off the huge pine tree at her house. We lugged the boughs home and arranged them in a galvanized tub, wedging them in with stones. It was very poorly proportioned to say the least and not at all sturdy. We had no electricity for lights, so we clipped on a dozen or so wax candles in holders. Hazardous! Absolutely. But with supervision we were allowed to light them for maybe ten minutes.

Gifts? I received a small rubber doll, no joints or curly hair, but with clothes lovingly made by my mother...and in addition, a bracelet and an orange. Not much, you say, but the joy, the wonder and the awe were there.

Bill remembers receiving, basically, clothes...and one year, a sled! Another year he remembers going to New London with one whole dollar to spend on gifts. He bought one white handkerchief for his dad and a small tape measure for his mother. He can't recall what he did with the "change."

In Sunday School this quarter we are learning about "world views." I do wonder what ours was in 1934. We lived a simple life, unpretentious, but we knew that all our family and friends lived in much the same way. We were surely poor, but it didn't matter.

Our expectations weren't very high, but we did so look forward to the holiday season, the Christmas music, the family circle and hearing the Christmas Story once again.

Louise

CONCERNS ABOUT TAKING CARE OF BILL
Letter to Bill's Family
2010

Because I'm finding it very difficult to verbalize what I'm thinking, Molly has urged me to write down my feelings, my thoughts—and to try to tell you what I'm experiencing, if I can.

For a year-and-a-half I've helped Bill cope with his diminishing quality of life. He has been the love of my life for nearly ten years, and I have wanted to give him my best, always. However, somehow, I'm finding myself in a struggle at this time. Physically, I'm struggling. I think I'm not very good at doing the needed hands-on care in my 86th year. I'm probably expecting that I should be able to do all this just as I have always faced everything in my life. However, it is in the emotional part of my being that I'm in trouble. And this is hard for me to *admit* or *accept* because I have faced a lot of adversity in my life down through the years and have always hung in there before. Now I find myself berating myself constantly because I'm not coping as I would like. I'm finding it so hard to make *decisions*—to make arrangements for more "day" help to stay with Bill, so I can do errands. I put off making phone calls and telling family and friends what I need. All probably because I don't quite know myself. Hopefully, you all will understand what I'm trying to convey.

Molly discovered that I was *not* making the decision to go to church this morning and she made arrangements with Linda in order that I could go, then came and got me. I fought my emotions through the entire service—through the music, which always lovingly touches my heart and through the warm and loving comments and hugs from our many good friends. On the way home in the car, I just plain cried and finally allowed myself to give in and give up my struggle of continuing to "sit on" my stress and hoping maybe it would go away. The sermon was based on Philippians 4, regarding "finding contentment in every situation." I knew the scripture was about accumulating "things," but it added more to my tension and the feeling of "indigestion" I have suffered with off and on since mid-June.

I've always tried to find a way to solve a problem. I try my best to "right" whatever situation—to get it "fixed, cleaned up or cooked." But I can't seem to get a handle on my feelings at this time. My resolve to keep Bill with me is still in my heart. Where do I go from here?

With love for you all,

Louise

CARE-GIVING FOR BILL
In His End Time
October 19, 2010

The last six months of Bill's life will be indelibly etched in our minds and hearts as his path was a slow road to the end. Only God knew the length and depth of the final days of his journey. He left us September 26, 2010.

In all that time he never spoke a cross word, nor did he complain audibly about this being his lot in life. He went through it with the attitude of "I just have to get through it." In the latter part of May he was hospitalized with a bad bout of Enteritis, followed by much diarrhea—not an easy time for him, for either of us. Each week, maybe each day, he lost both weight and ground, very slowly. And the Beattie family knew that time was running out for Dad.

I found myself remembering when Jim Conery was in the same stage of life, when he, too, was coasting downhill. And because I had not been able to see Jim through the end times at home, Jim went to Kingston skilled-nursing facility and died there March 18th of 1996. I have carried deep regrets over this and I was sure I could do better by Bill. So when Bill became just barely ambulatory—even with a walker—in May I vowed that I would see him through to the end. However, I didn't realize the sleep-deprivation that would be involved for me, nor the physical effort needed to pull him up on his feet and in and out of bed. His four children came and took turns staying nights, but even then I had trouble sleeping and became exhausted as I was on-call all day, making it difficult to get out even for errands. I was both physically and mentally exhausted. I don't know if I have ever in my life felt so badly "jangled," so very much *not* in control.

First, trying to keep his ever-changing medications straight shattered my confidence and Linda, Bill's RN daughter, so lovingly took over the meds for me, for us, filling the pill boxes once a week. Soon I realized that I was just overwhelmed. My kids had a meeting and Bill's likewise and Linda decided that with her siblings' help she would take over his care. In two days' time she revamped her home to make her dining room his bedroom and to meet all the requirements for taking care of an invalid. I don't know how she did it. In addition, she set up the scheduling for the family to help with his care. On July 21 the move was made. It was a sad day. I didn't know what Bill was thinking—he never told me. As Linda and Mike loaded my frail Bill into Linda's car and Don and Dreama stowed all the equipment into their truck I felt I had really failed him.

The time had come to pass the baton. It was time to pack up the transport chair, the commode, the clothing, blankets and bedding, the gauze and wrappings and ointments required and to try to get past my deep regrets.

And so began the final two months of his life. No one could have received better care than the care Linda provided for Bill. She adjusted her life to the very slow speed of his day-to-day life. Don, Jim and Sandy took turns, each staying about one night a week and Linda did the other four. With a baby monitor under her pillow she listened for her dad's every move and there were many. Except for two days, I went every day in the 60-day period. I did what I could to help to take care of Bill and did my best to see that Linda and her Mike could get out for part of the day. I baked cookies and pies and brought a few casseroles and tried not to make waves in this well-run operation. I asked only that I could be home by dark, in doing so hoping I could avoid the deer crossing the road at dusk. I got very used to the round trip of 14 miles. The bulk of the work fell to Linda. She loved her dad and did a fantastic job. I will never forget it.

Bill slept a lot in the new "lift" chair that was bought soon after his arrival at Linda's home. He watched the Indians play nightly and slept and slept and slept. Linda was so very patient with him and stayed up until he said he wanted to go to bed. She always gave him choices in everything, whether it was with food, bathing, dressing and sometimes even with medications, always striving for what would give him the most comfort, cause the least stress. That was her number one goal: providing comfort for him. She sat on the edge of the bed in the middle of the night—many nights—asking what he would like to do, what she could do for him. In the course of the 60 days she told me that she learned many things about her dad that she never knew before, now fond memories for her.

Often I sat in the transport chair beside him and held his hand. He really couldn't talk or didn't feel up to much conversation, but I knew how glad he was that I was there. Linda told me that he would often ask her when I was coming. I always got a big smile when I came and he would always tell me he loved me when I left. He would even watch the sun go down and be concerned if I was still there at dusk. He still wanted to protect me, it would seem.

I read my "My Bill" letter to him one day about a week before he died. He made no comment, just tucked it under his green John Deere tractor blanket. Molly read the letter at the funeral and referred to it as a love letter. Linda told me that he did have it out again, but I know he was probably past actually reading it to himself. I trust he was left with the sentiments in his heart.

One thing that was so dear to me I need to record in order to remember. One morning when I got there early I went into his "bedroom" at Linda's, and Bill was awake sitting on the edge of the bed. I sat down beside him and he said, "Wrong woman." For a second or two he thought I was Linda, and then he smiled a big smile—a little joke between us.

Mike, who was so very helpful, could get him to smile at the table. He could talk "tractor," cow dehorning and general farm-things— things that were of interest to Bill. One day he provided Bill with a video of old tractors. In the final days Mike helped greatly with the lifting and positioning.

Linda has a lovely big deck which Bill had helped build when her house was built and he was wheeled out there every sunny day. He did enjoy so much the sunshine out there and watching the woods creatures, deer and woodchuck, playing out on the huge lawn, not the mention the wealth of butterflies attracted to the butterfly bush and all Linda's lovely flowers! The fresh air and peaceful time on the deck was a big plus for him. He even got a little tan on his bald head.

On Saturday the 25th of September he was not having a very good day. I kissed him goodbye at 7:30PM and talked to Linda in the garage for a minute before I left for home. She told he was going pretty fast. About 11:00PM he had one of his ever-more-frequent, episodes of very difficult breathing—more Albuterol and oxygen were given, as well as the very helpful Roxanol. Shortly after, or during this breathing episode, he lapsed into a coma. Don and Dreama were there. Don was on-call for the night-duty at Linda's and they stayed all night. At 6:00AM Sunday morning Linda called me to tell me that Bill was in serious condition, the end was imminent—and said Mike was on his way to get me. The labored, rough breathing was with him and the end was near. The Beattie family gathered in.

I called Molly and she and Glenn arrived shortly, my good support. Some had some tea or coffee, a bit of breakfast, and we sat in the room with Bill and talked about family remembrances, in low-key, quiet conversation. We knew that several of our church congregations were praying for Bill and for us all at that very time. Someone, I think it was Linda, said we should read the 23rd Psalm. Glenn produced it on his smart phone and read it for us all. Then Linda asked that we all join hands and pray the Lord's prayer together and we did. At the "amen" I looked at Bill and realized that the breathing was rapidly lessening and in a very brief, few moments he breathed his last. In a second or two Linda, who had her fingers on his pulse, softly spoke, the words "He is gone!" It brings tears to my eyes as I write this—sad, but I felt it was all so right. It was his time to go. The blessed man had fought the good fight. The Victory was won! No more suffering, no more pain. He had reached the other side.

Linda called Hospice, who had been called in 3 weeks earlier, and a representative from that organization came shortly. I think it was this very kind lady who called Dr. Vore and then Heyl Funeral Home—Bill's choice, made the day he was interviewed by Hospice and taken into the program. I need to make note at this point that Hospice was very kind to Bill and also were very helpful to the caregivers, too. They were very supportive and provided us with all the things we needed to make things easier for Bill, for Linda and for us all, as well.

It is my feeling that we are becoming aware of more and more people who are choosing the dying-at-home process. I wonder what the statistics are on this. Not many families could come up with what it takes to do it all this way. The Beattie family is to be commended for the way in which they cared for their dad, especially Linda who organized it all so well. Even though exhausted, she told us she would have done it all again. There is much love and respect in this family.

I went with the family when arrangements were made at the funeral home to select the casket and later to pick out the flowers for the family, agreeing completely with their selection in regard to both. We organized his obituary together. I selected his clothes, the grey suit that he wore when we were married 2-10-01. I ironed his good white shirt and as I finished I kissed the inside of the breast pocket knowing it would be right over his heart.

Death is so final! I'm finding it hard to move on—to find my way—to keep busy. Being fairly well acquainted (I thought) with "anticipatory grief," it was my thinking that I could, possibly, get by fairly well in the grieving process, but not so. His empty recliner chair and the empty bed brought tears, but especially the empty place at the table and my thoughts of holding his hand while saying prayers at mealtime and also when sitting on the edge of the bed at night, our nighttime prayer. All hard to get past. He never talked a great deal, never raised his voice, but still the house is now so very quiet. Something I will have to get used to. I'm working on it.

Today, Sunday, two weeks after his death, I made a trip to the Ruggles Cemetery and took a wreath. What a beautiful fall day! The sunshine was so warm and the leaves were gently raining down over the grave site. I felt sad, but at the same time at peace with it all. A good man, a good father, a good husband, home at last. I will treasure our nearly 10 years together.

Louise Beattie

MY BILL
Written and Read to Bill before his Death,
Read at Bill's Funeral by Molly
September, 2010

We met after church one day—a grieving man suffering greatly from the loss of his wife of 48 years, the mother of his four children! As I shook his hand and told him that he had my sympathy—for I, too, knew of loss—he couldn't say a word. The tears were falling—all the joy had gone out of his life. How does one start to walk on alone, sit in a quiet house, all alone for the first time in his 76 years?

The next Sunday he came back to church accompanied again by his youngest son, Don and Don's wife Dreama. With his tears still falling, I asked "Was it any better this week, Bill?" And he shook his head in a silent "no." Years of togetherness—and then suddenly a barren, lonely, oneness—causing a deep-seated pain that wouldn't go away.

Bill and I met again at Hospice, that great program that allows death with dignity at home but also helps the loved ones walk through the "lost" times—a mine field where in seeing other couples together, going places, having fun, remembering the anniversaries and shared heartfelt times just breaks your heart. I remember how in the middle of a hymn at church—while holding the newest great-grandchild his wife Miriam would not see in this lifetime—his tears suddenly flowed again.

The months passed and after much heartfelt conversation he asked me if I would like to go out to eat with him. My first thought was, I can't go down this path again. However, I took a deep breath and said "yes." I thought, if he takes me to Lynway, EVERYBODY will be so alert to the fact that we are going out!! But Bill surprised me with dinner out at The Amish Door in Wooster, a favorite memory for us.

Then one day Bill asked if I would like to take a ride down into the southern part of the state to see the fall colors, a drive he had made just the day before with a load of cattle. We went, we viewed the trees in all their fall splendor and we talked and we talked. We discovered that our backgrounds and "raisings" were very similar, that we also had our big families in common and knew many of the same people.

He brought me roses on "Sweetest Day." He came in his work clothes with his State Farm work-cap in hand and he asked if he could kiss me. I was 76 years old, but I felt for that moment a bit like 16 again! A man of few words, not given to chatter or boasting. He made me feel like a queen.

The months rolled by—Bill liked to come to supper at the condo and I started to ride on the cattle truck every trip he took. I got to know the cattle barns at Creston, Bucyrus, Kidron and Mt. Vernon and all the little eating places along the way. Bill wouldn't allow me to actually help load the cattle, so I became the gate-holder. The cattle today are a bit crazy in comparison to the little docile Jerseys of my farming childhood memories.

We were married February 10, 2001 at Christ Community Church by Pastor Jeff Powell. Our guests totaled nearly 100 with 75 of them being our combined families. All our grandchildren made it to see us married except John Keiffer, my eldest grandson in CA. After a short weekend trip to The Inn at Honey Run down in Holmes County—a wedding gift provided by our combined nine children—it was back home to the condo and back on the cattle truck. We never had an argument, because we both know so well what starts a fight and we just talked it out until it was resolved and we were in agreement.

Open-heart surgery for Bill in November of 2001 made for difficult times, and I witnessed the closeness of his devoted family as they gathered around his bedside and in the weeks of recovery. Bill's family made me feel so welcomed into their circle. Bill's cattle-hauling days were coming to an end. How hard it was to give up doing what was his "life" for years. Not easy to sit around in a condo when you would rather be loading up at Dave Sigles—cattle broker—in Homerville and heading to Mt. Vernon with a load of cattle.

His kids refer to the "evil eye" that he could give if he was displeased by any of their wrong-doings or bad behavior down through the years. They would sometimes tease me and ask if I ever got that "evil eye," but I never did. He was a man of few words not big on "small talk" or standing around and visiting after church. He would never make a great shopper in a million years. He loves word puzzles, the Indians, the Cavaliers and old Columbo shows.

This man has given great meaning to my life for I know he loved me. In fact, he has made me feel "cherished," a magnificent word that all too often doesn't make it into many marriages. I wouldn't have missed this life with Bill for the world—and I'm so glad I said "yes" that day when he asked if I would go out to eat. I will miss holding his hand in church—praying together with him daily—praying for the safety of our big, extended family and for our combined circle of mutual friends. I will feel the void. I brace myself for the loneliness that will suddenly be in my life again.

We will meet again! God has planned this for us in His wonderful plan for salvation and life eternal! Hallelujah!

Louise Beattie

WILLIAM (BILL) BEATTIE'S SERVICE AND BURIAL
October 30, 1923–September, 26, 2010
Written September 29, 2010

On the inside lid of his light-blue coffin was stitched the scene of a winding road with the words "The Journey" beside it. How appropriate for Bill with all the miles he drove to fetch cattle from all those farms and then to deposit them at various sales barns, or the miles involved driving the water truck to fill swimming pools and cisterns, accompanied sometimes by old friends, family, often with a grandchild or two asleep on the seat of the truck with their heads cushioned on a pair of rolled up coveralls. Don, the youngest, was only two years old when he started to "ride along." No seat belts or restraining seats for kids in those days. Bill's life was a long journey of hard work—day by day—doing what he had to do to make a living for his family.

Today we buried Bill beside his beloved wife, Miriam, the mother of his four children, in the Ruggles Cemetery. The sun was shining. The temperature was perfect for Ohio in September. The "Color Guard" of the Ashland American Legion Post 88 provided a 21- gun salute, followed by "Taps," done on an electronic trumpet, I've learned. It was hard to hold back the tears at such a time as we honor a veteran of this country, this very special veteran in our lives.

But allow me to go back to his death three days before, on September 26. It was Sunday morning following a very difficult night. His breathing became very labored on Saturday evening and somewhere before midnight he drifted into a coma never to regain consciousness. Linda, Don, Dreama and Mike, Linda's special friend, saw him through the night. At 5:45AM Linda called me to tell me that Mike would be coming to get me as life had become very tentative for Bill. Linda managed his final day of care in the same loving way she has done for the past several months. The family gathered in. Molly and Glenn arrived and they added support—especially for me—to the family circle gathered in Linda's living room. Loving stories were told around the room as we did our best to keep the faith and our emotions in check as we listened to his labored breathing in the on-going struggle.

Bill and all the family were being supported by many friends in several congregations at that very hour. It was suggested that someone should read the 23rd Psalm which Glenn did, and then we all bowed our heads to recite the Lord's Prayer. After the "amen" all were silent and we watched his breathing start to level out, slow, and then stop. Sad, but actually awesome! In a moment he was gone. A good man had left us, crossed over to the other side. No more pain and suffering for Dad, for Bill. A representative from Hospice arrived. We were given all the time in the world to say our "goodbyes."

I can't say enough about how well Linda took care of her dad. She has told us that it was a wonderful experience, that she learned so much about him and his life, things she had never known before. His mind remained quite clear all through his months of decline. He treated it all like, "Oh, well, I just have to do this." He went through it all with never a whine or a cross word. He still had a good sense of humor and he appreciated so much all the "care" going on. I'm sure that was not an easy thing to do, this man who didn't like to have others do for him!

One morning I went early. I slipped into his bedroom and sat down on the edge of the bed beside him, and he said "Wrong woman." And then gave me a big smile. At first glance, he thought I was Linda coming to help him in the middle of the night. Just a little joke between us. Mike was the perfect table companion with Mike keeping Bill entertained with just the right kind of talk. By the way what would we all have done without Mike's quiet, compassionate presence? Linda's loving manner, plus skilled nursing abilities along with family help, made for a great team. Mike said one day that he thought the Beattie family should write a book on "How to Care for Family Members in End Times." How true!

Yesterday, Tuesday, was a full day. Two sessions of visitation—2:00 to 4:00 and also 6:00 to 8:00. Lots of family were there during the evening sessions. Grandchildren and great-grands of the Beatties and likewise for me, too. So good to hug all these grown up "kids" and to see them all so well-launched in their lives.

The day that Hospice did their intake interview with Bill they asked the question "had he considered which funeral home he would prefer to use?" I was surprised to hear them ask this pointed question, but I would guess it is all a part of them heading a patient realistically down the road that leads to death. She then asked which minister he would prefer, to which he promptly answered, "My sister-in-law, Sonja Bender." Pastor Bender's husband Don was a brother of Miriam's. Sonja had presided at the service for Miriam eleven years ago and she provided a beautiful service for Bill. Her words were perfect and so comforting. Pastor Mike Futrell, from our church, assisted, by reading the obituary and also various scriptures selections. Molly read what I had written about Bill and our marriage. She called it a "love letter." It was actually entitled "My Bill." Dreama had some very nice comments about Bill and about the good man that he was, always. Linda spoke of her dad and his association with each of his grandchildren and also had wonderful words to say about her dad and taking care of him. She ended with praise for Mike and his support of her. Don Bender then told of his summers of working for Bill on the farm, making hay etc., and what a good person Bill was to work for and with. He said he had lots more to say, but Sonja told him he had to be brief. He admitted it was dangerous to give him a mic.

Pastor Sonja closed by singing a song—unaccompanied. However, the name escapes me at the moment. I think that someone she knew had written the song and it was based on the scripture, "My peace I give to you." Words and names often escaped me these past few days.

It was a long day, but a very special day. I was happy to see several relatives of mine, four of the Martins from Michigan—and Beattie relatives from out of state, Jeremiah and Stacy Johnson from Arizona, plus Travis and Amy Turk with little Alisa from Indiana.

At the time of Miriam's death Bill had been very "put out" because the Sheriff's Dept. had failed to provide an escort for the procession to make the turn off from a very busy Rt. 224 into the cemetery, and he told them so. The funeral home representative, Tyler Heyl, remembered his unhappiness with the way it was mishandled. They did it perfectly this time!

After the burial at the cemetery we went down to our church where the ladies of the church had prepared a nice dinner for us all. A dinner is a nice way to enjoy a time to visit with family and friends to unwind after an emotional time for us all before heading home.

Many times in life we find ourselves having to say goodbye to ones we love. This was one of those times. Bill's quiet spirit, his honest approach to life, meant so much to me, to everyone who knew him. No fussing, no lamenting about his lot in life. He was all for "just getting the job done." Even in dying he was resigned to working through even this very sad and challenging time, the end of life. I can imagine that those conversations between Linda and her dad in the middle of the night were most comforting to him, to them both, no doubt. He always smiled when I arrived and I felt loved and very much a part of the family.

And so I march on alone in life, again. However, I have learned a bit more about how better to cope with adversity. I will need to find more things to do, more ways to keep busy. And so I will take a page out of Bill's book. Just get on with the job and "git'er done." It is strange but that was also my own dad's approach to life. Fix what is broken, clean up the mess made, hoe out the weeds, fix the fence, see the job finished! At 86 I might have a couple more years—only the Good Lord knows! I salute my Bill. His presence in my life made my life special. I'm so glad I said "yes" when he asked if I would go out to eat with him that day, way back in the year of 2000! A man of few words, with great integrity, always honest and fair. We all will have a void in our lives. Bill Beattie will be missed by many. And so—we, too, must all travel on, each on our own "journey."

Blessings always,

Louise Beattie

LETTER TO WALTER BROWNSON
November 13, 2011

Dear Walter,

Ah, yes, the years have rolled by! After listening to your excellent talk honoring the Veterans at the Nankin Church this morning I just thought I might go back in time for a minute. Is 59 years right? It seems to me the years during which I wrote to you each week when you were serving in Korea were 1952 and '53. I can't remember very much of what I wrote or what you wrote in return. Guess I should have kept the letters. Mostly I remember that it was a very busy time for me; however, I always felt a real pull to "get a letter off to Walter"— to heck, for a moment, with the kids hanging on my skirt, needing attention, running noses and challenging voices.

I'm so glad I shucked off minor responsibilities at Christ Community Evangelical Free Church this morning to be on the same page with so many of our Brownson family to attend Nankin Federated Church, to see and hug some longtime old friends again, but most of all to hear you speak. You did a GREAT job! It was a history lesson, as well as providing some very good thoughts and words concerning the various branches of the service. You did it so well—your timing was great—your sincerity front and foremost. I know in my pew there was hardly a dry eye in the group. Thelma was moved with the remembrance of Dom's passing, of course (like we all do when we think of those we miss so much.) Tina and I tried to be stoic as is our nature, to try to keep control. Rick was fighting his emotions right along beside Margaret whom I know was struggling, too.

I do hope that Betty could at least hear some of what you had to say. It must be so hard for her to attend events she knows are important and yet can take in so little of what is said because her very impaired hearing. "You could hear a pin drop"—to be sure. You had us all in the palm of your hand. I know it took effort to put it all together in your mind and then to deliver it as you wanted to do. It is so nice that NFC makes important the honoring of our veterans. Few churches do to that degree. You are so right—we are safe because all of you gave so much. So many gave their all, their utmost, for us all! Thanks to you (and Dick Bland, too—good man) we all took home many heartfelt thoughts to ponder as the days go by. I'm glad I was there.

Love,
Louise

A MOST UNUSUAL DAY
March 27, 2011

My senses and thoughts are heightened by my somewhat emotional state these days as I ride the ups and downs of Cancer verses Chemo. Today it was one of those almost euphoric days for me. I have experienced this strange, perhaps elevated, sort of happiness in prayer at bedtime and now today it happened again. I must write the events down before my thoughts lose some semblance of order or they will slip completely from my mind.

Yesterday I had experienced physical difficulties in regard to post-chemo distress—one being extremely low blood sugar—quite intense—and it was not a good day. However, this morning I got up knowing that I was feeling so much better, not nearly so droopy and I made it to both Walmart and Aldi's with energy to spare.

In the afternoon came visitors, very good friends of mine from my church—Bonnie Graves and Dianna Hall bringing some beautiful flowers and lively conversation. We enjoyed some heartfelt sharing of thoughts mingled with fun as well. But I need to relate the unusual thing that happened.

Bonnie was mentioning the Sunday School class she and Ron are presently team-teaching on the Minor Prophets and happened to mention a wonderful scripture from Micah. I asked what it was and she picked up my Bible and looked it up and read it to us.

> He has showed you, O man, what is good.
> And what does the Lord require of you?
> To act justly and to love mercy
> And to walk humbly with your God.
> *Micah 6:8*

After she had finished reading the scripture,—simple verses, really, yet so profound—she told me that they were already underlined in my Bible. And then I noted from my marginal notation that Pastor Jeff Powell had preached from this same scripture on April 29, 2001. An interesting connection thus far. We then spoke of what a good message it is and how it applies to our lives today.

Less than an hour later as I resumed reading from the present book I'm in--just fiction--entitled *Leiv's Will,* by Dale Cramer--I came upon that very same, identical scripture and I was totally amazed to see it twice in a matter of maybe only minutes. In this book, Amish in background, an adult son Will, rejects his Amish faith and his Amish background leaving many "sins" behind and the utter wrath of his Old Order Amish father who is now in his end times living in the "dawdi haus"...a harsh man who shuns and hates his son Will all his adult life. Will wonders how he can ever regain a son's status while living an "English" life style and find forgiveness with his father. He ponders greatly what God had in mind for his life and then one day, on the kitchen table, he sees his wife's Bible open to the 6th chapter of Micah and reads this very same message, the one we read just today. That was when he makes his decision that he is the one who needs to lead in the love and mercy concept of forgiveness. I thought it is amazing that I should read this — almost within minutes of our discussion —sort of like a "GOD THING" which I'm experiencing by chance more often recently. Perhaps everything is being made much clearer to me as I'm on "My Journey "... down my path through cancer and aging.

To act justly — with love and mercy — and to walk humbly with your God...that really says it all. Just further glimpses of what God has for me in my remaining time, perhaps.

I just had to write this down while it was all fresh in my mind.

Louise Beattie

SO, HOW DO I LOVE YOU, TINA?
2011

Dear Tina,

As I'm putting together these collections of my writings over the years, I can't seem to locate a letter written to you in the 1999 era. Records do get mixed up or misfiled sometimes. So I'm writing another to you this year, 2011, which is really "YOUR YEAR" anyway. When you and Rick bought your first home in Mansfield did you every dream you would be where you are today? Involved with three of your "boys" in the wonderful business of the Olde Parsonage and in the restoring of the John Fluke Home—not to mention all the various houses you have built or remodeled over the past 42-plus years? Now you and Rick are ready to progress on into the "addition" phase of that wonderful house of your heritage. It will be great to see it all as it progresses on into your dream home. The entire Fluke family watches with awe as each stage of the venture takes place.

And now you and Rick have gone back to the old home church—Nankin Federated—after all these years. Do you feel like you might have come full circle—with all those memories of living 16 years in the former Methodist Parsonage right next door to the church—those years of your growing up in the village. Playing in the park—learning to ride your bike, dodging the trees—playing on the "All Veterans Monument" in the park—Nankin Grade School—trips to the post office to get the mail and to Funk's store for a loaf of bread. Not many kids today have memories like you kids have—of a "safe and secure raising." All the village kids played outside until dark and the hunting horn drew you back home. It was the part of my life I wish I could have lived over at a slower pace—all those years went by way too quickly. Little League days, Mapleton sports, cheerleading, graduations and weddings. It all happened way too fast.

I marvel at your strength and the purpose of your life, Tina. When Rick said he felt he had one more house restoration in him at age 64, I doubt if you ever considered anything else but "let's go for it." To gather and burn brush for days last spring would have defeated most folks at the start. To have refinished all the woodwork—to have lugged all the tools and equipment up and down those tricky stairs—to have put together in your mind's eye all the colors—all I can say is "what a feat—what a talent!" And look how it turned out—all beautifully ready in time for the Fluke Reunion of 2011. What a wonderful addition to the whole weekend. For all the cousins of my generation it has been so much fun to try to relive our visits to the house 60-70 years ago with our dear lady, Aunt Chloe, taking us around the house with her. For me, my special memory was going upstairs with her once when she showed me all the flowers she was drying on the floor of one of the bedrooms. I was so impressed—seeds for next year. Not to mention her carnival glassware on the dining room table or her believing "no spot on the table should go unfilled—with a dish of jam, pickles or something."

I would guess that for many at the reunion—especially the young folks—it was the first time they had really "connected" the dots of the Fluke Family History. Oh, yes, they might have heard the history but only vaguely did they make any real association with their ancestors. It has become so much more "real" to them now, seeing the house as you and Rick have restored it. They probably couldn't quite understand how it all came to be with Philip and Mary leaving their home and relatives in Pennsylvania and venturing into this wild land in Ohio, covered with trees—dealing with Indians and the wolves at the door of the cabin. Strong people—people of insight and vision. A strong work ethic by all the generations involved made it all possible. Philip, John, James and Gene Fluke—what outstanding, hardworking, good, moral men!

Your own family: What an accomplished, handsome family you have produced and all very successful in their own right—plus all your beautiful, bright grandchildren who surround you. You are so fortunate that they are all so close by. The drums of our heritage beat on and toll out the message of our ongoing heritage. Just imagine this all—50-60 years hence?

This has been a milestone year for the both of you. Take time to enjoy your efforts of this past year as you progress on into the next phase of the project.

Blessings and love to you both, always,

Mom

FLUKE REUNION, 2011
Labor Day Weekend

Once again we meet—the gathering of the Fluke clan. What a weekend! This year we had the added benefit of celebrating the restoration of the JOHN FLUKE HOME. Rick and Tina McFrederick purchased the home along with 10 acres of the original farm in 2010, working all fall, winter, spring and summer to bring the house back to its original splendor. The timing was such that we could all be part of the celebration of this accomplishment. The Fluke family had the great privilege of the "unveiling" of this magnificent house, built in 1877. More about this later.

In July, the planning committee met to make plans for the weekend-to-be at the Sycamore Hill Farm—Glenn and Molly Smith, owners—on Labor Day weekend, as usual. Their farm is located one mile to the west of the John Fluke home, now the McFrederick home. (Before I go further, I need to say that Glenn and Molly graciously hosted this event, and we all very much appreciate their efforts.) Some of you reading may not know of the history of these two farms. Both have been in the Fluke family for many decades. For many of the family, it will all be etched in the memory because of childhood visits at the farm, starting when it belonged to Grandpa Gene and Grandma Mary. It became so clear to me, this year especially, how much it meant to all of the family who had this opportunity.

Back to the planning day. We had felt that we just might, perhaps, cut out a few things that were on the 2009 agenda, but soon found that we were adding more instead of cancelling any. It proved impossible to find time to make all these events happen. Maybe we can save some of them for "next time."

On Tuesday the volunteer group began to arrive and to tackle the list of things to do that would be helpful to have done before the reunion could get underway. I'm going to mention names here, hoping to avoid missing anyone who participated in these "sweaty" jobs. First arrivals were Bill Martin, grandson of Gene and Mary Fluke and his son David from Denver (the next generation), alone with Brian Oberst from Michigan. Shortly after, David Drouillard, husband of Liz Martin (grand-daughter of Gene and Mary Fluke) arrived, also from Michigan. They were joined by David Evans from Texas (grandson of John W. Fluke.) In addition, Liz Drouillard and Sheila Martin aided Molly greatly in the pre-union preparations.

In the first couple of days there was much "zero-turn" mowing of lawns, brush hog mowing of sod waterways and repair on one of the bridges at the pond area—all with Glenn as the overseer. One of the most interesting projects (to me, anyway) was the building of a short flight of steps to attach to the rear of the hay ladders, making the wagon more easily accessible to those who love the hayrides. Interestingly, the steps came out of the old Chick-Hog-o building—old native timber from the farm woods. Earlier, Glenn had viewed, somewhere, "hay wagon steps" and put this on the list of things to do. It was a bit of a challenge as the lumber was over 70 years old. All the efforts of the aforementioned men working on these projects were so appreciated by Glenn and Molly and also the clan. Many thanks to them all for their efforts in the extreme heat of the entire week. It was interesting in this day and age how the various crews communicated—at the pond or at the barn—by cell phone. Like, "Hey, bring me the 'chuck' to the drill," phoned from one worksite to another. It was fun for Helen and me to watch everything from our front-porch-swing viewing area.

I also wanted to mention the wonderful Kline family—Randy, Janna and Nate—who helped in so many ways through the entire reunion. They are Molly and Glenn's close friends. Nate was the winner of Donald's drafting set in the "Bucket Auction." He was *so happy*—he really wanted it!

Friday Morning—The tent arrived along with the porta-pot and things were taking shape. The work crew resurrected Grandma Mary's double-drainboard sink from storage, placed it in the backyard and attached the garden hose, making it a great place to wash off some of the heat and dust of the day. The kids loved it. A few times they turned the hose on each other but no one really minded, since it was so hot.

Friday Evening—The reunion officially started with a gathering at the home of Margaret Welch, granddaughter of Gene and Mary Fluke, who lives only a mile away from the farm. Margaret had put much time and energy into this whole project. In addition, she has helped Rick and Tina, no end, in all the phases of the restoration of the John Fluke Home. She was also on the planning committee for all events...and then volunteering to take on the Friday evening happening. She entertained us all on her beautiful lawn. Her chickens were of great interest to all.

Saturday Morning—The sun came out with the promise of another really hot day. The first scheduled event for the day was the celebration of the completion of the restoration of the John Fluke Home. It was now nearing 10:00AM, and the hay wagon was loaded up for the trip down the connecting road from the farm to the Fluke home—what a happy crew! We were all met with a large sign in the front yard indicating that the John Fluke Home was built in 1877 and now restored and owned by Rick and Tina McFrederick. My guess is there were perhaps 50 people gathered on the east lawn, all of us greeted by Tina who gave a welcome to all the family and friends from the front porch. Margaret also spoke, adding some history of the home and the work of the restoration process. Rick was also there on the steps to the new front porch (a special project of his.) We were all invited to tour the house, and we entered through the magnificently-restored, carved, double front doors. My generation, the great-grandchildren of John Fluke, have many childhood memories of being in that home and being entertained by our delightful Aunt Chloe. You would have needed to be on the tour of the house to really take in the accomplishments of Rick and Tina. I can't do justice in telling you of the beautiful blend of colors—the original wood floors and woodwork—the appointments and furnishings, mainly from Rick and Tina's previous home in Ashland. The modern kitchen combined with the furnishings all in keeping with the late 1800's era was amazing!

It was to time to go back to the Smiths. Back on the wagon, back to the fun and games. At this time I do want to mention our first-time-ever guests at the reunion, Stu and Hillary Ratner from Detroit, Michigan. Hillary is a descendant from the John W. Fluke family. How nice to have them with us.

1:00PM—Our catered lunch arrived! It was not easy to feed over 100 people in the heat, but our good friends Barb and Larry Bates did just that. The catered meal was beautifully prepared and presented—and also very tasty! Desserts were brought in by family. At the end of the day, the record-keepers estimated that over 50 gallons of water, iced tea and lemonade had been consumed!

The Martin Connection directed the first of the games and competitions: the Gator obstacle course. The extreme heat cut down on the competitive activity. Fewer signed up for the Gator obstacle course this year, much the same for the Corn Hole Tournament. Apparently, it was too hot—97 degrees—to stand in the full sun and toss the bags. Matt and Erin Johnson were winners of the Gator race.

The children's scavenger hunt was listed on the schedule of events, but was over quickly. Some of the kids found some clues ahead of time and, therefore, won the game before some of them were back from a Gator ride. All the kids quickly descended onto the pile of candy—the prize.

Like everything else, the cost of the reunion has climbed. The cost of the rental of the big tent has gone up. Porta-pot also. Not to mention the catered food. All this is valuable, necessary and worth every penny. The "Bucket Auction" was established in 2009 to help raise money to cover the costs, and we repeated it this year. No recording of the intake of this auction is available as yet, so I don't know our financial status at this writing. The auction does take a big block of time out of the day and ran late into the dusk this hear, requiring flashlights to read the ticket stubs. Any solutions or suggestions?

The Fluke Family Circle/Honoring of the Elders—At the time of this event there were seven remaining members of our generation of Flukes, the great-grandchildren of John Fluke, children for Gene and Mary Fluke: Donald Fluke (and wife Pepper,) Emeline Fulmer, Helen Helvenston and myself, Louise Beattie. Plus Marilee Evans and Gloria Horn, children of the John W. Fluke family. Molly Smith planned this event. We seven were asked to sit in chairs set in a circle, back-to-back. And I thought, "We are strange group to attempt to play some version of Musical Chairs—especially at our ages!" However, the entire reunion clan made a huge circle around us. The parents of the little ones had all been given little round tokens, each decorated with a heart, very pretty. The parents slipped the "gems" into the little ones' hands. I tried not to become emotional, but suddenly my grandchildren and great-grandchildren were offering me their delightful, heart-warming love, telling us all that they loved us. At the end of the Fluke Family Circle, Molly presented each of the seven of us with a framed-art picture of the "Mill Stone" so long in the front yard of the farmhouse. In the photo the mill stone has a floral arrangement in the center, plus a printed message at the bottom of the picture. The words, below, are something to be cherished! *May the Lord bless you and keep you. May the Lord make His face to shine upon you...and be gracious to you. May the Lord lift His countenance upon you and keep you in perfect peace."* So unique—so very much "Molly." We were all so touched by this event, and I'm sure the little ones were in the process of building memories, too. Many thanks to Molly for the loving space in time for us all.

Corn Roast—A huge bonfire—perfect corn—a mighty yummy affair. The was held in the north pasture. It is fun to line-up and wait for that ear of corn, all the better if it was a wee bit burned. The corn nearly cooked itself in the heat. Bob, Gini and sons Matt and Dan hosted the event. David Marin was also a big help.

Talent Show—Something was added this year. I'm sure we have many talented persons in the gathering— a few signed up. Glenn opened the show with a 'trombone impression" of the National Anthem with everybody accompanying him on kazoos. Rodd McFrederick and his 14-year old son Leif played several saxophone duets. Great job! Followed by Erica McFrederick who sang a Taylor Swift song with some variations, unaccompanied, very moving. I was surprised when my son Bob played his guitar and sang a song for me, his mom, entitled "A Song for Mom," with words of appreciation and love. I'm guessing that more will sign up for the talent show next time. A nice addition for the day. Molly, Bob, Gini and Ann Keiffer put together this event. Gini also lined up the "Minute To Win" game held just prior to the Talent Show. Willing participants made it really fun.

Dancing!—Matt Brownson was our "for real" DJ for the occasion. What a great addition. He set-up on the front porch. At the close of the talent show Matt cranked up the volume a bit, and my three daughters, Ann, Tina and Molly boogied. I simply couldn't stay seated and asked Tina to help her old mom up on the stage (porch), and I had SO MUCH FUN. After my past year of losing my Bill, followed by the diagnosis of cancer— which was defeated—I was ready to celebrate! My goal since last November was to make it to the reunion—so, DANCE I did!

Memorial Service—The last event of the day was the Memorial Service at the pond. The hay wagon was loaded up once more and by some way we all got back to the pond. Everything was dark and so peaceful there by the calm water. Lynne Ritschdorff led us in the nostalgic time of remembrance. The name of each person who has gone on before was read, as an individual torch was lit for each one. Tiny paper boats containing lighted candles were launched on the pond. What a sight—not a sound—not a word was spoken. Then John Azoni played guitar and he and his wife Laura sang, "It Is Well With My Soul." Our hearts were filled with memories and our eyes with tears, as many—of all ages—felt the depth of the moment. This has become an important time for us all as we remember our departed loved ones. Then it was back to the farm and off to find rest for the night. For some, it was the end of the reunion and time for final goodbyes for the weekend. For others, it was just time to get some rest to be ready for our final morning at the Sycamore Hill Farm.

Sunday Morning Breakfast—Liz and David Drouillard provided a wonderful breakfast for the 30-35 people gathered together, great food under our faithful green-and-white tent. There was a light drizzle—a nice change from the extreme heat of the previous day. The chairs were placed in a large circle and our open "remembrance" time began. Many have stated that this is the most meaningful time for them, the best time of the whole reunion. So the stories began. For many of the cousins it was a time to share experiences of their time spent on the farm on summer vacations and their utter joy in spending time with Grandparents Gene and Mary Fluke, not to mention the colorful times spent—and enjoyed so much—at the Krause home just up the road. In the circle you could hear everyone, even those of us with less-than-perfect hearing. What a joyful way to end the reunion of 2011. Then it was time to get on the road. It was hard to say goodbye, hard to end this wonderful reunion.

So we wrap up this year and wonder what the next reunion might bring. We are all feeling that this one can't be topped in the future—but we always say that. What a privilege to be part of this great family, whose strength and fortitude led us all, in part, to be who we are today. Not many families are fortunate to have the quality of strength in their heritage. Philip and Mary Fluke showed great courage to leave their family connections in Pennsylvania and head to Ohio in 1816 to make a new life for their own family. This year we had a wonderful addition of seeing the John Fluke Home restored to its original splendor, thanks to the insight and hard work of Rick and Tina McFrederick.

May all be blessed and continue to gather together in the years to come.

Louise Fluke Beattie

LOUISE MOLLY FLUKE — A SONG
The Song Bob Sang for Me
at the 2011 Fluke Reunion

Louise Molly Fluke
born in the spring of 1924
A shy pretty girl
from Orange Township
Religious and gentle, humble
and kind as a person could be

She loved to sing in the silo
Loud and inspired
her head tilted down keeping time
Would work in the field after supper
ignoring the hour
Hoping her dad would say
well done

And she loved to drive
that team down the road
Though they couldn't see
while they were pulling the load
She'd turn to the barns
and give the rein to go
And they'd already know

She raised five but 2 missing
no time for suffering
beans and the corn yet to freeze
nights alone because of
the hunting, a practice or speeches
but Friday nights seemed to
—bring back the glow

And she never said oh Lord why me
She was raised in a faith
that was strong and we see
She still grabs the team
and heads back up the road
She'll never let go

And she never said oh Lord why me
She was raised in a faith
that was strong and we see
She still grabs the team

and heads us back up the road
She'll never let go

For Louise Molly Fluke
Marvelous woman- we are so blessed to call her "my mom"

Bob Brownson

...I'M JUST SAYING

Thoughts on Cancer, Technology,
Facebook and Old Folks
October 1, 2011

This past year—2010/11—has proved to be quite a year of change for me. I became a widow for the third time, losing Bill in late September of 2010. And in just a few weeks I learned that the dreaded word "cancer" was to be mine with chemo-infusion treatments in the months to come. There were many things to learn and to adjust to as I headed into the latter part of 2010 and 2011. I was already learning to live—to adjust to life alone—again. And then along came this new challenge.

I made a decision to take a firm grip on life—to learn all I could about cancer—more specifically about Non-Hodgkins Lymphoma. I turned to my faith—prayed for strength and upped my attempt to be as positive as I could. And I wondered what help I could be to other people with newly-diagnosed cancer. People started bringing me names of cancer patients to pray for and to write to. This all helped me, and I was hopeful that somehow my words of loving support might be of help to others. After five months of chemo, I was told my cancer was "under control" and I would have six months "OFF" from chemo. Nice words. The six months are up now, and I'm ready to start back on four weeks of chemo to keep the "beast" at bay—followed by another six months off. I consider myself truly fortunate.

During this six months, I have made some gains and a couple of inroads into the modern-day technical world where my generation finds so much confusion and frustration. My second husband, Jim Conery, who died in 1996, used a computer in his daily work for Myers Pump, but he had a firm rule: "Don't touch my computer"—meaning, me. Anyway, I thought that if I did try to use it the ONLY information to come forth would be in regard to Sewer Lifting Stations and related water-moving projects. I didn't touch it.

After Jim was gone, I decided I would like to have a computer of my own. It opened up a whole new, wonderful world for me. How great it has been to regularly exchange email with my brother Donald in North Carolina and my sister, Helen, in Florida. In addition, it provided me with a better means to attempt to write my thoughts from time to time.

I've had a cell phone for several years, but used it basically for emergencies—like in being on the road with Bill hauling cattle to various sales barns and knowing that in case of a breakdown, help was just as close as phone contact with any of our combined family members. Except for the time we got stuck in deep snow in an Amish man's driveway in Holmes County. We didn't need to call the family. Two young Amish fellows were delighted to hook their team of big Belgian horses to the truck and pull the loaded trailer out to the plowed county road. I could imagine the chortling laughter that night at the Amish supper table as they told of hauling that 4-wheel drive Chevy truck with its loaded trailer out of the snow with their Belgians.

In the fall of 2010, Glenn and Molly took me to the Verizon Store to upgrade my cell. I was still quite cautious and asked only for a bit more than the "emergency only" concept, but said I did want to try my hand at "texting." With much nervousness I chose the slide-out sided phone. I felt that would be easier for a beginner, like me. I did learn to "text"—found I loved it. But I'm not very good with all the "lol's," not knowledgeable regarding all those standard abbreviations that the kids use when texting in all gathering places, in restaurants, even in church or just across the room!

And then, more recently, I ventured into Facebook. I'm feeling my way through that maze—again trying to learn the lingo. My generation just isn't into this either. I felt it might be a good way to keep in better communication with my 15 grandchildren and maybe a few of the older ones of my 40 great-grandchildren. But then again, I'm not sure I really want to know what all they are doing all the time. In addition, I do wonder how they find the time to check in with FB—to communicate so often—in their busy lives. I do admire their sense of humor and their pictures. I would much prefer that they would use their own pictures in their profiles and not in such exaggerated, crazy poses. It is interesting to know when some go out on business trips—whose kids are to have surgery—and who is having a birthday—and who is reaching the various milestones in their chosen fields of work.

My sister, Helen, tells me she feels like she is wandering around out there in cyber space without a clue as to where she is going. In my first week on FB someone (not family) wrote in that they didn't feel that old folks should be allowed on FB. Hmmm....

I have yet to put my picture on my home page and can't quite decide who all I want to be my "friends." I really liked it when my California Ann set up a "family group." That seemed a really good idea, especially since we had all been coming down off a Fluke Reunion "HIGH." I put a couple of family things on the "group"—spelled everything correctly—and didn't attempt any fancy abbreviations. I told about Sara and Don and the kids, home from Colorado to visit, and mentioned Molly and Glenn's upcoming anniversary. Only one tiny response was posted on our "family group"—so apparently the kinfolk didn't give a hoot about the McIntyres' being home from Colorado and they thought "so what" to the Smiths many years together. So—I'm just saying—no one has written on my "wall"—"back fence" or anywhere else since. I must have broken it all some way. Maybe "old folks" should just stay off FB, as the guy said.

I'm just sayin', folks.

P.S. This is meant to be "funny."

Louise Beattie

NEW GARAGE AND APARTMENT PLANS
AT THE FLUKE FARM
Letter of Explanation to the Family
April 16, 2012

I know that all of you must be interested in the plans for the garage/addition taking shape at the farm. My computer refused to allow me to make them into a document and email them to you—so we will rely on the good old USPS to pick this up tomorrow and deliver this to you.

One side of the enclosed drawings shows the garage and addition alone—drawn up by Molly—giving basic dimensions, etc. The other side shows the architect's drawing and positioning with the house. It is big! The apartment is a really nice size for me or whoever resides there in the future. There will be a basement under the apartment and attic space above the garage. Molly says the attic could be for young boys sleeping there in years to come—or it could be storage. The garage you will see now holds two cars and a larger space for Glenn's truck. I'm sure he will always have a BIG truck. It is in his blood!

The architect has provided several views of the house and garage, also showing how the buildings will be joined. I'm not going to try to send the others—very interesting, though. Due to the fall or slope of the lawn to the west of the now-gone old garage, the apartment will have to be two steps below the garage level, but they are working this out. As you can see, the kitchen and the living room of the apartment are really "one." In addition, there is the bedroom and the bathroom with a shower—I haven't used a tub for years—with a stacked laundry unit in that area. The total area will be quite adequate for me.

The outside will match the house. The trim will be very nice—cupola on the garage—fancy carriage doors on the garage—nice windows. The porches will join in some way.

Comforting for me will be family—Molly and Glenn—close by. And nearby will be Rick and Tina and Bobby and Gini. I will pay a monthly rent and enjoy free gas heat and a hookup to M&G's TV "dish," etc. In a way, I will miss my home of 22 years here on Avalon Drive, as it has been very good to and for me. However, when the time comes, it will be good to have another place to go. I will reserve the nursing home route—well, only if I experience a "bad" stroke and NOT death.

Long-range plans call for moving the corncrib/granary to the pond and fixing up the old "Chick-hog-o" building—complete with new siding, a large overhead door that will allow storage space for the camper and better use of the good space in that building—now sort of lost space. As I said these are LONG-range plans—things that M&G want to do in the future. All will make the place more valuable. Our dad might be horrified—maybe?? But he might be quietly proud of how the next generation praises his work of the 1937 era as being solid enough to move and keep using. Not many of us can leave behind what we have built with our own hands 75 years ago. He left his mark on the farm in so many ways in his lifetime. Is it 116 years since his birth?

With Rick and Tina's restoration of the John Fluke Home and with all the plans for their addition…and then plans for the Eugene P. Fluke farm—some completed, like the house renovation—and more things to come, I would say the next generation, beyond my own, have done a great job in the restoration and upgrading of both farms. It takes a great deal of money and MUCH hard work to keep on this upward path. I salute them all!

This will be a busy summer on Township road 782—at both ends of the road. Probably good that it is not a REUNION year!

Love,

Louise

MOTHERHOOD—RAISING MY FIVE
A Letter for My Children
January 25, 2013

For some time Molly has been asking me to consider writing about the raising of my five children. And so for the benefit of my remaining four children, I'm going to attempt to write some of my memories. The problem for me with writing about things in the past is that I'm inclined to pick out various times in my life and wish I could change a few things. But then I know that no one is perfect and as a young mother I did the best I could. With little money, few modern conveniences and—for many years—a very real lack of plentiful water. In addition, I've often thought that it would be so helpful to have the knowledge one gains later later in life in the early years, busy, busy days for me. Five children, born in nine years, represented much loss of sleep and many diapers, but also many joys. My children are still the most important individuals in my life. I think of death, and at 87, I know it might not be too far away. I feel ready to leave this life but I "tear" up when I think of leaving my children. You all are truly my reason for being—my biggest accomplishment in my life and my greatest blessing. I am so proud of each of you.

I miscarried my first pregnancy at about 3 months—a boy. Dad and I were living at the farm east of Ashland with your dad's folks—Grandpa (Frank Brownson) and Grandma Ruthie. Dr. Martin came to the house after Grandma Ruthie had called him to tell him I was having trouble. Afterwards, he told me I had "picked a flawed apple off the tree," but that wasn't a big help to me. It is my usual nature to try to take things the best I can without an extended time of prolonged grief. I've always felt the need to carry on the best I could, especially for all those around me—to try to show strength in difficult times.

Ann was born July 21, 1945—8lbs. 3oz. at Samaritan Hospital. We were living at the farm. In those days, mothers spent over a week in the hospital. On the 7th day you could dangle your feet over the edge of the bed...and the next day you could get on your feet...and the following day you could go home or to "your mom's" for two weeks. I'm not sure if this was valid thinking, but it was supposed to prevent future back problems. I don't think it worked for me.

Because of the lack of decent water at the farm, I carried cistern water down a hill to the house to wash Ann's things. Every drop was precious. Water left after her bath in the bathinette was used to do the initial rinse of the diapers. Can you imagine how long this all took compared to just taking a fresh diaper from the delivered package, all these years since? *Disposable* diapers came later. The family washing, Grandma and I took to the "Soap Bubble" in Ashland—Ashland's first laundromat—where we would load every washer and hope no one else came in. Imagine, neither of us drove, so someone had to take us there and come back and pick us up with our baskets of wet clothes. Everything was dried at home, on the outside clothes line, even in freezing weather. The diapers would freeze stiff before you could get back into the house. Gradually everything dried or was finished drying on the back of chairs or even ironed dry. In those days we got groceries no more than once a week. Again, someone took us to Ashland and then picked us up. Strange, but I don't remember much of this—the grocery buying. However, we did grow a lot of what we ate. It was at the farm that I learned to bake pies. Grandma Ruthie was a wonderful "quantity" cook who enjoyed making everybody "comfort" food.

Dad—whom I will refer to from now on here as Bob—started his degree in education in 1945 when Ann was just a baby. All this was made possible by Bob's parents. I think they were very happy for us to live with them. Plus, I think your Aunt Betty to some extent helped him to make the move to go to college. I know she "challenged" him to go for it—his heart's desire! The first year on the farm we lived right with them—Grandma and I cooked together, and we all ate at the same table and shared everything. The second year, Grandpa built on a kitchen for us, and in addition we were given two downstairs rooms for a living room and bedroom. The new kitchen was cold—too far from the stoker furnace which provided really nice heat for the rest of the downstairs. So Bob bought a wood/coal cook stove. I've always said it saved my life. The oven door hung open most of the time—it wasn't the best "baker," but the whole tribe loved our kitchen and most evenings were spent there playing cards and popping corn—lots of laughter and fun. I might add that at that time there were eight of us living in the house. Bob's parents, his brothers Walter and Jimmy, his sister Mary Lou, Bob and I, plus little Ann.

I want to say at this time that I really loved living there for those four years. Many folks over the years have groaned as I told about our time there; however, I found it a wonderful life in spite of the water problems. Bob and I were married Oct. 16, 1943 and were living on College Blvd. It was Grandpa who was determined to buy the farm. Grandma Ruthie said she wouldn't go unless we went, too. So the Brownsons all moved to the farm in the spring of 1944. Grandpa promptly went out and bought two Guernsey cows. Not a one of the Brownsons could milk a cow, so I milked until Walter (Mickey, in those days) learned how. He, at 14-15, was the real "farmer," not Grandpa. Grandma tended the chickens. The young folks were in school. Grandpa ran a milk route in town. And Bob went to college. Ann loved her nearly four years there. Grandma was so good to her—loved her so much. Ann would eat her evening meal at our table and then slip out our back door and rap on her Grandma's door with a cheery, "Here my is for supper"...to Grandma's delight, I might add.

Ann was always a child with a great imagination. When we lived in New London, she had two imaginary friends who came every day to play—Steedy Oby and Orrie Potts. They came in a green pickup truck and sometimes I almost felt they were real—actually there. She always loved "words" and later in life they became so important to her in the form of her poetry and writing.

Bobby was born at Samaritan Hospital while we were living at the farm. He arrived early in the morning of August 20, 1947—9lbs. 4 oz.—the easiest birth, even at that size. I think I was given ether in the hall and that he might have been born before the doctor arrived. I had canned three canners full of green beans the day and night before. Each canner required three hours of cooking on the hot stove, not counting the preparation time. (Bob had picked all the beans, I'm sure. He loved to garden.) Bobby was a good-natured baby—a good eater—just ate and grew. As he grew, he became a very organized boy— always on time and totally prepared—wonderful qualities at many levels for the great teacher he came to be.

Father Bob graduated Cum Laude from Ashland College in 3 ½ years while teaching History and Math at Jeromesville in the afternoons. In addition, he coached the basketball team there. We considered moving to Jeromesville, but didn't leave the farm until after Bob graduated from AC. We moved to New London where he taught and coached football, basketball and track at New London High School.

It was the late of 1948 when we moved to New London—first living at the Crippen place one mile east of New London. It was a remodeled house, okay, except it didn't heat too well—the furnace was in the garage—and again the water supply was not the greatest. Thinking back, I do wonder how I was able to launder all those gym towels for the kids in sports at New London High School. It was a small business— a very small business! Towels were dried on lines in the garage. That worked, the furnace was in the garage, remember! The athletes each had to pay five cents for a clean towel, but all in all it was not a good venture. Though I do believe Bob, with the profits, bought a top coat which he needed badly. He always needed clothes. He did so hate to spend money on anything like that and would wear things that other people gave him. In later years, while he was teaching and coaching at Ashland College, he was given many colorful jackets by Jack Myers. They were of high quality but very bright! Even a red one, many gaudy plaids, the talk of the football season. I often said I wished that Jack had lost some weight as they were all a bit too ample for Bob.

Bob's tenure at New London was most successful—many winning seasons. He was named "Coach of the Year" for small high schools in Ohio in the fall of 1951. We all enjoyed our time there. K. C. DeGood, the Superintendent, was a great mentor to Bob.

Ruth Virginia (Tina) was born April 5, 1949, overdue by three weeks and weighing 9lbs. 3oz. (When we moved to Portsmouth in 1952, she became "Tina," which I'll tell about later.) At the time of her birth we were still living in the country at New London. She cried so little that I became concerned she might have a hearing problem. Both Ann and Bobby played under her crib, and she didn't make a peep! However, she was okay—just non-complaining, not upset over noise and conversation. We moved into the village of New London in the fall of 1949 in a house on Coleman Court, purchased from Forrest and Ruth Motter, longtime friends of Grandpa and Grandma Brownson. It was located on a dead-end brick street. A wonderful place for the kids to play and to learn to ride bikes. Ann started school in New London. The only kindergarten in town was a little private school run by a local doctor's wife. It didn't seem to work well, and we felt Ann would be better off at home. The ladies "helped" the kids way too much—Ann got so she couldn't even put on her own coat and boots.

The next year Bob took Ann to the New London Grade School to start first grade. She had a really difficult time starting school. She did NOT want to go—cried, vomited and threw her lunch box out on the lawn. Again, I didn't drive so her daddy took her, and he was so distressed. However, she had a wonderful teacher and finally settled down. Her teacher told her dad that she thought Ann was having a really hard time "cutting the apron strings" from me, her mama. I didn't quite agree with that assessment, but didn't really know why she was so fearful and upset.

While in New London, I miscarried for the second time, at about 4 months, in March of 1950. This time I went to the hospital. It was a rough time with much hemorrhaging. Another boy with many challenges, especially because this baby had an open area on the top of his head. Again, I took it as best I could with the realization it was possibly for the best.

After four very successful years in New London, Bob applied for the head football coaching job at Portsmouth, OH. Wages were certainly different in those days. He was probably making about $2700, annually, in New London. When the Portsmouth Board of Education asked what it would take for him to come, we mauled it over for several days and he finally sent word that he would come for $4200. He was pleasantly surprised when they hired him in at $4400, a pretty good wage for those days. We moved down to the Ohio River on Bobby's birthday, August 20, 1952. I was criticized by other coaches' wives, because I (we) left the first after-game party too early (11:00PM) and because I didn't drink! Guess they couldn't see that we had just moved and that Frank's arrival was just a few weeks away. Bob set them all straight through the coaching staff and principal, etc. I never really cared for Portsmouth except for my really good friend, Helen Gardner, mother to two of Bob's excellent lineman on his football team.

As soon as we moved into our home in Portsmouth, little Ruthie skipped off down the street—it was safe to do that then—knocking on doors—just saying "hello." When the neighbors asked Ruthie her name, she said "I'm teeny," because Bob used to refer to her as teeny. The neighbors thought her name was Tina and it stuck. Sometime later Bob came home from school for lunch one day and saw her selling flowers to neighbors—like "door to door." He was horrified and told me to get her home. They were actually weeds from the vacant lot close by and indeed the neighbors were buying them. Tina was an entrepreneur long before her time at the McFrederick's store The Olde Parsonage.

Ann started the second grade in Portsmouth with the help of a friend we met at the summer camp where we lived for our first six weeks—not far from the Ohio River. No housing was available at the time of our move, because the Atomic Bomb Plant was being built just north of the city. She finally adjusted well to school—loved to read and, in time, became a "Brownie," also.

Bobby started the first grade at the same time. He was very stoic about school, didn't seem at all rattled about going. They both had a rather long trek down Fourth St. to get to their grade school. One day, early on, he turned the wrong way when leaving school in the afternoon and walked part way downtown until he realized his mistake and back-tracked toward home.

The house we finally got into after our stay at the summer camp was a victim of the great flood of 1937, and we were told that the water had been in the upstairs of our house at that time. After that flood the levee was built along the river-side of the town and it never again flooded. The football stadium and practice fields were separated from the river by the levee. The previous coach had not won a single game. So it was a good place to go—no way to go but UP. Bob's first year was a winning year and in the second one, his boys went undefeated. Bob was named "Coach of the Year" for the state of Ohio a second time. This time in the division of "larger high schools."

Frank arrived November 18, 1952, born in the Portsmouth General Hospital. He arrived 4 weeks ahead of schedule and weighed only 5lbs 4 oz. He had such very tiny legs and arms the older kids said he had "wiener legs." He was so sleepy. It was hard to keep him awake enough to eat. But he grew! In adulthood he was about 6 ft. 3in.—the biggest of all the kids. Both Bobby and Frank played in Little League for Nankin and both played football at Mapleton High School. Bob as quarterback and Frank, later, as center. Bob played all three sports at MHS. Ann and Tina both were cheerleaders for Mapleton. Tina played trombone in the band—Ann sang in the choir. Frank played tuba. Molly has always said she was no athlete, and I think she had seen enough of all that goes along with cheerleading that she didn't want to go that route. She has always been quite artistic. She can put together anything—curtains, pillows, etc.—great with a camera, making her "Love Letters" framed pictures, plus inventing a most helpful game for kids, "Responsibuilders." In addition, she is the best organizer of anything. As Fluke Reunion organizer, she is just fantastic.

Molly presented herself early also. We were living in Portsmouth. Bob had accepted the football coaching position at Ashland College, his Alma Mater, and we were all set to move back home. On the morning the moving van was scheduled to arrive to move us back, I woke up realizing that my "water" had broken—actually, it was leaking. What a morning! Luckily, I was all packed so we took off as soon as we could get the kids up, and we headed home. It was 8 weeks too soon. I wondered if we would have to stop in Columbus or at a hospital on the way. I had no idea how this would turn out. We had already bought a house in Nankin, and we made it all the way there. In fact, I sort of "leaked" for a week. Suddenly I had a wrenching back ache, and I realized this baby was on the way. When we got to the hospital, I was told that there was "no life." I tried to brace myself for this possibility, even though I thought I had felt "life" in the past few hours. After a whiff of gas and/or ether, I woke up to hearing a baby crying, and I was told, "You have a little girl." She was okay. Fortunately, she weighed 4lbs. 3oz.—not too bad for being 7 weeks premature. She spent her first month in an incubator at Samaritan and was finally allowed to come home when her temperature would stay up to normal and she weighed five pounds. I pumped milk for the month she was in Samaritan, and Bob took it to the hospital every day. She battled anemia for her first year, and it took her the better part of a year to catch up.

I learned to drive, at Bob's insistence, shortly after Molly was born. We drove a one-year-old Ford station wagon and Bob was telling me he wanted to buy a new one. I was not in favor of a new car—thought our year-old car was good enough. Then one day he came home with the new station wagon, tossed the keys on the kitchen table and said, "Now, I want you to drive." I finally got the picture. He saw that in the near future the kids would be involved in many things, and he wouldn't be able to see that they got to all these events. So I took my test and passed with no problem. The test was given at the Luray Bowling Alley parking lot. I can still see Bob holding little Molly in his arms with Frank hanging on his pant leg, fussing, while I took the test. He told me that he was praying that I would pass! I loved that buckskin-and-tan colored 1954 Ford wagon, and I drove it for years, to Mapleton for all sorts of events over many years and to Terrace Lake to swim—wherever the kids needed to go.

Our sixteen years living in Nankin was a good time for us as a family. The only negative was Bob's poor health. It was so hard for him and for us all. I have written about this elsewhere, so I won't dwell on it now. We bought our home in the village of Nankin from "Bun" and Ethel Jelly who had worked on the house for a whole year before we bought it. It was nothing fancy, but it served us very well. It was formerly the old Methodist parsonage and right on edge of the nice park—a great place to raise a family. There were several families living in homes bordering the park—good people, excellent playmates. My five would call it their childhood home. It was a short walk to the Nankin Grade School, to the basketball hoops, the grocery store, the post office and right next door to the Nankin Federated Church. All of our gang played in the park—all day and into the evening until parents called the kids home for supper. Then it was back out again until the call to come home to go to bed was heard.

But childhoods end. Did I enjoy this time enough? I've always said that I wouldn't want to go back and live my life over, but I do wish I could have slowed down a bit the years we lived in Nankin. Bobby learned to ride his bike in New London—Ann may have learned there, too, and I know that Bobby teased her a lot as she was attempting learn to turn her bike around in Mrs. Stall's driveway. He was only five, and she was 7. Tina learned to ride her bike riding around the park once crashing into a tree. It didn't take her long to master it, though. All five kids learned to drive while in Nankin. We would set up various buckets and brooms in front of the house when someone was learning to "park." Everyone made it. Other teenage driving took place around the park. One time Ed Lacey from Nova "backed" his car around the park at least ten times. We always thought he was perhaps trying to impress Ann.

I wish I had read more to you all—played more games with you—done more spontaneous things—and baked more cookies. I wish I had managed to save—and launder Frank's old duffle bag, the one he fell down with in the Shaum-poo while on his village trek. He cried over that when I felt it just HAD to go in the trash. I couldn't save Molly's kitten, the one that fell in the septic tank drainage, nor Frank's baby ground hog that he brought home one day. He wanted to keep it (inside.) I told him to "take it back where he found it," to which he tearfully told me its home "was all plowed up," and I felt bad for him.

Our circle was broken. Frank died suddenly on March 15, 2004. Such a shock for us all. I think that Frank, an electrician, was working on a job, perhaps in Mt. Vernon. He drove to work in the morning. He didn't feel well and came home during the day. Sherry came home in the afternoon and found him a very sick man and took him to the Samaritan Hospital. They did everything they could for him, but couldn't get him stable enough to be life-flighted to Cleveland. He died of Sepsis Pneumonia at 8:30 P.M.—a great shock to us all. His funeral service was held at our church, Christ Community, and attended by so many. He had many friends and co-workers who all thought so much of him. He is missed by so many.

Hindsight—our understanding after events—doesn't help me now all these years later. I've just figured out that it took just 30 years to raise you all. I wouldn't have traded it, any part of it, for the world. You all are my PRIDE and my JOY—and like I said—my reason for being. It was a good journey.

A grateful mom,

Louise Beattie

INVISIBLE IN AGING
January 28, 2012

In my younger days, I rushed through my busy years raising a family with all that entails. Cooking and cleaning, spending hours at my old Singer sewing machine. Making everything from "crop tops" to cheerleading outfits and prom dresses, plus three bridal gowns, with coordinating dresses for all the attendants, as the years went by. It was work, but also fun, too. I would burn the midnight oil long after everyone else had gone to bed. Most of this was for my three girls. My sewing was partly to save money; however, I derived great satisfaction in being able to make reasonable, respectable, one-of-a-kind dresses for the girls. I felt needed and quite "visible."

Three particular sewing items stand out in my memory. One was Tina's prom dress in her senior year in high school. It was made of sheer fabric, a very bright, bold print on white. It was totally bright! And then Tina asked me if I could line it with an orange fabric, so it would stand out. I did, and it did stand out! Another project was Ann's pale-ivory, satin wedding dress with a 12-inch band of very expensive lace at the bottom. We were copying something from a bridal magazine. However, in order to have the lace match the dress I needed to tint the lace. This required dipping it in a tea solution! Ann and I both wrung our hands over the Maytag as this was accomplished but we did it. Tina's wedding dress was white crepe with princess lines. Her pill box headpiece tended to slip off her shiny hair. Then there was Molly's lovely, ivory, cotton wedding dress in rather an old-fashioned design, with a cocoa-and-white cotton print for the attendant dresses. As their mom, I found great satisfaction in all these sewing projects for my girls.

And then there were years of school events to attend, sporting events to watch, special programs, milestone events in the lives of my five. I was busy, but I enjoyed it all. I volunteered to make cookies, head the "ways and means" committee work for the PTA. I later took on the fund-raising project for Mapleton, via banquets and smorgasbords, helping to make thousands of dollars to help pay off the new football-field complex. These were some of my best times in life—to be both needed and appreciated. And yes, quite "visible."

At age 50 I was given the opportunity for a bit more education beyond high school. The administration at Ashland College suggested that my husband, Bob, who had serious health issues, might benefit from acquiring some additional credit hours by taking course work aimed toward a Doctorate in Education. He had always loved to go to school. Bob enlisted my help to go along with him—for me to drive us to the University of Akron. We registered for courses—Bob signing up to take course work toward a Doctorate, while I contemplated what I could possibly handle. Since I did have some experience in Food Service Management, I signed up in that field, hoping that I might be able to combine it some way with my many volunteer hours at fundraiser banquets and smorgasbords. I hoped it might be possible to work something out like teaching it vocationally once I had a degree. Bob dropped out after a few weeks and several hurried trips back to Ashland and Samaritan ER. However, I hung in there and finished the year. The year at the University of Akron was a plus for me. My grades were good and the experience gave me more self-assurance, something I really needed. But it became clear to me that my days of Food Service Management were really behind me at that point. I needed employment—a paycheck. From there on, I worked mostly as office manager in various doctors' offices, and then at the Registrar's Office at Ashland College, retiring from there in 1986. I felt I was in the mainstream of life, contributing and needed, and again, "visible."

In October of 1975 I lost my first love, Bob, a great teacher and successful coach—a gregarious, outgoing, colorful man who gradually lost the battle of life. He was only 52. His struggle with depression was unending. His last 16 years were so disheartening for us all.

So, at 51, I was alone in my life. I built a new house, rather small, but just right for me. And then along came Jim Conery, a widower, a very successful engineer for Myers Pump, a longtime friend of the Brownson family. We married in 1986 and I moved to his home. In 2000 we moved to Ashland into a newly-built, very efficient condo. Jim died in 1996 of Congestive Heart Failure (CHF). I later met Bill Beattie at church, a kindly, good, quiet man. We married in 2001. We enjoyed nearly 10 years together before he, too, died of both CHF and Chronic Obstructive Pulmonary Disease (COPD), in September, 2010. This was a very sad time for me, alone again for the third time in my life. I've struggled with the loss of Bill greatly in the past year. As a result of loneliness I have felt that I am in some way becoming slowly "invisible."

Sometimes I wonder why I remain. At 87 I'm left with too many unoccupied hours in the day, without enough to do. I know that I should hunt for things to do—to volunteer, to go out, to visit people. I find myself putting off leaving the house, even to go get groceries. Sometimes I blame it on the weather and that does have something to do with it. But I should be able to get beyond it. I can't think of things I really want to do unless they involve family or church. My big family totals 72. It is hard to actually be truly acquainted with my 41 great-grandchildren, though I see such interesting individuals developing in this group. I look at them with pride; however, I feel I don't really know most of them. It isn't always easy to bridge among the three generations.

Did I know my own ancestors, my grandparents? All my great-grandparents were gone before I was born. I knew and was fond of my paternal grandfather, James Fluke, a fun-loving man, a part-time farmer and part-time politician. My paternal grandmother, Mollie Fluke, died when my father was 12. My maternal grandfather Rev. Charles Swan died when I was 4 years old. I was baptized by my uncle, Alfred Swan, the day of my grandfather's funeral. I do remember my baptism, but I do not actually remember Grandpa Swan. However, vivid in my memory is my maternal grandmother, Rhuy Swan. She was a very loving, strong lady—a college graduate, a missionary who also acquired a medical Doctor's degree before leaving for China and the mission field in the late 1800's. She taught me to sew when I as 10 years old. I've thought of her so often over the years and felt blessed by her influence in my life. That wonderful connection with her was so special to me. At 85 she wrote her life story—in history form without opinions—little about how she felt about her life. She was certainly not invisible to me. I remember her kindness, what she wore and the nice odor of her bedroom and her personal self. It could have been lavender.

I look at many things in life and feel that the elderly are much on the outside of so many things. This "electronic age" is nearly beyond the comprehension of my age group. Many in my age group refuse to even give it a try and end up scoffing at all of it. I'm not really current with present-day trends and gadgets, those that upgrade and change almost daily. Maybe it has always been that way for the elderly. I simply can't keep up with all my grands and great-grands, even by name. I do like texting and I'm working at mastering Facebook. I'm fairly efficient with email and find that I love to write my thoughts on the computer—a wonderful outlet to record thoughts and memories. I do enjoy the email method of communication with two of my remaining siblings. We are all three in our 80's, but we run everything by each other, family history, politics and health issues and find it all to be both comforting and comfortable. Otherwise, it seems best if we older folks quietly and respectfully "attend" but do not try to "project" ourselves or our ideas. Should I even want to?

I've battled Mesenteric Non-Hodgkins Lymphoma in the past year with treatment consisting of two kinds of chemo. It was, and still is, classed as non-curable, nor will it ever go into complete remission. However, it is in "control" and that is good. The other day I made a trip to Mansfield, by myself, to the Cancer Center to have my "port" flushed. It was my "adventure" day. I ate at Chipotle—I do love spicy food—and then did a little shopping. Not too successfully, I might add. Few stores seem to have what seems "right" for

80-year-old ladies. I like nice clothes, shoes and jewelry and think I make fairly good choices. But many of the current fashion styles make me cringe. I know the bulk of the shoppers today are very young—bare midriffs and short skirts are for them. I do hope that Alfred Dunner hangs in there for some more years.

Television is so often of more interest to younger people. The "virtual" shows distress me, as do the political things, especially all that we have to go through every four years to elect a president. Comedy is such a waste of time, for me. It doesn't bring me joy and that is what I want to experience. Documentaries of all kinds are good. I'm also glad there are so many books out there—books to suit everyone's taste. My Kindle is nice. My children got it for me when I started chemo. A nice form of reading to take along on "infusion day." However, I still find that I like to actually hold the real book in my hand and, in truth, I don't really like to pay $12 to read what I, perhaps, might find at the local library for free. Another "old" concept of mine, no doubt.

These days I'm invariably the oldest in the room at all gatherings. It is as it should be. But I notice that seldom is conversation directed toward the oldest ones. This does not happen in my family, where I feel included—it is just in other places. Granted that Seniors for the most part don't hear very well and that is one reason we seem not to be called on for much interaction; we do not quickly "get the drift" of the topic of the moment or we are a couple of steps behind the younger folks. It is difficult to try to catch-up in the middle of a discussion.

I feel respected and honored within my family, as well as at church. However, time changes things and health diminishes. I'm no longer able to able to lift a "loaded roaster" or carry the chairs as I did in my younger days. But this is noted in my eyes only. I'm not expected to do the manual stuff of life. Is this how I measure my worth? It shouldn't be.

When I was a little girl I thought it was sad that older people didn't get to go sled riding or tramping in the snow. What I didn't realize was that they didn't want to and really weren't able. The "chills" of life are felt more—the aches of aging backs and joints are felt more keenly. That's just part of life. I've resolved that it is within the individual person to try to take more part in the happenings of the day. For me, I find it hard NOT be "on the committee" in this latter part of life. Some would rejoice in this! I pray for enlightenment and discernment in my life, striving for contentment and the wish to seek more opportunities to find real joy in my life. I know that responsibility is mine. I don't want to be a cranky old lady.

Just this afternoon I answered my door to find a leader from my church's youth group along with two boys from the group at the door. They were bearing a large bowl of fresh fruit—for me. Surprise! They had had some sort of scavenger hunt gathering the fruit—enough to fill five bowls to be distributed to the elderly of our congregation. It was a contest between the boys and the girls; how it worked was not totally clear to me. But I was one of the recipients of the results of their fun activity. I'm taking back my words. I'm really not "INVISIBLE." Being lonely should not necessarily cause me to feel that way. It is all up to me, to take my place in life and interact! The choice is mine. Writing all this has all been a valuable learning lesson for me in seeking to feel more "visible" through my own efforts.

Louise Beattie

A LOVELY ANNEX HAS BEEN ADDED
TO THE OLDE PARSONAGE IN ASHLAND, OHIO —
QUIET, PRIVATE, BEAUTIFUL ACCOMMODATIONS

Call Ahead—Reservation Needed Due To Frequent "No Vacancy" Sign
February 25, 2012

On Tuesday morning, February 21, 2012, the Milliron Waste Management truck pulls up to the Olde Parsonage dumpster, slides the truck "arms" into the dumpster and lifts it up over the truck. Imagine the total surprise of the driver when a guy falls out—down onto the truck windshield! The guy was alive but shook up. The driver gets him to get into the truck, but the fellow gets back out, says he has to retrieve his "stuff," which he does and then takes off. (It was noted that he was of Indian descent, as in India.)

Fast forward to Saturday morning. A snow has fallen in the night and the McFrederick guys are ready to open up the store for the day. All are out shoveling snow from the parking lot. In jest, Luke raps on the side of the dumpster, yelling, "Wake up—it's time to get up." And out pops this same guy—with his backpack this time. Jake, ever ready with his cell phone—he does take more than take Taco Bell pictures—takes a picture of this early riser! Luke is calling, "Stop—we can get you a hotel room." The guy doesn't stop. Rick is calling 911, for the police, then all the owners of the Olde Parsonage take hot pursuit across the fields to the south of the parking lot. Rick nearly grabs the guy's jacket—but the dumpster-dweller gets away. Now all are running in full chase—Joe speeds past them all. However, this wiry, crafty guy outruns them all and is heading for Cabit Cove. Wow! Such intrigue!

The Ashland Police arrive. They search out the trail to Cabit Cove and determine that said dumpster-resident, last year, lived with his family in Cabit Cove. The parents moved to California, but the son didn't want to go with them. So he stayed behind! Where? In the dumpster? Who knows how long he has been making his residence there. Even after the rude awakening by the trash-hauler on Tuesday morning, the guy returned to his great accommodations, even though it just might be a tad on the chilly side.

Now we all know that the Olde Parsonage deals only in high-quality stuff, so no doubt an accumulation of foam and really nice comfy trash was inviting to this "stay-in-Ashland-at-all-cost" fellow.

Do you suppose he returned there tonight? Is he in the dumpster now, already sound asleep? Maybe he just loves to hear snow falling on the dumpster roof!

Reporting Granny
L. Beattie

MY HERO IN HIS HEYDAY
February 8, 2012

I was in my Sophomore year at Ashland High School, a B+ student, not very sure of myself, a bit shy and a "bus kid" to boot! I wonder why the schedule-makers put the bus kids all in the same classes. Everyone in my English class, taught by Miss Sprague, rode the bus. I never learned the purpose for this arrangement—or if there was a purpose. However, it did make us feel a bit segregated to some degree. I never really had a "best" friend. I was kind of a loner, always.

And then along came Bob Brownson! My life changed.

It was basketball season—the heart of the winter of 1939. Imagine my surprise one day when a classmate in study hall, Betty Brownson, one day asked me if I was "allowed to date." Apparently, her brother, Bob, wanted to ask me out and was enlisting the help of his sister to find out if I had parental permission before he would ask. I really didn't know if I was allowed this teenage rite of passage! I was 15 ½ and knew I needed to ask at home and see if I was "allowed." That evening at home, after chores, I asked my dad if I could go out with this boy, Bob Brownson. Of course Dad asked "Who is he and what kind of a guy is he?" Bob was in the Junior class, the same as my brother Donald. Both were very good students and in some of the same classes. Donald came to my rescue and vouched for Bob. I produced a picture from the Ashland Times-Gazette that showed Bob playing basketball on the AHS team. I got an "okay" and gave my answer to Betty. With this all verified, Bob then asked me to meet him after the next basketball game.

His interest in me had apparently begun the summer before when he saw me with my family at the Farm Bureau. He recognized me as a Fluke because my brother Donald was in the family group. The Farm Bureau was then on South Street in Ashland. He noted this family "gathering" as he rode past on his bicycle while on his "ice cream bar" route. He told me at a later time that he really wanted to stop and give me an ice cream bar that day, but he quickly decided it would be a bit hard on his profits for the day if he had treated the entire family!

I don't remember who took me to Ashland High School to the basketball game, but it was probably my mom. She was always good about getting us to "town" if there was something we really wanted to take part in.

I remember I met Bob in the hall with his parents and family just outside the auditorium. I was so nervous. Little did I know that night how closely my life would be entwined with this family in the years to follow. His mother, who later became a very special person in my life, wore a hat and I got the impression she was really tall—kind of a large woman. However, I later realized that she was pregnant for her youngest child. Just imagine, 17 years between the brothers—the oldest and the youngest. Apparently, the night I met them was quite a special occasion and perhaps Bob's first venture into dating, as Bob's Dad allowed him to drive their very new, dark blue 1939 Desoto for this "first date."

We must have had a Pepsi and hamburger at the Sanitary Dairy restaurant after the game—everybody went there. It was very snowy that night, and I was worried that we might get stuck in the snow and no doubt Bob was, too. I was very tense. He told me later that I sat quite close to the passenger door and carefully wore my gloves—very proper. So that date started us on a four-year journey of dating—for the rest of the basketball season and then on through the summer, followed by football season and beyond.

I recall being down at Myers field, after football practice, the team practiced there then. I don't know how I got there. I didn't drive. But one thing I remember was that when Bob got in his car, or maybe his dad's car, he complained about being nauseated and completely worn out from practice. I remember feeling a bit confused as to why a high-school boy would feel sick from practice. It was just a bit of a "flag" to me, and I did notice that the rest of the team didn't seem that exhausted. Bob was the "center" of the team, so he naturally didn't get the same glory as did the ball carriers. That didn't seem to bother him, though. I knew absolutely nothing about football in those days. Little did I know that it would become our life, our so called "bread and butter" some eight years in the future.

Bob was academically in the top ten of his class and had many friends. He had a good sense of humor, although I will admit that sense of humor did have a bit of a bite to it sometimes. He loved school on all levels and read a great deal, especially books on history regarding the American Indians, books on Germany and World War II.

In the summer of 1940 Bob found a 1908 Model T and bought it for $8.00. That made for a fun summer. I don't know what happened to it except I think he later sold it for more money than he paid for it. I do remember that several teenage drivers did give it a pretty heavy workout that summer. Close to Bob's grandparents, down in Holmes County, there is a small country road with a very steep hill where the old adage was you had to *back* your Model T up the hill in order to make it. Bob had to try this—successfully, I might add.

We went to Chippewa Lake Park on several occasions. I remember riding the roller coaster three times in a row, not that I really liked it, but it was the thing to do. We danced in the ballroom which I think later burned. All in all it was a very happy period of time for me.

We spent time at various homes, just teenagers messing around. Tom Wiley was also in the class of 1941. I recall going to his house with a gang of kids. I remember being there one Sunday afternoon and being involved in games in the yard—lots of fun in hot sunshine. Later Bob put his arm around me, gave me a hug, or a couple of them, and I discovered that my arm had this great odor of boyish sweat on it. I didn't wash my arm that evening. I'm getting to like this guy a lot. I'd tag along when he would go to play "barnyard" football out at the Fulk farm. This was where Bob's younger brother Mickey [now, Walter] about age 12, got the "wind" knocked out of him, and I realized that this farmyard brand of football, without any protective gear, could be downright dangerous.

I attended my first Brownson Christmas Eve party on Grant Street in probably 1940. The Brownsons were a family who had a lot of fun. Santa came, though it was sort of late in the evening. Bob's dad (the kids' Grandpa Frank) and his brother Bill ran a milk route in Ashland for years. Grandpa Frank would play Santa for several of the families on their route, once even walking a real live pony into the living room of Dr. Martin's home—"Santa's" gift for the doctor's daughter. After his "route friends" had been visited by Santa he would come back to the house to the delight of the kids, all dressed in his red-and-white suit and fake white hair and beard. Grandpa had a great sense of humor, making for a hilarious evening. I felt fortunate to be a part of this family even in those days.

We danced at a place known as Pelitts, provided especially for the high-school kids of that day. It was upstairs, somewhere on Main Street. We danced to a juke box. How heady for this little country girl. I loved to dance, but Bob wasn't too crazy about it. He really didn't like to do anything unless he was good at it! There were "noon" dances in the girls' gym at school or movies you could watch in McDowell auditorium, as well. At the end of the school day Bob would often walk me to the school bus and would sometimes slip me a candy bar. I've always loved chocolate!

Bob graduated from AHS in 1941 and through the efforts of his Uncle Gar he hired on with Western

Electric in Cleveland. He didn't like the job, nor Cleveland. And I realized that he hated to be away from his family...and me too, I think. He would "hitch" rides home on Friday nights in order to make it home in time to be the "timer" for the home high-school football games.

I graduated one year later. Bob asked me to marry him during graduation week and gave me an engagement ring. I was so excited and I accepted. Dates and times get a bit hazy after some seventy years. I don't recall how long Bob worked in Cleveland. I went to work immediately after graduation, working for Dr. Boignard in his office. I was receptionist, cleaning person and assisting "nurse"—all at 17 for the wage of $17.00 per week. I lived at the Business Women's Club on Cleveland Avenue. In those days, girls who were working didn't own a car, nor did anyone take us to work, so when you worked in town you had to find a place to live. In the summer, my sister Elinor and I shared a room there. We would sleep on the screened-in sunporch, second-story, over the front porch of the club. Bob would take the last Greyhound back to Cleveland on Sunday night, and he would have the bus driver toot the horn as they drove by the club. I felt special. He wrote me post cards and letters each week.

In October of 1942 I left the doctor's office and went to work for Faultless Rubber Co. "cementing" lifebelts for the Navy for $.43 cents an hour. It's now 1943–Bob was working in the testing department at Myers Pump. In the spring of 1943, I quit my job with the lifebelts and went home to help my dad on the farm. My brother Donald was in the service and Dad really needed help. I worked at home on the farm until the fall of '43. When the harvest was over, Bob found a job for me at Myers Pump working in the nozzle dept.

Bob's Aunt Hazel died suddenly and her husband was asking the family if anyone wanted to buy his furniture, all of it, for $500. We hadn't really talked about a date to get married. Somehow the offer of the furniture made it all possible. In later years I found myself wondering if it might have pushed Bob into marriage before he was ready. In my times of questioning my worth, I've wondered if Bob might have wanted someone more academic than I. But maybe not. In later years he would buy me really nice jewelry, once an Opal necklace and another time a string of pearls. His notes were very loving and appreciative of me as both a wife and mother.

Bob was not in the service, and I think this was a great cross for him to bear. All his buddies were scattered all across the globe fighting for their country. Twice he went to Cleveland to attempt to enlist, but both times he was sent home, rejected because of a chronic, dislocating shoulder issue, an old football injury. "Four F" guys—the military classification meaning you were not acceptable for service in the Armed Forces due to medical, dental, or other reasons—were not very popular. I felt sad for him in this.

We married October 16, 1943 in the home on College Boulevard where we were going to live, the house that had formerly been rented by his Aunt and Uncle and where the furniture was located. It was good to be married and to belong to each other, to start our married life together. Bob was now, at this point, working in Loudonville at the Flexible Bus Co.

Early in 1944, Grandpa Brownson wanted to buy a farm. It seemed the thing to do in the war years. Bob's mother, Grandma Ruthie, didn't really want to take on the venture but said she would go if Bob and I went, too! We moved—all of us—out east of Ashland on Rt. 250. I found myself pregnant in February. But a miscarriage was threatening, and I was told to stop working. I did miscarry in March. It had been a really tough winter for me. However, there was never a dull moment—so much to do, but through it all I enjoyed the "togetherness" of the big Brownson family.

Ann was born July 21, 1945. And shortly thereafter Bob started classes at Ashland College. His sister, Betty, challenged him to do what he really wanted to do and, I think, may have even helped a bit financially. An extreme shortage of teachers in this war-time period made it possible for Bob to teach History and Math in the afternoons at Jeromesville High School after taking classes in the morning at Ashland College. He was hired as Basketball Coach as well. The pay was very small ($70 per month.) However, by living with Bob's folks for free and with the small salary from Jeromesville, it was possible for him to make his dreams a reality. He finished college in 3½ years, graduating Cum Laude. I was so proud of him. Son Bob was born August 20, 1947. Upon graduation, Bob was hired by the New London School system as teacher and coach of football, basketball and track. While in New London, Tina was born April 5, 1949. Frank was born soon after we moved to Portsmouth, Nov. 18, 1952. These were very busy years for us all.

However, these were good years for us. Our four years at the farm were good to us and for us and made it possible, after Bob's degree in teaching, to be able to get out on our own. In August of 1948 we moved to New London. Our four-year stay there was "as good as it gets." We made many friends there—many wishing he would stay there longer. An "all-wins" season in 1951 made it possible for Bob to be hired on as the Portsmouth High School football coach. After another "all-wins" season in Portsmouth down on the Ohio River in 1953, it was back to his Alma Mater, Ashland College. Molly, our last baby, was born June 23, 1954. Her birth coincided with our move back home to Ashland. We bought a house in Nankin. Our home there would be the childhood home of our five children. It was a great place to raise a family.

Hired as the Football Coach at Ashland College in 1954, Bob was, again, very successful. For the third time he received the "Coach of the Year" award, this time at the small college level. The previous ones were given as the Coach of the Year on the small-high-school level for the Wildcats of New London and then the larger-high-school award as football coach for the Trojans in Portsmouth, OH.

Bob Brownson was a gregarious man who had great rapport with his many teams over the years. He was a much sought-after speaker at athletic banquets all over the state of Ohio. In addition, the Ashland College students sometimes waited several semesters to get into his very popular Educational Psychology classes.

He left us all too soon. I've often wondered what goals he might have achieved had he not been brought down by poor health.

So, I choose to remember fondly the good old days—Bob's heydays—his glory years, for they were great years for our family, for his children and for me as well. I will always treasure the memories of our first 20 years together. I wish I could have slowed them down a bit, savoring the successes and the joys of that heyday period in our lives.

May Bob rest in peace.

Louise (Brownson) Beattie

MY 88TH BIRTHDAY—THE SOIRÉE
May 26, 2012
Written on June 1, 2012

When Molly told me not to come to the farm until 6:00PM last Saturday night I wondered what was happening! She knows that if she told me dinner was at 6:00 her mom would be there by 5:00. So I waited and twiddled my thumbs until the appointed hour and drove to the farm.

What a surprise! As I rounded the curve in the driveway, I realized that a table was all set under one of the Maple trees in the front yard. Little did I know that it was elegantly appointed with all the nice things of my life, my era. My heart was so touched by all the thought and planning that had gone into making this memorable event so special. The family had contributed to the total staging of my party, marking my 88th year in this old world. What an evening!

Over the table a chandelier from the Olde Parsonage was hung from a tree branch with an electric cord brought out from the house to the tree to power the beautiful hanging light. Molly had provided a damask-like, pastel, muted-color, print tablecloth with lace panels bordering both ends of table. The table was set with my wedding dishes, dishes given to Bob and me as a wedding gift by my parents, Gene and Mary Fluke, in 1943. I had given them to Molly years ago. They were in perfect keeping with the table linens and all the table appointments. Daughter-in-law, Gini, added a nice touch by providing her sterling silverware place settings—gifted to her over a period of several years in her youth, by her parents.

Molly had placed a white daisy in each folded napkins—so pretty. A beautiful bouquet graced the center of the table, with peonies and other flowers from her garden. Candelabra graced the table along with water glasses and also small goblets, brought by Tina, for a bit of wine to celebrate the occasion. The chairs were an assortment of old Methodist Church chairs and maple chairs in keeping with the "bygone days" theme. The chair selected for me was a beautiful, old-fashioned, "antiqued" green chair with lovely spring colors on the floral print seat. Two beautiful ferns, on stands, graced two corners of the table. Truly, all of this was awesome to me, and Molly, knowing me so well, knew I would be thrilled—and I surely was! I'm so glad that Molly and Glenn took pictures during the evening—very helpful in remembering the party and in explanation to others, not in attendance.

The food was fantastic. Chicken Marsala, a recipe from Sara McIntyre's Colorado cookbook, was perfect for the occasion. The old covered tureen—from my dishes, usually filled with mashed potatoes in my day—held wild rice. In addition, there were green beans with carrots and bacon, a tasty aspic salad, a tossed garden salad and French bread completed the menu. Everything was perfect for the occasion. For dessert Molly had made her wonderful pretzel-and-raspberry specialty. I was toasted by the gang with some wine made by Rick. It was quite tasty and very festive.

Happy birthday was sung and gradually the sunlight faded into dusk. The hanging light that had added to the glow all through the meal became even more beautiful as the sky darkened. A light, warm breeze was blowing all evening—with no mosquitoes, most unusual! We sat for four hours talking and laughing, enjoying a delightful evening. It was a perfect evening, which was referred to as a soirée, an "evening party." I doubt that it can ever to be duplicated! I felt truly blessed as I was surrounded by my family. Ann would have loved to be there with us in the family circle We missed them—Ann and Larry. How nice it would have been if the circle could have been complete.

Earlier Ann and Larry had sent me a handsome door mat emblazoned with "GRANDMA LOUISE." It was given especially for my entryway at the Dawdi Haus—my soon-to-be-apartment on the farm. A neat gift.

At the close of the evening, Bob and Gini, Rick and Tina, plus Glenn and Molly gifted me with wireless head phones. My hearing is not what is used to be and they are proving to be a great aid in amplifying sound and words—making everything more audible and more clearly defined for me. Netflix, sent to me by Ann and Larry, will be enhanced by the headphones, where everything from English accents to the sound of horses' hooves and the chirping of the birds become so much more pronounced .

It was a birthday to remember! I think I have always been a bit a tense when "Happy Birthday" is being sung to me—always a bit embarrassed. This time I found myself fighting tears. At this special party I felt some of the same thoughts popping up, but this time my emotions were coming from a thankful heart. I felt my usual bit of unworthiness, but also great gratitude as I was surrounded by my loving family—and in addition feeling all the years of memories flood my heart and soul. It is said that "pride" is a sinful thing, but I feel that is not so when it is in watching the lives of my loving, "giving" children. Contentment, comfort and joy are with me in these remaining years.

By the end of the summer I will be leaving Avalon Drive and my 22-year stay there. They have been good years; however, I'm looking forward to moving back to the farm and enjoying life in the Dawdi Haus, a wonderful opportunity provided for me by Glenn and Molly. What an exciting summer this is turning out to be, starting out with this super birthday party that my "kids" presented to me in such grand style. As you can tell, I'm still enjoying the glow of the delightful evening. The memories of this beautiful evening will be with me for all time. I'm truly blessed!

Louise Beattie

WILD ANIMAL INVADES ESTES PARK, COLORADO
February 28, 2012

Everybody knows of the serene beauty of Estes Park, this legendary town in the Rocky Mountains, just north of Denver. It has always been known as an elite town—a place of distinction—not only regarding its beauty, but yes, also its rules and regulations. And yet from time to time the huge elk, as a herd, stroll down the main drag and everybody just stops and waits for them to cross or get to where they are headed in their leisurely jaunt.

However, it became a bit more "wild" last Saturday night. Glenn and Molly Smith were visiting the McIntyres in Estes. In Don and Sara's split-level home, Glenn and Molly always occupy the lower-level bedroom. The high winds howled around the house all night and Glenn—ever on top of things—thought he might have heard other noises in addition to the wind. In the morning when he looked out their bedroom window which is right at the head of their bed, he saw a dead animal along the foundation, half-hidden with mulch and debris. It proved to be a young elk and Don surmised it was probably the kill of a mountain lion. **Excitement mounted!**

On Sunday morning Sara walked out on their elevated deck to toss some water over the railing and looked down into the face of a mountain lion—looking back at her!! She stifled a scream and hurried back inside. Now the males of the human pack took over. A motion-detector camera, used for viewing the movement of game in darkness, was installed by the carcass. Night fell—friends were invited in to keep this vigil. Don and Sara's friend, Byron, who has a mounted mountain lion head in his living room I've heard, was there with his family. All gathered in Glenn and Molly's bedroom.

SUSPENSE! Sure enough, the lion returned to his kill and was "feasting" away–gradually becoming a bit ticked with the light from Glenn's camera phone aimed at him. I'm viewing this indoor lion hunt via Facebook later on Sunday, intrigued by the whispered murmurings of those gathered for the viewing. With admonishments of "get down, Lena" and "be quiet," it was very exciting, even though it was many miles away. I'm sure the motion-detector camera was activated, but that video was to be left for a viewing next day.

The assembled group was awed by "nature" up close that night as all gathered their little ones in a close embrace. One piece of window glass can separate us from the beasts of nature? Amazing!

I got to be in on the lion story via social-networking and share it with you. In this modern-day age of technology, it is amazing to ponder how we process the happenings of the day. The social network of the country keeps us all so well connected. It is almost like being there in person. My attempts in trying to keep up with the almost daily advances in this technical age are not very effective—I'm so behind. However, I do enjoy being in the "know" on these exciting happenings near and far.

Yesterday, 2-27-12, during the shootings at the Chardon High School in Chardon, Ohio, the use of this same social-networking kept many students safe and in touch with their parents and families through texting! The "towers" were jammed with phone calls—the texts went through.

Louise Beattie

FIRST FROST OF THE SEASON
IN SYCAMORE VALLEY
October 26, 2012

As I sit on my porch swing on my new front porch and look down into the valley I have viewed my entire life, I'm filled with memories intertwined with my thoughts of today. I'm filled with thoughts of my life which began at birth, on the farm next door, the Rudy Place. By age three I was living here, on the Fluke Farm—growing up here and taking life so much for granted. Our neighbors were all poor, and all of my classmates knew the pinch of the depression. We Fluke kids had no idea what wealth might mean, except for the occasional box of clothing received from our rather "well-to-do" Cleveland relatives. We were light years away from the electronic age. We took what came along, living in the world of FDR and the New Deal. The dreaded word "foreclosure" was scary in our lives. Our world was quite small. I grew up within a strong family circle, a hardworking family but with little in the way of frills.

Let me describe my valley. Two giant Sycamores grew in the valley along the former lane where they remain today, side-by-side, all these years later with their ever-larger, spreading white limbs still embracing the winding road used so little in the long ago and now quite a busy highway. Though I had known them all my life—and thought them to be huge trees—it was to be in this time—in my 88th year—that I really got in touch with them again as I viewed the entire valley from the vantage point of my swing on my wonderful porch—facing west with a wonderful view of the entire valley.

Glenn and Molly built a perfect Dawdi Haus for me this summer, and I moved back to the farm in late August. What a joy to sit on the porch and view again this wondrous place of my childhood—reliving my memory of the games we played in both the south pasture (for the horses) and north pasture (for the cows). Our imaginations ran wild as we played in the creek and tramped the lay of the land, talking and acting like storybook characters. We walked the "cow paths" and rode imaginary horses—always flashy, fast steeds—as we rounded up the cows every afternoon for evening milking.

My 19 acres of woods, that I can also view from my porch swing, is of so much interest to me this fall. The Maysville Lumber Company is presently "harvesting" the woods. The Ash trees of this area of the country are dying—many are already dead, the rest are dying—but of these, both the dead and dying, many are still somewhat salvageable at this time. All in all there are some 250 trees that will be harvested and head out for Maysville in Holmes County. I can sit on my swing and listen to the Big Boss chainsaw cutting the wedge into the tree—followed by the pinging of a couple of smaller plastic wedges being driven into the "V' to hopefully determine the best direction of fall. And then the final roar of the last cut and down comes the tree crashing to the ground. I know from what son Bob has told me that if it goes down with a solid boom it has not crashed into other trees on its downward path—the optimal way to fall. These lumber men are a rare breed. Such dangerous work handled so skillfully and carefully.

And then as I sit here and view the effects of the "first frost" of 2012 I'm realizing that I never took real interest in the first frost as a kid. Oh yes, we put our shoes back on again, and the cows were brought back to the barn to stay after grazing in the "forty" all summer—forty acres of pasture, that is. The tomatoes turned mushy in the garden, and we started picking corn by hand and tossing the ears into the wagon. The growing season had ended, but I didn't take great notice of events—like frost on the windows—or on the pumpkins—or an extra blanket on the bed at night. It all just gradually happened.

However, this year I've really been touched by this phrase, "first frost," and realize so clearly how it all corresponds with my life here and now—back home on this same farm after all these years. The frost has curled the rhubarb, nipped the red raspberry bushes the little great-grandchildren have circled all summer to find the ripe and tasty berries ready for the picking. The back yard Locust trees are shedding their little leaves, and it looks like yellow snowflakes raining down on the Hostas plants already going to sleep for the winter.

It is now that I'm struck by the fact that I, too, am experiencing the coming of the "winter" of my life. I think I am way past the first frost; however the changing of the seasons reminds me of the life cycle. My life is drawing to a close. I write this not regretfully but fully realizing that I'm weary. I'm losing my "zip and zest" for life by degrees.

I'm reading Kay Warrens' new book, *Choose Joy—Because Happiness Isn't Enough*, and I'm learning that joy is deeper than happiness, lasts longer than excitement, and is more satisfying than pleasure and thrills. Life is no picnic. There are many ups and downs—some very sad times with seemingly little possibility to experience joy. However, I'm realizing that joy is often our choice. Real, true "JOY" is ours to seek—to look for—to make happen.

Tonight at the Halloween party at Jake McFrederick's—after an all-family affair of "Trick or Treating"—I watched two-year-old Ridge Bernard squat down in the driveway, put one knee on the ground, and hunker down to tell the assembled group in the driveway all about "hunting." He did it in his very own little droll style, all about shooting a muzzle-loader gun—priming the gun—loading the gun—aiming—pulling the trigger. And then he went on into a discourse of how to call a buck deer—making the proper sounds. When asked how did he call a doe, he said, "We don't call a doe." He paused after each phrase he uttered—not for effect, but just his natural style. We all understood his "story"—it was easily understood. He did not do it like he was showing off. It was just like he was telling an old hunters' yarn as he hunkered down in the driveway. It was priceless to witness this little fellow do what seemed to be fresh out of his daily life experience. We all felt spellbound by his very serious story. It was a little corner of joy in this great-grandma's life!

The cold winter winds will soon be upon us, but I'm snug in my Dawdi Haus surrounded by family. I'm ready to face the "winter" of my life in my warm and comfortable home.

Louise Beattie

THE CHOICES WE MAKE
February 13, 2013

In each day of our lives we are faced with "choices," from the time we are toddlers, through our growing-up years and on into old age. It is at this point in life that I can look back and ponder how these choices have affected my life...for good or for bad. Sometimes choices that seemed rather insignificant at the time have a huge bearing on how we face the road we travel.

As a toddler, I sucked my thumb...actually both thumbs, either would do, and I bit my nails as well. No doubt the thumb-sucking was somewhat comforting to me with my shy nature, likewise with the nail-biting I added to the mix. I won't say these were actually "choices" on my part; however I was often admonished by my mom to stop both nasty habits with words like, "You will ruin your teeth." The thumb-sucking didn't end until I started to school—peer-pressure, no doubt. The nail-biting, l gave up some years later when I worked in a doctor's office where I washed medical equipment. Different from barn work to me, somehow.

As a youngster growing up on the farm, I followed the family rules—learned to milk cows at 10 years of age—turned the "separator" to separate the cream from the milk—drove the team of horses in the fields. There was no TV and until I was 17, no electricity—with little outside, social influence requiring the serious choices faced by the teenagers of today. For the most part, I think I rather automatically followed my parents' wishes. I made their choices mine. I asked my dad if I could attend the regional basketball tourney for the *second* night. He said "no." I was dating Bob Brownson who played on the Ashland team—victorious in the first game. I didn't fuss or argue about my dad's decision. You would have to understand, my dad was *not* a sports fan in any form. These were the smaller type of choices I encountered earlier in my life—decidedly easier in the 1940's than today. In truth, I really didn't think very deeply about these decisions or making proper choices. No doubt the teens of today spend little time reflecting on choices! Neither did I.

Little did I know in those years, my growing-up years, that I was gradually learning skills to better meet the much bigger decisions coming in my life. No one knows what might lie ahead in life. The finesse needed to stretch a very small paycheck in order that Bob might acquire a college education, was huge. Family assistance was lovingly given. Bob loved to go to school and made every semester-hour count, graduating in 3 ½ years, with honors.

Serious illness followed for Bob, coupled with major surgery and ongoing depression. This was a very bleak period in all our lives. However, it was during this time that choices had to be made at every turn. Bob's health deteriorated to the point where he could no longer make decisions, and I experienced the shock of knowing that I had to step up to the plate and attempt to hold the family together. However, it was also in this worrisome time in my life that I found the true meaning of compassion for others. Through the heartbreak of pain, loss and loneliness during that time, I witnessed, as well, others also coping with adversity that was overwhelming.

Seldom does a family escape the trauma of health issues today. We all experience loss of life within our family circles. We all feel the connection of the wars of the world, some going on for years, taking the lives of so many young people. Add to this the frequency of the diagnosis of cancer and heart problems which cause much sorrow for us all. I'm ever reminded that God is in charge. However, I firmly believe that He expects us all to provide a listening ear and comfort to others suffering distress in whatever way we can, whenever possible.

Good choices! So important! How do we learn to make the right choices? Even for our very young children it is important that we teach the meaning of compassion in words and ways they can understand. It is so important that parents take time to explain why bullying is so painful and its effects are so long-lasting. Parents are given such an awesome responsibility in raising children. No "how-to" booklet comes with this needy little bundle! The problem is, often, young parents have no idea of how to lovingly teach the moral excellence needed so badly in their children's lives as they grow and mature. Grandparents have the awesome opportunity to help change little lives. Other adults within the family and community circle can also take up that opportunity.

Our lives are often the sum product of the choices we have made as time goes by. I'm now in my 89th year and there are still choices for me to make and for my contemporaries to make as well. We see so many who are so unhappy and rudely negative in their later years. I believe that what a person experiences and the attitudes one accumulates in life may very well spell the choice of attitude they will live by in old age. Too often we see Seniors take on the role of victim, voicing negative thoughts to everything they don't like or agree with. No doubt illness and dementia to some degree are the cause of much of their lament, and this must be considered in assessing their behavior. I'm so aware of all the comforts I have been given by Glenn and Molly as I have come back to the farm—the place where I grew up—where I sit on my swing and look at my valley—and enjoy my life in the Dawdi Haus. I know all this has been a big plus to me, and I am very grateful and realize how few in their old age have benefits like this.

Some big choices in my life:

What if I had said "YES" to the management of the fabric store in Ashland when offered to me in the 1960's? I said "no," but I wondered if it was a big opportunity missed. Now I know I would have hated it. What if I had said "no" to Bill Beattie when he asked me if I would go out to eat with him—the man who made me feel cherished in my later years? And what about the big choice I made in 1972 when "SALVATION" was offered to me at a Bible study? My "YES" that night changed my life forever. I'm quite sure that God is somewhere in all our major decisions. We often fail to realize or recognize His input, so valuable to us all.

Louise Beattie

SECRETS IN FARM LIFE
Protecting the "Girls" from "Man Talk"
June 9, 2013

As the planning for the Fluke Reunion, Labor Day weekend, 2013, is taking place, many emails are passing back and forth among the cousins. And various individuals are thinking of things they would like to see take place as the family revisits the farm...as we celebrate our heritage and remember growing up on the Fluke farm or remember visiting as grandchildren in summer. Everyone has different thoughts and feelings as they examine their own individual memories.

This morning in an email to my daughter, Molly Smith, our coordinator for the event, arrived an interesting remembrance from Cousin Molly Fluke Evans, forwarded to all on the reunion email list. Her dad, my Uncle John, trucked livestock from farm to market in the by-gone days. Cousin Molly recalls that she and her sister, Gloria, had to be very careful as they recorded the phone calls instigated by the farmer who called in to request that his "animal" be hauled to Cleveland on a certain day, at a certain time. The "gender" of said animal was not spoken by the caller...but referred to as "the animal"...purposely, as a nicety, out of regard for "frail girls." When Uncle John arrived home he would return the call and find out the gender of said animal...asking if it might be a bull, ram...or perhaps steer, cow etc. The caller's thoughts being that the word "bull" or "ram" should not reach the girls' ears. As I recall, we used these words without a problem on the farm, but apparently many "gentlemen" of the day did not feel comfortable in using such defining and, therefore, sensitive words when speaking to the adolescent female.

All this made me remember my early years in the Fluke barn. At ten years old I was assigned "my cows" to be milked in order, morning and evening...followed by the leading of the horses, Fanny, Polly and Becky to the watering trough. However, watering the "bull" was off limits for girls...and rightly so for safety's sake...all rather mundane in farm chores it would seem, but not okay for "girls." When Uncle John would arrived at the Fluke farm to pick up a cow that was deemed "off to market"—probably it meant "without calf or she didn't catch" or some such breeding terminology—Dad would quietly say, "Louise, go to the house now." Sometimes I think Uncle John would have a helper riding along and Dad did not want me to be involved in or hear any "man talk." Remember, I was dressed as a boy, in overalls. No frills in the barn.

We girls were not to be in the barn when calves were conceived or born...not right for girls. Of course, I'm sure Dad realized that once in a while we were in the barn when he wasn't, where we got the concept of an unassisted calf-birthing in an accidental sighting. For boys, I believe this all was considered "manly," all a part of the rights of passage to manhood.

All summer long I drove the blind team, Fanny and Polly, in the fields as we loaded the loose hay. It came up the "loader" onto the wagon where Dad carefully loaded each pitchforkful with great precision. As the load filled, I climbed higher up on the cross-pieces of the hay ladder in the front of the wagon where I carefully spoke, audibly, to the totally blind team...stopped them at each little ditch with a "whoa" and then eased them on their way with a "get-up." (In recent reading of the old English customs, I learned in that country the men would say "walk on" to their horses.) I took great pride in doing my jobs. However, when "Threshing Day" would arrive...my favorite day of the summer ...when the big steam engine arrived to thresh out the grain, wheat or oats...Dad would say, "You stay at the house today, Louise." At the house Mom, (Grandma Mary to you kids), explained it to me...and it very nonplussed me...the "why" of this. She told me that Dad didn't want to me to be subjected to "male talk" and no doubt he didn't trust completely the age 13- or 14-year-old neighborhood boys participating in the threshing. I was crushed at Dad's ultimatum for the day. Dad didn't really explain in detail the "what or the why" of things. And if he did explain...it was only ONCE. You grandsons who came to work with him will well remember his few words spoken as you got your instructions as to how to approach the "fitting of a field" or the process of the bailing of hay.

Were all girls more protected in those days...or was it that the Fluke brothers, Gene and John, were protective of their children? They were the best of brothers, fathers, grandfathers and men.

I've enjoyed this little venture back into my memories this morning. It is a good to do just that from time to time...to remember the rolling land, the seed planting and the harvest, and especially the men and women who filled our lives with the defining, good principles of life itself. We have all been blessed many times. On Labor Day weekend we return to the farm to remember the days gone by and the good people who helped chart our lives.

I'm blest to be living here again in my 90th year...to sit on my porch and view my Fluke Heritage!

Louise Fluke Beattie

FLUKE REUNION, 2013
Labor Day Weekend

The long anticipated event has come and gone...all the voices raised in laughter and song are stilled...the patter of little feet on the porch outside my Dawdi Haus door, likewise. It is quiet here on Sycamore Hill...all evidence of the three glorious days has disappeared. Gone are the motorhomes that arrived the Wednesday before—motorhomes of the Martins and Drouillards from Michigan who made up the crew that lent many hands and hours of assisting in readying the farm for all the Flukes! Except for those actually involved in the preparations, most have little concept of all that goes on in the couple of days preceding the reunion.

My estimated guess is that some 124 attended on Saturday, exceeding the 100 in attendance in 2011 on the "big" day. The weather was perfect for all three days...warm and sunny. Our good fortune holds...no rain, ever, for all the Saturdays of the reunion held in this Labor Day weekend format since 1981. We sweltered in 93 degree heat at the 2011 event. We were so happy, this year, that the weather was so cooperative. Everyone enjoyed a great day. It just needed to be longer...more daylight hours.

The event officially started with a wonderful evening as guests of Rick and Tina McFrederick who entertained us with an outdoor buffet set up outside the front door of their beautifully-restored Italianate Style home, built by John W. Fluke, for his wife Elizabeth, in 1876. Perhaps some 60 attended, and we were privileged to view the reenactment of "John W. Fluke and wife Elizabeth" arriving at the lawn party. The stately couple came strolling up to the lawn from the road... delightful, even to nearly duplicating John's white hair and unusual beard. It was a perfect evening for all who attended.

Saturday morning: The tent, tables and chairs, and the porta-pot arrived, the tent set up and the porta-pot neatly positioned between the two silos...everything was in place...we were ready to go! Things got off to a fun start with fishing at the pond to the delight of the kids, supervised by Gini Brownson and Don McIntyre. At the same time, some trooped down to Rick Krause's farm to view his 4-helicopter-motor, "pulling" tractor. They got a peek at all that POWER before Rick stowed the tractor in its very own semi-trailer, ready to be trucked to a big "pull" competition in New York State.

During the morning the "Bucket Auction" was set up...tickets sold...all to help defray the expenses of the reunion. Donated "family" things and a variety of interesting items were brought in. I'm not sure that everyone understands the need for this. Money is needed to fund this weekend...thus the auction. Proceeds from the auction, plus donations, help to cover the expenses.

At 11:00 everything goes into full swing. I've lost the sequence of events, but, as usual, the hay rides began...over hill and dale...down the old cow lane...always a popular, fun time. On either side of the lane there was towering field-corn. Wasn't it beautiful? It has been a good growing year on the farm.

The "Gator Ride" competition took place in the pasture next to the barn...however, I don't recall the winner. It seemed the "Gator" was in constant motion all day...every day...morning and evening... some nighttime rides as well...all ages included.

A delicious, catered lunch was prepared by Barb and Larry Bates and served under the tent. It is great to have the meal prepared...off-site. Thanks, Barb and Larry!

An interesting added attraction this year was named "Lost Arts." This was an attempt to show...especially to the younger folks...how the basic chores of the by-gone days took place...how bread was made, how it was kneaded and baked...how wood was split for stoves...how the laundry was done, outside in the yard, long before the modern methods of today. A couple of hand-cranked ice cream makers...the old fashioned way to make ice cream...turned out some delicious treats for the enjoyment of all ages. All agreed "Lost Arts" was a winner. Many worked very hard to create this glimpse of the "Old Days." Our gratitude to ALL who revived the lost arts of yesteryear.

Another one of the lost arts I might mention was the "tatting" demonstration, done with a little shuttle, using thread to make little loops and circles. This handwork demonstration, used long ago as a decorative trim on hankies and ladies collars, was headed up by Mary Fluke. Some laughter took place within the modern generation as they assumed at first that it just might be a "tatting" demo—as in TATOOING." Margaret Welch...during the planning session...said she wondered, for a minute, where she might find those stick-on tattoos for kiddies. A sign of the times, to be sure.

The little ones played in a kiddy wading pool filled with shelled corn. Trinkets were hidden in the corn...they loved it and went digging through the corn over and over. The trinkets...plastic creatures...turned up for a few days all over...even in the Dawdi Haus.

The Puppet Show was revived for this reunion, since both John Keiffer and Sara (Smith) McIntyre could be here to do their hilarious skit. There were events we didn't have time for and we do regret that...maybe next time? Margaret still thinks pony rides would be great!

A corn roast followed...also in the pasture south of the barn. It was a delicious treat for us all and a mighty "HOT" activity. Bob Brownson and family took on this extra-hot job.

After eating...again...we adjourned to the pond for the family memorial service, provided by the Ritschdorff family, honoring all who have died since 1975. A torch for each one we've lost was lit by a family member close in relationship to the departed loved one. And little white paper boats with a lighted candle inside each were launched into the water of the pond, each in honor of all those in the family who have died in the past 38 years. We sang and prayed around the pond, watching the glowing little boats...so meaningful to us all. It is always a quiet time filled with heartfelt love for all as we each remember our loved ones.

On Sunday morning Bill Martin called us all to circle around under the big Maple tree and we sang many of the favorite old hymns from our childhoods...treasured by all of us...especially those of us on the older side. Harmony rang out on Sycamore Hill. The "sing" was followed by a beautiful breakfast served under the tent...all of it provided by the Drouillards, Liz and David. We gathered for a time of visiting, but way too soon it was time to say goodbye to all the travelers...each getting ready to start the trip home. This is always an emotional time for many, but I think this time especially so for the remaining Fluke "kids," my siblings...four of us are still here. As our age increases, travel becomes more difficult. Mary Fluke, bless her heart, saw to it that her dad Donald and mother Pepper were able to make the long trip from Durham, NC. Helen flew in from Ocala...with Emeline joining us on Friday night...and I, Louise, live right here in the Dawdi Haus at the farm where I spent my first 18 years.

It has been a great privilege to be born into this strong family heritage. The far-seeing Flukes who braved the trip from Pennsylvania to Ohio by covered wagon to homestead here in the Midwest showed great fortitude. Phillip and Mary Fluke set the pace...took the venture in stride...as they made it to Orange Township...here in Ohio, their home to be...our heritage. In doing so, they blessed all of us.

Our Fluke Reunion President, John Fluke, declared us solvent in a short business meeting. Thanks to John for keeping our financial records. It was agreed that the next reunion, 2015, would, again, be on

Labor Day weekend...same place...the Sycamore Hill Farm.

You will note that in this writing I have used only a few names of those who helped in so many ways. I wish I could have mentioned all of you and what you did to make this wonderful gathering a reality, but it would just take up too much space and I am sure I would be forgetting many. Mostly, I have mentioned those who put forth much time, effort and expenditure for their phase of the reunion. Please forgive me if I failed to mention you. Without your efforts this reunion could not have happened. We, in the Fluke family, are so indebted to all who handled each successful and memorable occurrence.

There is so much I have not been able to include in this writing...some things humorous and some things sad. The sad thing is the recognition that we all grow older each year and it is difficult to think about "the next time—the next reunion." I'm well into my 90th year as I write this...I pass the joy of writing the account of the next event...to someone else in 2015. We are all grateful to Margaret Welch for her wonderful and heartfelt record-keeping and especially this year for her efforts and to her family also...for the compiling of *Written On Our Hearts*. Also, Margaret put together a time-line for the Fluke Family, complete with pictures and dates...a great addition. This was displayed in the garage during the reunion. Hope you didn't miss it. Much appreciation to Margaret for all she does in respectfully and carefully keeping the records.

How indebted we all are to Molly and Glenn Smith for providing this wonderful venue for our gathering together, as we recall our roots and connection to the Fluke family of the past...and remembering the generations before us with great pride. Molly and Glenn keep everything looking so nice and welcome us all to the farm for each reunion so graciously.

I know full well this reunion is a most unusual occasion as reunions go. Many friends have told us that our Fluke gatherings are so unique and they wish they could be a part of the Flukes. You then learn that some families never have had a reunion of any sort.

Truthfully there is no way to do justice to our fantastic three-day reunion. Our dear Aunt Bernice Fluke wrote a wonderful account of her memories of the Flukes many years ago. As I recall, she entitled it "You Had to Be There." How true!

Blessings to you all...Until we meet again.

Louise Fluke Beattie

LAUNDRY IN THE EARLY DAYS
Fluke Family Reunion, 2013
*Written for one of the learning experiences
about "lost arts" for the gathered children*

Philip and Mary (Summers) Fluke, our ancestors, traveled by covered wagon from Bedford County Pennsylvania to Ohio in the early 1800's. Philip came first and built a log cabin and then he went back and brought his family...his wife Mary, and 4 little children...to Ashland County. The family grew...a total of 11 children as the years went by.

So, how do you suppose they washed their clothes? I'm sure they all got dirty as the children played along the trail. No washing machine or dryer!!!

Here is what they had to do on "WASH DAY".

1. Gather wood along the trail to build a fire to heat water in a tub
2. Gather soap, wash board, everything needed to get the clothes clean (show homemade soap)
3. Scrub the clothes and rinse the soap out
4. Lots of wringing to get the water out
5. Drying took place on bushes or on makeshift clotheslines strung from tree to tree.

They would have done this all the miles they were on the trail. When they got to Ashland County where the cabin was already built, Philip no doubt put up a clothes line between the trees. However, the washing was ongoing year after year in the same way. Heating the water in the yard over a bonfire and going through the same procedure every time. It was a job that took all day.

This method carried on until some sort of mechanical machine was invented. My mother, another Mary Fluke (at this very house) had a washing machine with a gasoline motor. Now this lady was the GREAT-GREAT-GREAT-grandmother of all you youngest gathered here for this story.

Laundry has changed greatly since Mary Summers Fluke crossed through the wild countryside in the covered wagon with her little ones almost 200 years ago. It is much easier in so many different ways now.

This is the time to ask questions.

Louise Fluke Beattie

INSTRUCTIONS
What To Do Upon My Death
November 15, 2013

To Robert W. Brownson—Bobby
[Executor of the Will at the time of writing, later Bob and Tina became Co-Executors/Trustees]

My financial statement is separate from this. See "Financial" folder in blue file box.

My funeral is PRE-PAID—at Denbow-Primm-Kemmery. Ed Kemery and I have talked about this, but it has been several years ago. Probably when Frank died in 2004. I do not know if there will be other costs attached to this or not. See the contract with Allianz Co. Policy taken out 2-25-94—for Jim and me, plus Jim's son, Bill Conery, too. It worked well for both of them. Allianz Co. papers located in the "fire-proof" box on the floor by the computer hutch.

Be sure to use an <u>inexpensive</u> "cremation casket"—don't need an urn. You will know where to place the ashes—maybe some in your woods and maybe some at the pond. The family can decide.

Perhaps there might be a memorial service at the church with only an hour of "visitation" time ahead of the service. But it is all up to the family. Do whatever you like.

All important papers, birth certificate, social security and a copy of my will etc. are in the fire-proof box on the floor in my bedroom, to the right of the computer hutch. By the printer are notebooks, one for each investment .

I have no lawyer now. Briefly, mine was Daniel Finley with Harpster and VanOsdall, but he moved away. The official "WILL" should be in that office. Tina knows that office quite well. She would be a good help on all this.

I don't seem to have agents for my investment policies; however, I have left addresses and telephone numbers to contact both American Equity (an Index Annuity) and Columbus Life (also an Index Annuity.) I have no agent for American Financial. I receive statements only from that company. (A folder for them is in the navy blue, big file box.)

My ring, from Jim Conery, goes to Ann—valued at $2000. I gave it to her to wear, but she brought it back cleaned and polished for me to enjoy while I live. So, Ann is to have the ring and the $2000 taken off her inheritance. She agreed—may have suggested the arrangement [of having it taken off her inheritance.]

There is no property nor car to sell. Most of my things have been disposed of or given to family. I'm happy that so much of the "end of life stuff" has been done already. Our family history indicates longevity. I'm now nearly 90. Whatever will be will be!

Louise M. Beattie

CHRISTMAS GREETINGS, 2014

At Christmas we usually write of "stars and tinsel" and The Christ Child...and what it is all about. However, in my advancing years, I often find my thoughts turning, at Christmastime, to what my role in this world should be now. Often I feel concerned about what I really should be doing after my very busy years when my family required much input and participation from me in their lives, especially now in my 91st year.

No longer does my life require me to be the transporter of my kids to and from school for both practice and games...to all sporting events. No longer do I need to make outfits for the cheerleaders, or carry around hot food in "roasters" to help raise money for the Boosters Club at the local high school. In truth, now days my kids really need to transport me, their mom!

So, how do we, in our waning years, measure our self-worth? Seldom can we actually "see" it. However, when I take an in-depth look at my now-adult children's lives and see them all serving the needs of others in so many ways, I am happy and grateful. I believe that the encouragement of others is so important. Gift-giving at Christmastime is traditional. Gifting to those in need is a blessing to the recipient...and also to the gift-giver, as well.

I turned 90 in May and had a wonderful party hosted by my family. Ninety-some attended and it was a fun day. Another great-grandchild was added to my list in November, making the total 45.* All live in Ohio except for two in Colorado and one in California. I do enjoy living here in my wonderful apartment on the farm where I was raised. My dwelling is referred to as the Dawdi Haus, an Amish term for the older generation (Grandma) living in the little house, behind the big house where the younger generation lives.

In September I had a fall...fell over backward in the garage. No broken bones, but I did manage to damage my shoulder (torn rotator cuff) and really whacked the back of my head. I'm still in the process of healing. Healing just takes longer than it used to. I knit stocking hats for kids, make good use of my iPad for email, texts and watching movies. I get out to church nearly every Sunday. Molly and Glenn plus Bob and Gini and I are all active members of the same church. This makes it nice for me to find a ride. I no longer drive.

As we thank God for all the blessings of the past years, we remember our friends and relatives, those who have been a very special part of our lives. Memories were made...memories that bind us together and keep us concerned for each other. May 2015 be a special year for you.

Peace and Love!

Louise

* 49 great-children by the time of Louise's death

CHRISTMAS GREETINGS—
ALSO SOMETHING I NEED TO TELL YOU
Sent to Bill Beattie's Family
December, 2014

Christmas Greetings To You All,

It was great to be with you all Tuesday night. Good to see you all and catch up on your lives a bit. Lots of good laughs as the evening went by. Good to hear word on Ted and Sandy's cruise... Matt's successful surgery and of the progress on Ruth's house. I'm very concerned for Sonja, and of course, Don, too. The long weeks ahead will be so difficult.

I have something I want to tell you all...should have told you all Tuesday night, but I was too close to tears. I'm finding it so very difficult to go out at night. I hate it that I have to drag along a cane, and I should really have taken my Rollator/walker Tuesday night to help me from being so shaky and off-balance. I do hope the family will understand when I tell you how difficult it is for me to ask for help (except from my kids.) Therefore, I really need to let you all know that much as I enjoy being with you, I'm running extremely short on stamina and mobility and need to leave the Tuesday-evening Beattie circle. It has been great! You have all been so kind to me. I will remember the good times always and getting to be a part of the gang. Bill Beattie would be so proud of you all...his family.

The Christmas season is a time for joy for all the little kiddies especially and a time for remembering all the great Christmases in past years. A star shone brightly over Bethlehem all those years ago. Thankfully, it still shines on all God's people today.

Merry Christmas to each of you, and to your families also. May 2015 be a *great* year for you all!

Love always,

Louise

GRANDMA LOUISE AND LUKE MCFREDERICK
The Family Cradle and Grandpa Bob's Scrapbook
October, 2014

Hi Grandma,

I wanted to see if you have any history on this baby cradle. We were working at Mom and Dad's, and I am trying to put some history behind some of the items that have been in the family. I figure you were the expert for this one.

I also grabbed Grandpa Bob's old scrapbook and read the entire thing...every last news clipping and letter. What a collection of history and accomplishments. I admire your strength and dedication to your five children during long and busy times. It must have been difficult at times, but the memories that were created were priceless.

Hope to get a history lesson soon.

Love you,
Luke

Hi Luke,

What an interesting email from you. I love it that you care enough about family history to ask questions about the cradle. I wish there was a fantastic story to relate to you about a family heirloom, but the history of this neat piece of furniture is lost to me. Grandpa Bob bought it somewhere...don't know for sure, but I think it was a gift to me. I did love it...for sure...but in later years found it took too much living space and was a shin-scraper. It came into our possession when we lived in the Nankin house. It sat in our living room, the same room that held Grandpa Bob's picture above the mantel, the same picture that hangs at the Olde Parsonage, I believe.

One New Year's Eve I was getting ready to go to a party of Grandpa's old coon-hunting buddies and their wives—a party where I knew the men would sit in the host's kitchen and tell yarns about "treein' a BIGUN with old Buck," while the wives sat in the living room and talked of birthing, diapers and toilet training. I was irked, not really wanting to attend the party...and then my five kids got into a squabble. They fell into the cradle, the plant in the cradle got broken, and one kid even got a broken collar bone. I picture this all like it was yesterday. I always felt bad about being a bad mom...getting so mad at them.

Then came the day, years later, when Uncle Jimmy Brownson decided he wanted to buy the cradle...from ME. Over the years I really hated Brownson family haggling sessions. Fussing over money...making fancy "deals" and so forth. Jimmy wanted me to throw in a fishing pole of Grandpa Bob's in addition to the cradle. I'm usually a fairly passive person, but I remember I exploded and yelled at him, saying, "Remember, you are dealing with ME, not a BROWNSON!!" There was no deal!

When we made a move, maybe to the brown house in the woods, in 1972, I think, the cradle came into the possession of the McFrederick family. I don't remember just how. I think it was when the Olde Parsonage was still on Sandusky Street. I tell you this modern-day history, because I don't have the real history. It is a lovely piece of furniture. Maybe it is going into the "sale" stuff and it could have a history yet.

About Grandpa's scrapbooks...Can't tell you, Luke, how happy I was to hear you enjoyed those clippings from a by-gone day...Portsmouth, Ohio 1952-1953? The two years with the Portsmouth High School Trojans football team was a heady time in Grandpa's life...the heyday of his life. Maybe even more so than the Ashland College days which came next. I so often wish the Good Lord had allowed Bob more time to keep on shaping young fellows' lives...had given him more healthy years for that period of his life. He had what it takes to motivate guys with ability and even those with lesser ability. Few of his team members are alive today, but those who are, remember their playing days with Bob...in BOLD, BRIGHT colors...with fantastic stories to tell (with minor embellishments, as well, no doubt.)

There are several older books from Bob's Ashland High School and New London High School days. After all the years, they are a bit tattered...but held special now in your Uncle Bob's hands. When it was his turn to sit with me, his mom, during my cancer treatments, he brought along the scrapbooks in his possession. We both enjoyed them greatly during the three-hour chemo infusion time. I'm sure Bob would be happy to loan them to you, Luke.

These past four weeks have been difficult for me. The fall took a lot out of this 90-year-old body, so I'm a bit discouraged. Still have healing to go. I'm feeling my years. This has all taken a toll on my self-assurance, as well.

Wishing you the best always, Luke.

Love you,
Grandma

DONALD'S *SINGLETREE*
—REMEMBERING CHILDHOOD DAYS—
May 21, 2014

From: Louise Beattie <Imfbeattie@gmail.com>
Sent: Wednesday, May 21, 2014 3:14 PM
To: Fluke Donald; Helvenston Helen
Subject: Remembering our childhood days.

I have just finished re-reading "Singletree," Donald, and bless you again for writing this absolutely wonderful account of your memories of our childhood experiences of life...just what I needed to factor in before taking on my 90th year celebration. How in the world did you remember all the detail of so many "things" and happenings...the events in our lives? No way can I do justice to this account of growing up a Fluke kid. And yet it was all so familiar to me. I could smell the horses (loved their smell) the cows and, yes, even the sows chewing ear corn—and a memory of mine, spring clothes out of the camphor wood chest ready for summer-night wear. Playing in the ravine, the vine house, the kitty grave yard and the sugar camp site. When Molly takes me on a Gator ride back to the woods, I see in my mind the area and remember the non-thirst quenching, sweet sap...the steam in the evaporator...and Fannie and Polly plodding through the mud with the collection of sap.

There was SO MUCH to do...day in and day out...all year long. In the dead of winter there was always the important WOOD! How did Dad handle ALL that had to be done? Oh, yes, there was Forrest and our help down through the years, but I still don't see how he handled all the planning...the planting...harvesting and putting everything back in place. Sigh!

One thing I want to refer to but don't know quite how to ask my question or make my point. To you Donald: Your superior mind was developing all through your growing up years...details...how everything was made...but you had no inkling as to what you might BE or BECOME in your life. Did you think you might end up a farmer? Did you dread the thought? In reading through your account this time I noticed your reference to monotony and repetition in doing all these things over and over! Did you ever question the nature of this life...the purpose in your boyhood life? Of course, you didn't have a clue as to all that was ahead of you. Oh, my I'm getting in rather deep here, but hear me out...this is where my faith comes in. I think as this whole progression of events and circumstances was happening, your life was being guided and shaped by a higher power. I'm off my soap box now...back on my cow-milking stool.

We were all so fortunate to be raised by honest, hard-working people. Both Mom and Dad gave us the best "basics for life"...no frills...no travel/vacation or big dreams...but the really important stuff of life...how to make our way in life and to be good people! I felt the tears well up when you wrote of Dad and Grandpa Jim's "heart-to-heart" in the shop the day after the fire. What a terrible hurdle for Dad. It was good Grandpa was a kindly, understanding man. I'm sure our dad benefited gratefully from his dad's wise council. As Helen said after reading "Singletree" (the first time?) "We weren't poor...we just didn't have any money." How true! And yes, there had to be eggs and flour in the rivels [small doughballs in soup]...and did rocks sometimes rain down on us from the dynamite blasts when the "cut" went in? I'm just rambling here. I wish our "email threesome" could just sit down in a totally quiet room and talk about this trip down memory lane one more time...but then maybe it is best all kept in our hearts.

Love to you both,
Weezie

MY 90TH BIRTHDAY
May 26, 2014

In recent months I have thought frequently about reaching this upcoming milestone in my life. Ninety had always sounded really "old" to me...and here I am. I have reached this stage in life and it seems quite okay...even comfortable to me. For years I have realized that I was almost always the oldest in the room, be it in church or gatherings of any kind. The decades come and go...each a special time in life. Along with the years come joys and also sorrow and loss...all a part of life. So, I'm here in my Dawdi Haus... thanks to Molly and Glenn who wanted to see "Mama" in a safe and comfortable environment, thus making this cozy place mine. I can sit on my lovely back porch and view the beautiful flowers Molly has so carefully planted and cared for and also the valley that was in my sight all my growing-up years, the first 18 years of my life. I'm *back*...spending the last portion of my life...here on what is now Sycamore Hill Farm.

To those who might ask, "Did you have a party for your birthday?" I can only say...**you bet I did**! And it was a dandy! Molly carefully planned the event...spending much time on all the decorations...planning the food and all events of the afternoon. Her artistic abilities came through. For the invitations she used a picture of me in my Junior Prom dress...1941...with the invitation to the party on the back. Many exclaimed on how much resemblance there was between Erin Smith Johnson and her Grandma Louise at seventeen. There were 92 in attendance with many of them my own relatives...a few from the church...my Bible study group plus Pastor Mike and wife Dana...the Beattie family...my good friend Lova Lantz from Columbus... and friends from down through the years. I was blessed to have many of my 15 grandchildren here, plus a good representation of my 44 great-grandchildren who had a wonderful time playing games in the yard. Gini and Bob had put in quite a bit of time working out a lawn Bananagram (like Scrabble) game for the kids...plus Corn Hole and Frisbee. The kids kept busy inventing their own games as well.

The weather was perfect for the end of May; however, in planning ahead it seemed best to hold the party in the three-car garage. Molly chose an old-fashioned theme with beautiful, colorful tablecloths on the main buffet and dessert tables laden with all kind of goodies all catered and put together by Janna Kline...a good friend of the family. Janna made a most interesting cake that resembled a bee hive...iced in bright yellow with bees hovering (on wires) above the cake. There is no way I can do justice to what a handsome layout it was. Above the main table hung a wire "swag" on which Molly had placed a line of dollies edged in old-fashioned lace on which were centered the initials LMB, indicating "Louise Molly Beattie."

Molly had also put together five hanging parasols...one for each child of mine... from which hung a placard with Bob's and my wedding picture plus a picture...my favorite...of my five children taken in about 1957. On the other side was a sort of collage of pictures she had made for my 85th birthday, five groups of images depicting the things that were important to each of my "five" in their lives. The five parasols were spaced around the room. It is difficult to describe them to you, nor can I really tell you just how special they were. The effect was all so meaningful to me...tugged at my heart.

I was especially happy to have Betty Smith, Bob's sister, here, thankful that her daughter, Leslie, could bring her. It was Betty who introduced me to her brother, Bob, when she and I were both 15-year-olds at Ashland High School in 1940. Those attending the party from my generation...in addition to Betty...were

Glenn's mom Martha Smith, 92, from Bucyrus, accompanied by her daughter Jane...Arlene McWilliams, also 92, and Helen Manring, 86, both good friends from church. Noting ages might not be very polite, but this was an occasion where "age" was recognized. Also in attendance from my generation were my brother-in-law and sister-in-law, Walter and Edith Brownson.

Ann and Larry flew home for my birthday...their annual trip...and stayed with Rick and Tina. I'm sure the Keiffers enjoyed staying at the McFrederick bed-and-breakfast at the former John Fluke homestead...now owned by Rick and Tina and once again back in the family.

On Sunday evening Rick and Tina provided a lovely dinner for the family. Delicious wine and hors d'oeuvres—remember how Grandpa Frank Brownson used to like to refer to them as "horse deevers?" Wonderful food...both steak and chicken on the grill with all the trimmings. Gini had chosen three questions to ask us all (a wonderful idea.) I don't think we ever got beyond the first question which was, "What special thing happened in your life in the past year?" I'm not really sure about what the other two questions were, because it took us a long time to finish with the first one. It was a lovely evening, a grand birthday dinner celebration for this special birthday...a very gala and fun evening.

I wanted to give my family a gift to take home with them. Vainly, I suggested a picture of me...to be given to my four children...my fifteen grandchildren...and my forty-four great- grandchildren. I never knew my great-grandparents but did so enjoy looking at their pictures down through the years. Therefore, it was my decision to provide each one in the family circle with a picture to keep. I chose a picture taken from a church directory of several years ago. I wanted it to look not too ancient, but also hoped that they could see some resemblance to their grandma of today. Again this was all worked out by Molly. To each of my grandchildren's generation I wrote a brief note telling them how much their lives have meant to me...voicing my pride in the things they do. I ran this picture idea past Granddaughter Molly Bernard and asked if she thought it might mean something to her two children...Macy, 7 and Ridge, 5. She chuckled and said, "Ridge already has a picture of his grandfather, Roy Winland, on the headboard of his bed along with a picture of Roy Rogers and he kisses and prays for them both every night when he goes to bed." Think there might be hope for me to make it in that line up?

After recently finishing Rick Warren's *Purpose Driven Life* (for the second time) I'm pondering, again, the purpose of my life at 90. I'm losing ground...losing stamina...experiencing some loss in just plain "getting it" in conversation...maybe hearing loss? And the big one...no longer driving. All this does cut down on what I am able to do and how I can participate in social time and interactions. However, in these later years I have tried to be an "encourager" in life...applauding the accomplishments of others... recognizing their acts of kindness...their victories in academics and sports. In addition, I also try to be a support to those experiencing sadness and loss in life. I am finding it is easier to recognize these occurrences and events in the lives of others as I grow older. Probably in aging there is more sensitivity to the ups and downs in the lives of others, as well. In the quietness of my life here, there are, no doubt, fewer distractions coming from the fast-paced world.

I am comfortable and cozy here in the Dawdi Haus...well looked after by family. My time to go might be near...only God knows. I would like to stay as independent as long as I can...to "maintain" myself...attend to my personal needs and sit on my swing and watch north Ashland County folks roll by out on the road, to work, to school and home again...to enjoy the birds...the nest-building and the flowers blooming everywhere.

Two majestic Sycamores stand beside the old lane...have been there all my life. I have always wondered how and when they came to grow in that exact spot. Somehow their sturdy presence there in the pasture gives us all a claim to our deep-rooted Fluke heritage...established here in Orange township dating back to the early 1800's.

It was a **wonderful** birthday! As the matriarch of this wonderful family I feel great pride in the lives of these eighty-some people. I am truly blessed!   Louise M. Beattie

MY THOUGHTS ON
THE PURPOSE DRIVEN LIFE
by Author Rick Warren
April 30, 2014

Having recently finished a study of this book...for the second time...I am thinking that I really need to put some thoughts together, assessing what the book has meant to me, what I have learned and experienced in the process.

In my adult life I have often wondered, "What am I here for?" Had I ever truly pondered that question in my decision-making when I was younger? Perhaps...once in a while...but surely not in any depth.

So here I am with my Bible Study friends digging into the thoughts brought forth by Rick Warren in his book, looking at our life journey with the idea of a purpose. Warren lists five reasons for being:

1. You were planned for God's pleasure.
2. You were formed for God's family.
3. You were created to become like Christ.
4. You were shaped for serving God.
5. You were made for a mission.

First of all, the real purpose of our life is far greater than for our own personal fulfillment, our peace of mind, or even our happiness. We were born *by* God's purpose and *for* His purpose. In our self-centeredness we begin making it all about "us." It is only in God that we discover our origin...our meaning...our purpose...our significance...and our destiny. As Christians, this is what we need to remember. We are not an accident...we are all in God's plan.

What drives our lives? Many are driven by guilt, fear, anger, resentment; some by materialism and some by the need for approval. This question makes us take a good hard look at our lives. I suspect that the latter one... approval...defines me. All my life I have wanted to please...not rock the boat...to stay calm in time of trouble...and to work hard to try to do my assignment well and finish the job—all done by learning through my own father's teaching and by his example. I realize, now, that basically....in earlier times...I looked to my earthly father for guidance...not to my Heavenly Father.

Learning and knowing our purpose helps us to motivate our lives. Purpose produces passion. Passion gives us a reason to keep going even in old age. Nothing energizes like a clear purpose in life to go and to do!

It also helps us all to better prepare for eternity. Our lives often become quite cluttered. Think of all the "stuff" we collect...our treasures and trophies. Somewhere on towards the end of our lives these things...once so important...lose their importance and end up unwanted and, ultimately, trashed.

The way we "*see*" life, "*shapes*" life. How we define life determines our destiny. Life on earth is a test...a short time compared to eternity. God continually tests our character, faith, obedience, love, integrity and loyalty. In addition, life on earth is a trust. Our choices in life often help to determine our end times. Our time on earth and our energy, intelligence, opportunities, relationships and resources are all gifts from God that He has entrusted into our care and management. How well do we handle these gifts?

We have a need to "belong"...to belong to a church family. We need, really need, to be in a church family circle, church fellowship which speaks to the needs of all within the circle...where we can unite and be of encouragement to one another.

There is a tremendous need for those who are willing to "serve." Service starts in our mind. Servants focus on others, not ourselves. This is true humility...not thinking less of ourselves, but thinking of ourselves less. Servants should think of the ministry of serving as an opportunity, not an obligation.

We are made for a "mission." God is at work in the world, and He wants us to join Him. My grandparents were missionaries in China for seven years in a very dangerous, stressful period in history. Sometimes I have questioned (to myself usually) how many natives they were really able to "bring to the Lord." However, I do commend those who "go" and serve.

What a great last chapter—"Living With Purpose."

A suggestion is made that that we write down a "Life Purpose Statement" for our own lives. This prompted my attempt to write this piece today. Hopefully I have recorded the essence of the book—though, for the most part, what I've written applies to me in my life.

This has been a good study, one that has helped so many all over the world, a study very helpful for all ages, easily read and understood. I am nearing my 90th birthday, a milestone in my life, years in which I have known both joy and sorrow. The losses in my life were difficult. I have tried to be a good servant, especially in trying to be an encourager to others in times of pain and suffering, applauding others in their times of joy and success, and praying for those who need God's intervention.

Louise Beattie

LETTER TO BOB AND BEV LEE
—My Longtime Friends/Neighbors/Former In-Laws—
October 31, 2015

Dear Bob and Bev,

What a great idea...a party to honor our good friends Bob and Bev Lee's anniversary and Bob's 90th birthday at the same time. As I write this letter I'm thinking of all the memories I have of you both and your family. Within the huge circle of friends surrounding you...all those gathered on this special day...what a wealth of memories has been accumulated by knowing you both. They could fill many pages and no doubt will.

You moved to Nankin and into that wonderful house across from the Nankin Elementary School—the school no longer there, all torn down, just green grass now. Little did I know that day that our lives would become forever entwined...that we would share grandchildren...or how much I would also enjoy our cup of tea together late at night. (And I never was a "coffee-get-together" type person before you, Bev). I loved the way you organized your girls to bake pies...my Molly included...and she was thrilled to be included...and not just one pie, but 5 or 6. I was so impressed.

How I admired your forging ahead to get your degree, Bev...your years of teaching and you and Bob adding to your already big family with the addition of Marsha and Jeff in the Nankin days.

How well I remember your kids at our house...Peggy laying down on the floor in front of the hutch retrieving our dog Thurman's tennis balls. No wonder he was always delighted to see her arrive. The girls' sleep-overs under the apple tree in the back yard. The "flood" of—was it 1968?—and the girls running back and forth across the park in the rain. The hours and hours the kids played in the park. How fortunate for the parents as well as the kids to have their own safe park to play in and ride bikes. I will always be thankful for the village park. The Veterans Memorial statue and the cannon will long be remembered by scores of kids.

Two more things I especially remember: the evening the freshly hung wallpaper slid down off the wall in heaps all around...the sound of it sliding was so weird. And I think it was Andy reading (forbidden, maybe?) the Readers Digest by flashlight. I can't remember, was it the night-reading or the flashlight that was forbidden? Oh, those were fun days. There were always great activities going on at the Lees'. The Brownson kids always wondering why we didn't do those fun things.

Bob, I have always admired your involvement in education and I can't recall ever seeing you angry. I remember your relating how you got through your undergraduate work on a shoestring and an old car...oh, well, I guess there were a bunch of us who managed the "old cars that wouldn't start in the mornings" era. I recall helping my Bob start his old car in the AM and his basketball boys' "pushing him off" to get the car started after practice in the PM at Jeromesville.

How wonderful that you both have been fortunate to have 65 years together. It doesn't happen often these days. I always admired that you did so many things *together*...back then and *still today*! Oh, how I have enjoyed your pop-in visits over the years!

Congratulations to you both.

May God continue to bless you as time goes by.

Love always,

Louise

THE SOUND OF MUSIC
And the Memories this Wonderful Performance Brought Up
about Ashland High School and McDowell Auditorium
February 23, 2015

In this winter, this snowy, cold winter, I experienced a delightful Sunday afternoon. This does not happen frequently at age 90. Tina, my daughter, and her husband Rick McFrederick invited me to this wonderful, emotion-filled day, which started by attending my childhood church in the village of Nankin, Ohio...the Nankin Federated Church...always a pleasure for me. This was followed by a trip to Peking Restaurant, one of my favorite places to eat. From there we went to the Ashland Junior High building and attended "The Sound of Music"...the last production of any musical to take place at McDowell Auditorium.

When this building was built, the auditorium was incorporated into the high-school complex. The wrecking ball will take it all down soon, after the end of this school year. It is the end of an era and sad; however, it is a very tired building. Think of all the feet that walked those halls in its 100 years existence, all those who attended or graduated from Ashland High School, and all those who taught and worked there through all the years. In the early 40's (my era) it housed 7th and 8th grades, in addition to four years of high school...some 1200-plus students at that time.

Rick and Tina's granddaughter, my great-granddaughter, Maya McFrederick, was a joy to behold in the part of Brigitta, the fourth child in the von Trapp family. The "full- house" approved with an exuberant, standing ovation. It was a colorful and exciting production...a large cast of many wonderfully talented young folks. I was glad it worked out that I saw the third and final presentation, the matinee of "The Sound of Music"...a happy yet tearful afternoon for so many teenagers as they closed out the McDowell Auditorium Ashland High School musical productions. McDowell has served Ashland well these 100 years.

In addition to enjoying the delightful musical it was also a very nostalgic afternoon for me to be in McDowell Auditorium at this last milestone event. For it was in February of 1940 that I had my first date with Bob Brownson who some years later became my husband and the father of my five children. Bob asked me to meet him in McDowell after the basketball game. I did...and that was 75 years ago this month.

I was a very shy, country gal coming in from Nankin by bus. Bob had his sister, Betty Brownson, ask me if I was "allowed to date." I wasn't yet 16; I had to ask my dad for permission. He hesitated a bit and then asked "Who is this fellow?" My brother came to my rescue to inform my dad that Bob was an honor student who played sports and had lots of friends. My dad gave his approval. So my mother drove me to AHS on the appointed night, and I viewed the game. I have no idea now what school we played, or who won the game. I was so nervous. I met Bob's parents in the hall after the game, more pressure. When we got to the car I was surprised that Bob's dad had allowed him the use of their NEW black DeSoto. Wow, I'm not sure about wartime-gas-rationing and how that all fit into the winter of 1940.

Actually Bob told me, at a later time, that he had "picked me out" at the Farm Bureau, which was at that time located on South Street. I was with my family; however, he spied my brother Donald whom he knew from attending the same classes at AHS and surmised that I was Donald's sister. Bob told me that he had wanted to give me an ice cream bar. Seventeen-year-old Bob was selling ice cream from his bike/ice cream business, but decided that it would be too hard on his profits for the day as he really should give one to each of the family group...so he rode on.

As I sat in McDowell, other memories floated over me. Like the movies that were shown in the auditorium during the noon hour...just a few minutes of a movie each day, so we had to be there the following day also to stay in the sequence with lots of westerns and movies involving trains. The sound always seemed to be cranked pretty high and the moaning whistle of the train often stayed with me. At times I could "hear" it in my dreams years after. I also loved the other noon-time events—when we were sent to the girls' gym and we danced to Pennsylvania 6500, String of Pearls and Slow Boat to China. Bob danced, but he said he wasn't very good...and he didn't like to do things he couldn't do well. I wasn't very adept either...never learned to Jitter-Bug. It was now the winter of 40-41. I was a Junior, Bob, a Senior.

In my Senior year, Bob worked in Cleveland and traveled back and forth by Greyhound. He came home for my last day of high school. I was ready to graduate, and he asked me to marry him. He gave me a ring, another happy memory. This was up on the balcony of the girls' gym. That was May of 1942. We married in October of 1943.

On my recent Sunday visit to McDowell, my attention was taken by the large brass plaque just inside the front entrance of the former AHS building. It noted that the building was erected in the years of 1914-1915, and I had to smile because my mother, Mary Swan, moved to Nankin in the year of 1915. She was the daughter of the new minister of the Nankin Presbyterian Church, and she rode the interurban (streetcar) to attend the NEW Ashland High School on Cottage Street. On the streetcar she asked about the boys in Nankin and was informed that Gene Fluke was the nicest boy, but he was in Columbus in college. After Gene finished the special course at Ohio State University, he returned to Nankin. Mary and Gene became acquainted and then married in 1920 after he came home from WWI.

I'm writing this basically for my children, but also for the younger generations, like our 16-year-old Maya's. Maya was so thrilled to have a part in "The Sound of Music" in 2015. She was bubbling over with joy, building her happy memories of a very special weekend in her life...one she will long remember. Writing has given me much pleasure in my last 20 years. I've kept a lot of records of dates and times and happenings at special occasions like this. It is my belief that happy memories from our youth can help sustain us in our later years.

Keep "The Sound of Music" in your heart..."Climb Every Mountain"...and live within the melodies of life. These are some of "My Favorite Things."

Louise Beattie

MY 91ST BIRTHDAY
May 26, 2015

If I am going to write an account of my birthday, I'd better get started...before I forget....easy to do at this stage in my life. It was a wonderful birthday. I told Molly I wanted only a small group this year...just my kids and their spouses. The actual party was held at Rick and Tina McFrederick's in their newly-finished garden/party area...fit for a king...just right for my family to celebrate Mom's 91st. Ann and Larry had emailed me some weeks before letting me know they were coming for the event, completing the "circle." They arrived here at the farm on Saturday morning and quickly made plans to take me to Chipotle for lunch, a favorite of mine.

The weather was ideal for the entire four days of my "birthday." The temperature was in the high 70's...with no wind...and it made for a beautiful evening party. The food was delicious. What a totally FUN evening...much "remembering" and laughter. For three hours we sat around the table bordered by the beautifully-planted shrub beds, there under the big trees...and, in part, thinking of our heritage along with my 91 years. A portion of the original John Fluke farm is now back in the family, thanks to Rick and Tina, the new owners. John Fluke was the great-grandfather of Tina—and all my children's generation, of course. So nice to hold the party on that beautiful lawn, reminding us of the building of this wonderful house by John Fluke in 1876, so special to us all.

The family presented me with a planter consisting of violets in three colors, beautifully arranged. Ann and Larry also got me an orchid and a large hanging basket of petunias. Molly and Glenn gave me a beautiful pot of pink begonias combined with trailing ivy. Molly told me they were for me, but she thought I might want to take them to Bill's Beattie's grave first...and I did. Ann and Larry saw to it that this happened by taking me to the Ruggles Cemetery the next day.

Sunday: Only Bob and Glenn went to church and Sunday School. Molly, Ann and I managed to get "one-on-one" visiting on various swings on either porch. Sometimes it is hard to find time to make this all happen, but we all did well this visit. The Keiffers took me to Bella Bleu's in Ashland for lunch on Tuesday before they flew back to California. What a great time we all had in these four very special days. "Till we meet again"...were Ann's words whispered in my ear before they left for the airport. She knows goodbyes are hard for me; we don't like to say goodbye anymore.

My "children" now are all older than I tend to think they are. Where have the years gone? Forty years ago, October 17, 1975, their father...Bob...my husband of 32 years...died, leaving part of our lives unfinished. I wish he could have known of the successful lives of his children...the loss of Frank...his 15 grandchildren and all the 45 great-grandchildren.* I wish he could have known all these most interesting kids, excelling in academics and some making a name for themselves in athletics. Maybe he does. The oldest two great-grandchildren have just recently graduated from Ashland High School...Bob's high school...where he excelled in both sports and academics. Like I said, what an interesting gang of young folks. Bob would have been delighted.

The year I was born, in May of 1924, was an extremely wet spring. In those days, farmers plowed their fields and fit their acreage with one team of horses, a one-bottom plow, and a disk or harrow to fit the ground. It was so wet that year that my dad had not been able to plow even one acre of his 100 tillable acres. Just think of this spring, 2015, in Ashland County, all the corn and soybeans are already planted and the first planted are already several inches high by May 26th...amazing! In my lifetime I have seen many changes! I have lived in the era that stretched from hand-milked cows to milking machines...from a time when hay was raked and hay-forks were used to pitch hay into the mow to a time when hay is baled and stacked...from "check-rowed" corn fields to drilled corn-planting with much higher yields...from "party-line" telephones with many people listening in to cell phones with all their many ways of communicating...just to mention a few of the changes I've seen. One can only imagine what will take place in the years to come.

No one knows how many years they might have on earth! In my 90-plus years I have experienced a blend of sorrow and joy. I have known "loss"...of three husbands and my son, Frank, when he was 52. However, I welcomed 5 children into the world, plus 15 grandchildren and at this point in time, the births of 45 great-grandchildren.* I am satisfied with my life. I have been very truly blessed!

Louise Molly Fluke (Brownson, Conery, Beattie)

*49 great-grandchildren by the time of Louise's death

LETTER TO THE FAMILY FROM HELEN
Prior to Fluke Reunion, 2015 (?)

Dear Family,

Louise suggested that I might consider being a part of the reunion celebration by sending some memories your way. What a thoughtful invitation! If you've heard a strange thumping sound as you gather in joyous celebration, think nothing of it. It's just my heart. I sent it up there to be with you in love and remembrance of those who have gone before us. Family, near or far away, has always meant more to me than you realize. When I moved to Florida 62 years ago, I replaced my given middle name (Margaret, which I loved) with Fluke, making it my legal name in honor of that legacy.

I consider it to have been a blessing to grow up on the land and in the buildings that surround you today. We were sheltered and nurtured by parents devoted to each other and to doing their best for us. The views from home still live in my mind's eye with total recall. The fields, the "40," the pastures and the family gathered around the table. Nankin itself but, especially, Nankin Federated Church, the grade school, Grandma Swan and her warm, welcoming home. Somehow these things have been an anchor in my life. Our parents gave us the greatest blessing any parent can give their child. They gave us a peaceful life...a life without quarrels, without vices and/or outrageous language...a life that let us know we were loved. I often wonder...how did they do it! Growing up and growing strong in our family was like being wrapped in one of those beautiful quilts Grandma made.

So...having said these things, may I offer a toast to those who have gone before, as they are missed and always will be. Our earth time is limited and each will go as destined. It is expected that reunions will soon be beautiful memories. So, until we meet again...in life or the forever after...

Peace and love to you all,

Helen

FLUKE REUNION, 2015
Labor Day Weekend

As I am attempting to write about our wonderful weekend I am reminded of Aunt Bernice and her lovely write-up of the Fluke family...years ago...her generation...entitled "You Had to be There." Beautifully done. It applies so well to this reunion just past. We did some new things, made some changes, as well, but kept many of the old and loving traditions from all the years gone by.

In late July " the cousins" met to make plans for the big weekend. It was a great meeting with everyone committed to approaching this with total honesty and with a generous heart. Liz became our leader and she did a fantastic job thru the entire event!

As usual, our reunion weekend started at Rick and Marti Krause's lovely home. They provided us with a beautiful meal served outside under a tent. Keeping a close eye on the threatening weather made us all aware of how fortunate we have been these many years in dodging the rain. One quick run with food from outdoors to inside proved only a momentary interruption. Round tables helped with conversation and soon after the meal the "cousins/boomers" got us rolling with laughter. A most fun evening was enjoyed by all.

New Tradition (I think)...7:00AM a 5K race...introduced by Laura Tvergyak and billed as "The Gene Fluke 5k Race." Seldom did I see my dad Gene Fluke run—though he walked many a mile and some in this race did, too. Laura's dad Bob Brownson helped her lay out the course. Many thanks to the four young mothers who really RAN the course, accompanying some 20 others all ages. Again, a lot of fun..I overheard one adult say he was suddenly overtaken by a small fellow wearing PJ's...7-year-old Raif Johnson, the youngest in the race. The sun was just popping up over the corn field and from my vantage point on the front porch swing I could see this variety of runners make the turn headed for the finish line. All the "mature" runners...the "boomers"... claimed to be winners in their own age category! Like Aunt Bernice said...you should have been there. There always will be 2017–time to get out your knee braces and running socks....time to join the fun.

By about 11:00Am the front yard was filling with sporting-events-type folding chairs. Our ancestors would question those strange chairs...in the old days dining room straight-chairs would have filled the bill.

Dinner was catered and served by Barb and Larry Bates...the family brought in desserts. Everyone got filled up, especially when the ice cream machine got fired up and cones and bowls dripped with goodness.

As the afternoon progressed much activity took place. Three different hay rides left the driveway filled to the brim all three times to circle the farm and take in the McFrederick area, too. Rick Krause drove Grandma Gene's last tractor, pulling the loaded hay wagon. This is all tradition, too. Some of us in the older generation grew up on hay ladders, a vital part in hay-making and the entire harvest season. Some of the boomer-generation were probably involved with wagons, too, though it might have been in hay-bailing time.

The little ones started off the yard games early. Two bushels of shelled corn were dumped in a "kiddy pool" which entertained some of the little ones most of the day. The shelled corn appeared everywhere when the cleaning-up took place. A bit was eaten and some sneaked to a doggie or two. Hope no one got sick.

The raffle was a success this year. Seems that the family-treasure items just might be staying put...right where they are. But a nice number of things for the raffle were brought in as the morning progressed. The kids were so distressed in 2013 over not really getting to be "in" the raffle. So this year some items were brought for their part of the raffle, suitable for them and their wishes. They seemed pleased with the items they acquired this year.

I don't want to get into the finances of the reunion, but I do want to make mention of the cousins'/boomers' most generous gifts of money to start off the 2015 reunion...readily accessible for payment of rentals of our faithful green-and-white tent and also for the porta-pot. All in all, from the donation jar and the raffle money, we have a cushion ahead of the 2017 reunion.

Our big regret of this reunion was the fall that Molly Fluke Evans from Texas (daughter of John and Peggy Fluke) experienced. It took place during our Sunday morning breakfast session at Rick and Tina McFrederick's. May Molly Evans have a good recovery and be on her trip home to Fort Worth soon. She was accompanied by her son, David, and her daughter-in-law, Eva...all three are so faithful to the reunion.

The reunion was well-attended. I estimate 40 for the Friday-night dinner at Rick and Marti Krause's....120 on Saturday noon (the most ever for Saturday)...and approximately 40 for breakfast at Rick and Tina McFrederick's on Sunday morning. Those unable to make it from the 7th generation were Donald and Pepper Fluke from North Carolina, Emeline Fulmer from Canton and Helen Helvenston living in Ocala, Florida. Poor health and the many miles to make it back to the farm are great levelers in whether some attend. We missed them all so much. Not the same, not having them here with us.

At 91 years I was the oldest one attending. But it's easy for me...I live here in an apartment at the farm—very fortunate for me, too. The youngest...first time reunion attender was Ellie Azoni, 4-month-old daughter of John and Laura Azoni. John is the grandson of the late Elinor Martin (Ellie to many). What a joy it was to hold little Ellie—granddaughter of my dear sister.

Louise Fluke Beattie

LOUISE'S FAVORITE COOKIE RECIPES
Often baked for the Sunday School hour at
Christ Community Evangelical Free Church

Included in "Mom's White Binder" and computer files were these four cookie recipes. What book by Louise wouldn't have something about cooking and baking and taste-bud-pleasing in it! Maybe you'd like to taste-test these recipes in your own kitchen, if you haven't already sampled them in Louise's kitchen or at the church, where they were always a hit. May these recipes and this entire book of Louise's writings leave you with a little bit more sweetness in your life.

Iced Sugar Cookies (With Lemon or Orange Icing)
1 cup of Crisco
1½ cup of white sugar
2 eggs
1 t. soda
1 t. baking powder
1 cup of milk
4 cups of flour
Salt
1 t. vanilla

Cream together the Crisco and sugar. Mix in two eggs. Add the flour plus soda, baking powder and salt, mixed in alternately with the cup of milk. The dough will be quite soft. Pat dough out on the floured counter top and carefully cut out the cookies. Don't be tempted to add more flour to the batter. In the process of cutting out the cookies more flour will be added.
Important:
Bake at 400 degrees for <u>6 minutes only.</u> I don't allow the tops to brown. The bottom of the cookie will be slightly browned. Frost when completely cool, using your favorite powder sugar icing recipe, adding a bit of grated lemon or orange peel and juice to flavor.

Magic Cookie Bars (Very Easy)
2/3 of one stick of butter
1 cup of graham cracker crumbs
1 (14 oz.) can of condensed milk (not evaporated milk)
1 cup (6 oz.) of milk chocolate chips (I usually use a bit more)
1½ cups of flaked coconut
1 cup chopped pecans.

Preheat oven to 350 degrees. Bake in a 9x13 pan (if glass, bake at 325 degrees.) Melt butter in the glass pan in the oven. Sprinkle crumbs over the melted butter, pour the condensed milk evenly over the crumbs. Top with the remaining ingredients and press down firmly. Bake for twenty-five minutes or until lightly browned. Cool and cut into bars. Makes 32 cookies.

Buffalo Chips

½ cup of butter
½ cup of Crisco
1 cup of brown sugar—packed tightly
1 cup of granulated sugar
2 eggs
1 t. vanilla
1 cup of quick rolled oats, (uncooked)
2 cups of flour (pack it down well)
1 t. soda
1 t. baking powder
½ cup of coconut
½ cup of chopped pecans
1 cup of Rice Krispies
½ bag of chocolate bits.

Preheat oven to 350 degrees. Cream the butter and Crisco together. Add sugar, eggs and vanilla. Mix well. Stir in the oats, flour, baking soda and baking powder. When well-blended, stir in the coconut, pecans, Rice Krispies and chocolate bits. I usually put in a bit more flour at this point as they may seem to be too moist and sticky. Make into balls and place on an ungreased cookie sheet (or try dropping them, whichever works.) Bake for 12 minutes at 350 degrees. Do not over-bake. You want them to be a bit "chewy." I usually bake a double recipe, making over 100 cookies. It "doubles" or "halves" easily. This recipe, as written, makes 50 cookies or more.

Toffee Bars

Preheat oven to 350 degrees.
Cover a jellyroll pan—bottom and sides—with foil. Grease foil lightly with butter. Cover the entire pan with a single layer of saltine crackers.

Bring to a boil:
One stick of butter
One stick of margarine
One cup of brown sugar
Bring these three items to a full, rolling boil and cook for exactly five minutes.

Pour mixture over the saltines and bake in a 350 degree oven for ten minutes. Sprinkle 1 pkg. (12 oz.) of milk chocolate bits on top and spread evenly. Top with ½ cup of chopped nuts. Refrigerate. Break into pieces and serve. Best kept in the refrigerator.

Louise Beattie

Thank you, Louise, for sharing your life with us...all the days we were together and on these pages. We loved you and always will!

Made in the USA
Monee, IL
06 December 2019